Invitation
to
Struggle

Politics and Public Policy Series

Advisory Editor
Robert L. Peabody
Johns Hopkins University

Congressional Procedures and
the Policy Process
Walter J. Oleszek

Interest Groups, Lobbying
and Policymaking
Norman J. Ornstein
Shirley Elder

Mass Media and American
Politics
Doris A. Graber

Financing Politics:
Money, Elections and Political
Reform, Second Edition
Herbert E. Alexander

Invitation
to
Struggle:
Congress, the President and Foreign Policy

Cecil V. Crabb, Jr.
Louisiana State University

Pat M. Holt
Former Staff Director
Senate Foreign Relations Committee

Congressional Quarterly Press

a division of
CONGRESSIONAL QUARTERLY INC.
1414 22nd Street N.W., Washington, D.C. 20037

Cover Design: Richard Pottern
Cover Illustration: Guy Aceto

Printed in the United States of America

Third Printing

Library of Congress Cataloging in Publication Data

Crabb, Cecil Van Meter, 1924-
    Invitation to struggle.

    Bibliography: p.
    Includes index.
    1. Presidents — United States. 2. United
States. Congress. 3. United States — Foreign rela-
tions — 1945- I. Holt, Pat M., joint author. II.
Title.

JK 573 1980.C7   327.73   79-27912
ISBN 0-87187-196-3

Foreword

Who initiates, implements, and ultimately controls the foreign policy of the United States? For most of the nation's nearly 200 year history, the president has generally dominated the making of foreign policy. From time to time, however, Congress has taken an increasingly independent and assertive role and, as *Invitation to Struggle: Congress, the President and Foreign Policy* convincingly demonstrates, the decade of the 1970s has been one of those periods of conflict. In this, the fourth book of the Congressional Quarterly Press Politics and Public Policy Series, the authors suggest how and why the traditional relationship between the president and Congress has been modified if not revolutionized.

As Cecil V. Crabb, Jr. and Pat M. Holt, the authors of this timely volume, point out, the past decade was not the first period of congressional insurgence in the foreign policy arena. Senators, charged by the Constitution with a central role in treaty ratification, have expressed a continuing interest in the conduct of foreign policy, and House members have also shaped external relations, primarily through control of the purse strings of government. Members of Congress have usually come together to assert their latent prerogatives following aggressive administrations or major wars. Thus congressional involvement in foreign policy, even to the point of seizing initiatives, has been strongest following the Jackson, Lincoln, Wilson, and Truman administrations, and most recently, after the Johnson and Nixon presidencies.

Nevertheless, by far the dominant pattern throughout our history has been a president in control, a Congress mainly passive. In *The Theory of Social and Economic Organization* (1922; trans. 1957), Max Weber suggested why this was the typical relationship:

> It is impossible for either the internal or the foreign policy of great states to be strongly and consistently carried out on a collegial basis. Collegiality unavoidably obstructs the promptness of decision, the consistency of policy, the clear responsibility of the individual, and ruthlessness to outsiders in combination with the maintenance of discipline within the group. Hence, for these and certain other economic and technical reasons in all large states which are involved in world politics, where collegiality has been retained at all, it has been weakened in favor of the prominent position of the political leader, such as the Prime Minister.

Examples of congressional acquiescence to presidential leadership abound in the realm of foreign policymaking. When the French were about to yield Dien Bien Phu in Indochina in 1954, Speaker of the House Sam Rayburn observed in the *New York Times* (May 14, 1954) of his Democratic colleagues, "We're ready to cooperate in a sound foreign policy." Rayburn, however, asked of Republican President Eisenhower that he make clear "what that policy is." The speaker of the House was simply acknowledging a long held tradition: in the main, presidents determine foreign policy, leaving Congress with the right to react, delay, and only rarely, reject.

Twenty-five years later, following on the frustrations of the Vietnam War and the catastrophes of Watergate, which led to the downfall of the Johnson and Nixon presidencies, Congress has reasserted its role in the making of foreign policy. Under President Carter, the struggle between the executive and legislative branches over foreign policy has remained in great flux. And these relationships will probably continue to be characterized by great contentiousness into the 1980s regardless of who is in the White House or the party ratios in Congress.

Hence the value of *Invitation to Struggle*. In this book, two knowledgeable senior observers of the process have combined to capture and share with the reader the central foreign policy themes of the tumultuous 1970s. Perhaps more than in any other decade in the nation's history, Congress has accepted that invitation, inherent in the Constitution, to combat the natural advantages of the president in the foreign policy arena. With its appropriations and foreign policy committees in the forefront, Congress has sometimes seized the initiative and almost never backed away from a major involvement in the implementation of foreign policy.

Cecil V. Crabb, Jr., who has taught courses in international relations and American foreign policy at Louisiana State University and other colleges, earned his Ph.D. at Johns Hopkins University. He is the author of numerous articles and books, including *Bipartisan Foreign Policy: Myth or Reality* (1957), *American Foreign Policy in the Nuclear Age* (1972), and *Policy-Makers and Critics: Conflicting Theories of American Foreign Policy* (1976). Pat Holt, the co-author of this book, contributes more than 30 years of experience as a reporter and congressional staff expert, including 3 years as the chief of staff of the Senate Foreign Relations Committee under Senators J. William Fulbright and John Sparkman.

Professor Crabb is the author of Chapters 1, 2, and 8. These lay the groundwork for understanding the current tensions between the president and Congress and analyze the future direction of American foreign policy. In Chapters 3 through 7, Mr. Holt, drawing upon his lengthy congressional staff experience, details the interaction between Congress and the president on such fundamental issues as consideration of the Panama Canal treaties, the Arab-Israeli conflict, support and maintenance of the armed forces, congressional oversight of key intelligence functions and, finally, development of the human rights issues abroad under recent Congresses.

What can be expected in the future? Edward S. Corwin, the preeminent constitutional scholar, whose observation provides the title of this book, suggests the most applicable guidelines, indefinite as they remain:

> What the Constitution does, *and all that it does,* is to confer on the President certain powers capable of affecting our foreign relations, and certain other powers of the same general kind on the Senate, and still other powers upon Congress; but which of these organs shall have the decisive and final voice in determining the course of the American nation is left for events to resolve.

At the change of a decade our country was faced with a series of unfolding crises: the freeing of American hostages seized by Iran, response to the invasion of Afghanistan by Russia, what to do about the continuing conflict over the price and flow of oil from the Middle East. We are indebted to Crabb and Holt for helping to make the processing of such events more understandable. In addition, they have provided another important set of perspectives to the unfolding but as yet unresolved struggle between the president and Congress over the initiation and implementation of foreign policy now and in the future.

Robert L. Peabody

The Constitution . . . is an invitation to struggle for the privilege of directing American foreign policy.

—Edward S. Corwin
The President: Office and Powers

Preface

On the eve of World War II, one of America's most eminent constitutional authorities, Edward S. Corwin, observed that the Constitution created an "invitation to struggle" between the president and Congress for control over the foreign policy process in the United States. Indeed, he continued, it made that struggle all but inevitable. Corwin's widely quoted observation — made while the United States was still devoted to an isolationist foreign policy — has lost none of its cogency in the intervening years. At the end of the eighteenth century, President George Washington complained adamantly about Senate opposition to the proposed Jay Treaty with England, and many legislators no doubt believed that "His Majesty" (as President Washington was sometimes called) was trying to exclude them from foreign policy decisionmaking. More than a century later, President Woodrow Wilson and the Senate clashed over the provisions of the Treaty of Versailles following World War I.

In no period of American diplomatic history, however, has the executive-legislative interaction in foreign affairs been more intense, more prolonged, and more momentous in its impact upon the nation's diplomatic behavior than in the period following the end of the Vietnam War. Inevitably, the roles of the president and Congress in the foreign policy process — and the nature of executive-legislative relations in external affairs — were affected by that traumatic episode. Other developments — like the Watergate scandal during the Nixon administration and the growing diffusion of power within both the executive and legislative branches — have fostered and intensified the struggle.

The post-Vietnam War period of American diplomacy is an era of transition. The process of making foreign policy decisions is changing almost as rapidly as is the substance of America's relationships with other nations. New, interesting, and highly significant forms of struggle between the legislative and executive branches of government have developed. They will undoubtedly have a lasting impact upon the conduct of foreign relations by the United States.

Invitation to Struggle was written primarily with two groups of students and general readers in mind. For those chiefly interested in recent American diplomacy, the study provides insight into important issues of contemporary foreign policy, particularly those arising since the Vietnam War.

For those concerned more with the process of American policymaking, three issues should be of special interest. First, the role of the president in foreign policy is examined. The problem of achieving unified, coherent, and effective policymaking among a widening circle of executive agencies — and of assuring the president's control over the activities of the executive branch — is a theme that appears in every chapter.

Second, our study focuses upon the place of Congress in external policymaking and on the significant developments on Capitol Hill that affect the legislative role of Congress in the foreign policy process. How have recent changes in legislative rules and procedures affected Congress' ability to exert its influence successfully in the sphere of foreign relations? How well organized and equipped are the House and Senate to function as partners with the chief executive in foreign affairs? What can be identified as the major and continuing impediments to a constructive foreign policy role by the legislative branch? These and other fundamental questions are considered in depth.

A third perennial and vital issue of interest to the student of American policymaking is the nature and influence of public opinion in the formulation and administration of national policy. The role of interest groups in both domestic and foreign policymaking has become increasingly influential and must be taken into account more fully than ever before by students of American foreign policy.

Particularly in the study of foreign policy, examples are necessary to illuminate the roles of officials and institutions in the American governmental process. Therefore, this book contains three general chapters and five case studies of particular events or policy areas. Case studies are most useful as learning devices when they are examined within the context of general political principles. The first two chapters (Part I) of *Invitation to Struggle* supply that perspective. In Chapter 1, the reader will find an overall discussion of the constitutional and historical powers of the president and of the role of executive agencies in the diplomatic field. Recent trends affecting the president's position of diplomatic leadership — like the progressively acute problem of uncoordinated activities by executive agencies, and the decline of the State Department's pre-eminent role in foreign affairs — are identified and evaluated.

Chapter 2 focuses upon the constitutional and historical powers of Congress in foreign relations. The current era of congressional militancy in external affairs can only be fully understood against this background. The forces inducing Congress to play a more assertive and independent foreign policy role since the Vietnam War are also briefly identified.

Five case studies (Part II) provide the basic data for our inquiry into executive-legislative relations in the post-Vietnam War period. Each deals with a noteworthy development or issue in recent American diplomacy and illustrates one or more important aspects of presidential and congressional authority in external affairs. For example, how have developments during and after the Vietnam War affected the ability of the United States to enter into long-term agreements with other countries? That crucial question is examined in our discussion in Chapter 3 of the new Panama Canal treaties. Or, what was the impact of the Vietnam experience upon traditional executive and legislative control over the armed forces, particularly with regard to the use of military force in behalf of diplomatic objectives? That problem receives extended treatment in Chapter 5.

In the concluding chapter, the post-Vietnam War era of struggle between the White House and Congress for control over the foreign policy machinery is placed in a more theoretical perspective. On the basis of experience thus far, what are some of the major consequences of this struggle for the ability of the United States to meet its responsibilities as a superpower in the international system? How durable are the causes of Congress' diplomatic activism? Conversely, what are the prospects for a revival of forceful executive leadership in diplomatic affairs in the years ahead? What kind of new balance may emerge between executive and legislative prerogatives in foreign relations? These and other fundamental questions are addressed in Chapter 8 (Part III).

The authors are indebted to many individuals who have contributed directly and indirectly to this study, and their assistance is most gratefully acknowledged. In particular, the authors wish to express their genuine appreciation to two members of the Book Department staff of Congressional Quarterly. Jean Woy provided encouragement, advice, and criticism at every stage; her assistance was indispensable. Barbara R. de Boinville supplied capable and essential editorial assistance in the production stage. Harriet F. Crabb read several chapters of the manuscript and made numerous suggestions for its improvement. Members of the LSU Library staff — most especially the head of the Documents Department, Jimmie H. Hoover, and his assistants, Roberta Scull and Gordon A. Saucier — as always were skillful and ingenious in assisting with problems of research and bibliography. Ms. Josephine Scurria and Ms. Angela DuPont typed successive portions of the manuscript, and their contribution is recognized with sincere thanks.

While acknowledging the essential contributions of others, the authors accept sole responsibility for any errors of fact or judgment that may be found in these pages.

Cecil V. Crabb, Jr.
Pat M. Holt

Contents

Contents

PART I

The Process of Foreign Policymaking

A unique feature of the American governmental system is that its powers are exercised by separate executive, legislative, and judicial branches. From the perspective of constitutional theory, these are often described as "equal and coordinate" branches of the government. In practice, however, their powers and influences are not equal — especially in the foreign policy sphere. The purpose of Part I — Chapters 1 and 2 — of our study is to provide an overall context within which congressional efforts to play a more influential role in foreign affairs can be meaningfully understood.

Throughout American history, the judiciary has largely been content to play a passive role in the foreign policy process. When the Supreme Court has concerned itself with foreign policy questions (which it does rarely), nearly always it has taken one of two positions. Either it has declared foreign policy issues to be "political questions" that are not susceptible of resolution by the judicial system,[1] or the Supreme Court has forcefully upheld the exercise of *executive power* in foreign relations.[2] Over the years, a series of Supreme Court decisions has thus reenforced the claims of successive presidents that in foreign affairs the chief executive is the dominant organ of government. Insofar as fears about the emergence of an "imperial presidency" have resulted from vigorous and unrestrained presidential leadership in foreign affairs, that phenomenon has received strong impetus from the constitutional interpretations of the Supreme Court.

Both the diplomatic experience of the United States and certain provisions of the U.S. Constitution dictate that we begin our inquiry by focusing upon the role of the executive branch in the conduct of foreign affairs. Although recent years have witnessed a new congressional militancy in foreign relations, the fact remains that the president is still in charge of American foreign policy. For the most part, Congress' powers are limited to telling the White House what it *cannot do* beyond America's borders. The power to decide what the United States will undertake in its relations with other countries — and to carry out specific programs like arms control or foreign aid or mediation in the Arab-Israeli dispute — resides with the chief executive. As we shall see in Chapter 1, every incumbent president has at his disposal a variety of instruments giving him an unrivaled position for influencing the diplomatic destiny of the United States. More than at any other time in American history perhaps, the nation's influence abroad depends upon presidential decisions

— including, of course, decisions to work collaboratively with Congress in the foreign policy process.

Congress is also assigned, in the American constitutional system, a number of responsibilities impinging directly and indirectly upon foreign affairs. In whatever degree legislators have felt in recent years that their views have been ignored by the White House, the American Congress has more power to influence foreign affairs than its counterpart in any other country. Along with its constitutional prerogatives, Congress has also acquired over the course of 200 years extra-constitutional powers and informal techniques for affecting the course of foreign relations. One tendency since World War II — the erosion of any sharp distinction between "domestic" and "foreign" affairs — has significantly enhanced Congress' influence. Chapter 2 provides an overall discussion of the formal and informal prerogatives of Congress in the foreign policy field. In addition, the forces that have produced a new congressional militancy in external affairs are identified and analyzed. Chapters 3 through 7 examine detailed case studies of congressional behavior with regard to selected foreign policy issues.

NOTES

1. Referring to the interpretation of a treaty, in 1855 a federal judge ruled that this was a "political question" and was not among the powers which were "confided by the people to the judiciary . . . but to the executive and the legislative departments of our government." See *Taylor v. Morton* 23 Fed. Cas. 784 (No. 13,799) (C.C.D. Mass. 1855) and an earlier case *Foster v. Neilson*, 2 Pet. 253 (1829).

2. Two landmark decisions affirming the president's prerogatives in foreign relations were the *Prize Cases*, 2 Black 635 (1863) and *United States v. Curtiss-Wright Export Corp.*, 299 U.S. 304 (1936).

1

The Executive Branch and Foreign Affairs: Locus of Decisionmaking

During the late 1960s, at the height of the Vietnam War, one of America's most experienced political commentators said, "I cannot think of a single major foreign-policy move any President wanted to make since the Second World War that he was unable to carry through because of the opposition of the press or of Congress."[1]

The diplomatic experiences of the Nixon, Ford, and Carter administrations provided considerable evidence that the once largely unrivaled position of the president in the foreign policy field was undergoing serious challenge. Yet any understanding of the foreign policy process in the United States must begin with recognition of a transcendent reality. The motive force — or, as we have described it in this chapter, the locus of decisionmaking — in foreign relations is the executive branch, headed by the president. The American chief executive is not only a national leader; more than any other head of state in modern history, the president has become a *world leader*. Policy decisions made in the White House can determine whether there is global peace or war; whether the United States has a favorable image in black Africa; whether regional stability exists in the Middle East; and whether the nations of the Third World have access to foreign assistance required for their development.

As future chapters will show, Congress plays an increasingly assertive role in the foreign policy realm — and some legislators believe it should become an equal partner with the executive in external decisionmaking. The quest is likely to be long and arduous. After two centuries of American diplomatic experience, the president has emerged as the "ultimate decider" or the "decision maker of last resort." [2] Despite challenges to this leadership position on Capitol Hill, the chief executive possesses constitutional powers and other techniques for exerting influence over foreign affairs that are unequaled.

BASIC DEFINITIONS

Before examining the constitutional and historical bases of presidential leadership in foreign affairs, a few definitions are needed. By *foreign policy*, we mean *those external American goals for which the nation is prepared to commit its resources.* This definition enables us to distinguish between the nation's foreign policy and a variety of hopes, visions, and dreams (such as universal democracy and perpetual peace) often espoused by American society. Unless the objective — such as deterring the Soviet Union, or protecting the security of the North Atlantic Treaty Organization (NATO), or assisting in the economic development of India, or preserving the stability of the Middle East — involves some application of the economic, military, intellectual, or other resources of the nation, it cannot be seriously viewed as forming part of its foreign policy.

A closely related term is the *foreign policy process.* This denotes a complex and often time-consuming series of steps by which officials in the executive and legislative branches formulate the nation's diplomatic goals and decide upon the most appropriate means for reaching them. To cite an important case from the nation's postwar diplomatic record, in a speech before a joint session of Congress early in 1947, President Harry S. Truman promulgated the "Truman Doctrine." The goal — formulated over preceding months by executive and legislative policymakers — was the "containment" of Soviet expansionism into vulnerable areas, such as the Mediterranean and the Middle East. Initially, the means employed was the Greek-Turkish Aid Program of 1947 providing economic and military assistance to these countries. In time, other means (such as the Marshall Plan for European recovery and the NATO defense system) were also utilized in applying the containment strategy. For the containment principle, as for all other long-term diplomatic strategies, its meaning and usefulness were periodically re-examined in the years after 1947.

Another concept which has come to the fore since World War II is *national security policy.* It includes those activities in the foreign policy field — as well as those in domestic affairs — designed to protect the independence and integrity of the United States. At its most basic level, national security policy is concerned with the defense of the nation against actual and potential enemies. Construed more broadly, it involves preventing threats to national security; collecting and digesting information about the behavior of potential enemies; creating and maintaining necessary military alliance systems; supplying friendly countries with arms aid; and taking other steps aimed at enhancing the security position of the United States under widely varying conditions abroad.

While the Department of Defense perhaps plays the most central role in national security policy, in the postwar period the Department of State — along with a growing number of other federal agencies — is also intimately involved. At least implicitly, American officials have become aware of Clausewitz's dictum that "war is the continuation of politics by other means."* One of the implications of this principle is the idea — highlighted by the concept of Cold War between the United States and the Soviet Union — that political and military relations among nations are opposite sides of the same coin. For example, political (or diplomatic) decisions sometimes lead to armed conflicts among nations; in turn, the results of war — and one nation's perception of another's military strength — crucially affect what diplomats are able to achieve at the conference table.

Awareness of these realities led to the creation in 1947 of the National Security Council (NSC), the highest presidential advisory agency for national security policy. The National Security Council is headed by the president. Its members are the vice president, the secretary of state, and the secretary of defense. NSC's operations are supervised by the president's national security adviser; President Nixon's choice, Dr. Henry Kissinger, is the most well-known national security adviser in recent years. NSC endeavors to blend diplomatic, military, and other relevant policy considerations into a unified national security policy for the United States. It is important to note that NSC is solely an *advisory organ* to the president. Ultimately, the decisions emerging from its deliberations are made by the president after considering the views of his advisers. A second significant fact about NSC in the postwar period has been the degree to which its staff, under the president's national security adviser, has emerged as a rival to the State Department for influence in the foreign policy process. (As we shall see, this development has introduced a new and significant source of conflict over foreign policy issues within the executive branch.) The third noteworthy fact about NSC is that it is a civilian-controlled agency. The president and his advisers may, and frequently do, request the viewpoints of military leaders about national security questions. But the fundamental American principle of civilian control over the military establishment is preserved in its membership and deliberations.

Another term that requires brief explanation is *diplomacy*. The concept is perhaps inherently and inescapably ambiguous and often causes widespread public confusion. At the risk of oversimplification, we may say that it has two primary connotations. Diplomacy can refer to *the entire range of a nation's external relationships* — from routine diplomatic communications between governments, to heads-of-state "summit" conferences, to the recognition of one government by another, to cultural

---

*Carl Maria von Clausewitz was a Prussian general in the Napoleonic period. After the defeat of Napoleon, he wrote a celebrated treatise *On War,* containing his reflections upon the relationship between armed conflict and the political process. For an illuminating condensation of his thought, see Roger A. Leonard, ed., *Clausewitz On War* (New York: Capricorn Books, 1968).

and scientific exchange programs. Alternatively, diplomacy can and often does have a more limited connotation: the resolution of disputes and conflicts among nations *by peaceful methods.* In this sense, diplomacy is a substitute for war and violence; or it is an effort to *prevent* the resolution of international controversies by reliance upon armed force.[3]

Traditionally, Americans have been suspicious of diplomacy and of officials engaged in it. In the public mind, diplomacy is associated with Old World political values and machinations held to be at variance with the democratic ethos of the New World. One argument invoked to justify the old isolationist approach to foreign affairs was that Americans lacked skill and training in diplomacy; hence in any encounter with experienced diplomats of the Old World, the United States would almost certainly lose! (This point of view was re-enforced by the results of several diplomatic conferences during World War II, like the meetings at Yalta and Potsdam in 1945, which many Americans interpreted as diplomatic victories for the Soviet Union.) This historic frame of mind unquestionably contributes to the poor image that the State Department usually has with the American public and with Congress. [4]

THE PRESIDENT'S CONSTITUTIONAL AUTHORITY

The pre-eminent position of the chief executive in the American foreign policy process stems from two broad sources of power: those conferred by the Constitution (including those "implied" from key constitutional provisions); and those that are an outgrowth of tradition, precedent, and in some instances, historical necessity. Let us examine each of these categories in detail.

Almost since the beginning of the republic, constitutional authorities have debated whether the Founding Fathers intended to make the conduct of foreign policy largely an executive responsibility, whether they meant for Congress to be the dominant organ, or whether they desired some kind of approximate balance of power between the two branches in the foreign policy field. Arguments are still heard pro and con on this issue, and the question will no doubt be debated in the years ahead. [5] Yet two facts seem beyond contention. The original intention of the founders of the republic proved to be a less crucial consideration in determining the outcome than numerous other influences, like the impact of forceful personalities upon the presidential office, the crises confronting the nation at home and abroad, and the decisions of the Supreme Court bearing upon the problem. Irrespective of what the founders desired, as a result of 200 years of American history the tendency has been toward executive pre-eminence in nearly every aspect of the foreign policy process.

Constitutionally, the position of the president in foreign affairs rests upon several important provisions. Article II vests the executive power of the government in the president. The presidential oath of office (Article II, Section 1) requires the chief executive to "solemnly swear (or affirm)" to "preserve, protect and defend the Constitution of the United States." The oath thus confers upon the president a unique responsibility for the preservation of national security.

Commander in Chief

The Constitution (Article II, Section 2) also designates the president as "Commander in Chief of the Army and Navy of the United States," including today, of course, the air force. In common with other constitutional provisions, this one has engendered controversy throughout American history concerning its precise meaning. Did the Founding Fathers intend that the president should merely function symbolically or ceremonially as commander in chief (much like the British monarch in modern history), leaving the determination of military strategy and the deployment of the armed forces to others, possibly Congress? (The case study in Chapter 6 focuses upon congressional prerogatives and claims regarding the use of the armed forces for foreign policy ends.) Or, did they (like President Franklin D. Roosevelt during the Second World War, and President Lyndon B. Johnson during the Vietnam War), contemplate that chief executives would actually determine military strategy and tactics, sometimes with momentous implications for the future military and diplomatic fortunes of the United States? [6]

American diplomatic experience has left no doubt about the answer. Successive presidents — following the precedent of Abraham Lincoln's administration perhaps — have interpreted their authority in this realm broadly and dynamically, and their position as commander in chief of the armed forces is clearly one of their most influential powers in the foreign policy field. The list of specific steps or actions taken by the White House under the authority of this constitutional provision is almost endless. Here we can do no more than cite a few outstanding examples.

As commander in chief, presidents since the Washington administration have time and again ordered the armed forces to carry out missions in distant parts of the world. Throughout its history, the United States has been involved in approximately 125 "undeclared wars" and other instances of violent conflict abroad conducted under presidential authority. For example, in 1846 President James K. Polk unquestionably (and almost certainly, intentionally) provoked Mexico into war when he ordered the army to occupy disputed territory along the Rio Grande River. In the face of strong congressional opposition, President Theodore Roosevelt sent the American navy on a cruise around the world. (The president's real objective was to impress Japan with the nation's naval power.) On his own authority, President Franklin D. Roosevelt ordered the navy to "shoot on sight" German submarines that entered the hemispheric security zone. And President Harry S. Truman personally made the decision to use two atomic bombs against Japan in 1945. In 1950, Truman also ordered American armed forces in the Pacific to resist North Korea's aggressive thrust into South Korea, thereby involving the United States in one of the most prolonged and expensive undeclared wars in its history.

Early in his administration, President Dwight D. Eisenhower threatened Communist China and North Korea with possible use of American nuclear weapons if peace talks in the Korean War were not successfully concluded. Beginning with Eisenhower, a succession of chief executives expanded America's military commitments to the government of South Vietnam, thereby in time virtually guaranteeing massive American involvement in the conflict between North and South Vietnam. In what was perhaps the most dangerous cold war encounter since World War II, President John F. Kennedy in 1962 presented the Kremlin with an ultimatum demanding the removal of Soviet offensive missiles from Cuba. In this context, Kennedy placed the air force on worldwide "alert," and he interposed the American navy between Cuba and Soviet ships which were apparently bringing new missiles to the island. Little doubt exists that Kennedy was prepared to *use* whatever degree of force was required to eliminate this Soviet threat. [7]

Relying upon the constitutional power as commander in chief, the president can take other steps affecting America's relations with other countries. It is the president's prerogative, for example, to *terminate military hostilities* with other countries and to enter into truce negotiations with them. At a later stage, the White House also initiates diplomatic negotiations designed to produce a peace treaty. A presidential decision *not* to employ the armed forces (as in President Jimmy Carter's reluctance to have the United States become embroiled in several conflicts in black Africa) can have a significant impact upon America's influence regionally and globally.

With the concurrence of the Senate, the president can appoint and promote high-ranking military officials; and on his own authority — as in Truman's widely publicized dismissal of General Douglas MacArthur during the Korean War — he can also relieve military commanders. While ultimate authority to determine the size and nature of the American military establishment resides with Congress, the president can and does play a crucial role in that decision. His annual budgetary message to Congress — along with countless other communications to the legislative branch, and the testimony provided by executive officials before congressional committees — usually have a decisive impact upon legislative attitudes and behavior.

To the minds of many Americans by the mid-1960s, White House reliance upon the armed forces to achieve diplomatic objectives — often with little or no consultation with Congress — symbolized the "imperial presidency." Limiting this presidential prerogative has been a major goal of those legislators who advocate a more influential role in foreign affairs. A noteworthy step in this direction was passage of the War Powers Resolution in 1973. (We shall examine this resolution more fully in Chapter 5.)

Treaty-making Power

Article II, Section 2 of the Constitution states that the president has the power "by and with the Advice and Consent of the Senate, to make treaties, provided two thirds of the Senators present concur." The ability of the chief executive to enter into formal agreements with other countries in the form of treaties — and less formal accords and understandings by means of "executive agreements" — is another influential tool of presidential leadership.

Controversy has always surrounded the meaning and requirements of this constitutional provision. What, for example, did the founders intend precisely by giving the president the power to "make" treaties? Did they mean that the process of *negotiating treaties* was an exclusively executive function? Or does "the advice and consent of the Senate" extend to the negotiation of treaties, as well as to senatorial consideration of them?

Again, whatever the constitutional arguments pro and con, American diplomatic experience since the Washington administration has answered the question. Successive presidents have taken the view that the executive branch "makes" (or negotiates) treaties, and then submits them to the Senate for its acceptance or rejection. In the post-World War II period, senators (and occasionally representatives) are invited by the White House to participate in the negotiation of treaties. This practice reached its zenith under the Truman administration, when Republicans and Democrats alike sought to achieve a "bipartisan" foreign policy. Nevertheless, the negotiation of treaties — and more broadly, all official negotiations with foreign governments — remains an executive responsibility.

Chapter 3 is devoted to a case study of the negotiation and ratification of the new Panama Canal treaties by the Carter administration. Consequently, here we shall attempt to gain only a brief, overall understanding of the president's use of this power to manage foreign relations. A prevalent source of confusion needs to be clarified at the outset. The process of treaty ratification consists of three distinct, albeit interrelated, steps.

First, the president's agents (the secretary of state or other high-ranking diplomatic officials) conduct negotiations with other governments, leading to an agreement that is formally embodied in a treaty. Only the White House can initiate such negotiations; and it has the power to terminate them when the diplomatic interests of the United States dictate this course.

Second, after the treaty has been negotiated and signed by the parties to it, the document is then submitted to the Senate for its consideration. At this stage, the Senate has several choices. After deliberation and debate, the Senate can *approve* the treaty by the required two-thirds majority. (Throughout American diplomatic history, the vast majority of treaties has received senatorial approval.) Conversely, the Senate can *reject* the treaty, by failing to give it a two-thirds majority. Alternatively, the Senate can take two other possible actions. It can attach *amendments* to it, as the Senate did to the Treaty of Versailles after World War I. It can also append *reservations and understandings* to it, clarifying or interpreting the treaty's provisions.*

Then, after the Senate has completed its deliberations, the treaty must be signed by (meaning that it must be acceptable to) the president. This is the third and last stage of the ratification process. It is thus incorrect to say that the Senate "ratifies" treaties. The Senate plays a key role in the ratification process, but in the end the treaty becomes the law of the land only when it is signed by the president. Throughout the entire process of treaty-making, the chief executive retains the initiative. The chief executive decides to undertake negotiations leading to an agreement; agrees to the provisions of the treaty; submits it to the Senate for its concurrence; and signs the treaty, thereby completing the ratification process. At any stage, the president may withdraw the treaty from consideration; or, as President Wilson did after World War I, the president may refuse to sign a treaty acceptable to the Senate, which the president believes contains provisions detrimental to the national interest.

Can a president also "terminate" an existing treaty? This question was posed by the action of the Carter administration in December 1978 when it recognized the People's Republic of China and concurrently notified the Republic of China (Taiwan) that the existing security pact with that government would be allowed to lapse. Predictably, Carter's action precipitated considerable public and congressional opposition. Since the security treaty with Taiwan had been approved by the Senate,

---

*An amendment to a treaty changes its language and provisions, thereby probably requiring its renegotiation with the other parties to it. Reservations and understandings specify the American interpretation of its provisions. For example, in several international agreements, the United States has specified that the accord does not supersede the Monroe Doctrine, under which Washington has historically protected the defense of the Western Hemisphere. In Senate deliberations on the SALT II arms limitation agreement with the Soviet Union in 1979, several senators insisted upon an understanding that the Soviet Union would adhere to pledges (given orally) not to expand certain components of its military strength. As we shall see in Chapter 3, in consenting to the new Panama Canal treaties, the Senate appended certain "conditions" to its approval of them. In reality, with the passage of time the difference among the various categories of changes has become increasingly indistinct.

some legislators were convinced it could only be terminated with the concurrence of the Senate or of Congress as a whole. Initially, this viewpoint was upheld by a United States District Court, which held that legislative concurrence was needed to terminate the security pact with Taiwan. But on December 13, 1979, by a vote of 7-2, the Supreme Court disagreed with this interpretation, holding that the president had the constitutional authority to terminate the defense pact with Taiwan on January 1, 1980. Four members of the court held that the controversy was a "political question" that was not subject to judicial determination, but had to be resolved between the president and Congress. [8]

Executive Agreements

In lieu of formal treaty accords with other countries, incumbent presidents in the modern period increasingly have utilized "executive agreements." Since World War II, such agreements have accounted for almost 95 percent of the understandings reached between the United States and foreign countries. While executive agreements are not mentioned in the Constitution, they have a venerable tradition going back to the earliest days of the republic.* During the past half-century, such agreements have been made frequently, and in the following cases they have had a momentous effect upon the course of American foreign relations: President Franklin D. Roosevelt's "Destroyer Base Deal" with Great Britain in 1940; several agreements arrived at with Soviet Russia and other countries by the Roosevelt administration during World War II (notably at the Yalta, Potsdam, and other wartime conferences); a series of understandings during the 1950s and 1960s between Washington and Saigon, promising American support for the government of South Vietnam; another series of agreements (beginning with the Truman administration) according to which the United States assumed a de facto commitment for the security of Israel; a widely publicized oral pledge by the Nixon administration to Hanoi, calling for massive American assistance to Southeast Asia in the post-Vietnam War period; understandings arrived at by President Carter and Chinese Deputy Premier Deng Xiaoping, providing for cultural and scientific exchanges between the two countries. These are leading examples of a president's reliance upon executive agreements to achieve diplomatic ends.

According to one estimate (and estimates vary widely), between 1946 and 1976 the United States signed 7,201 agreements with foreign

---

*Constitutionally, a distinction can be made between a "treaty" and an agreement (or "compact") with other countries, although the differences are not always legally and practically clear. An "executive agreement" is an understanding between heads-of-state; it may be either written or oral; and many agreements ultimately require congressional approval (as in providing funds for their implementation) before they can become effective.

countries (excluding over 60 "secret agreements" that the State Department reported to Congress between 1972 and 1977). [9] No presidential prerogative in foreign affairs perhaps has generated such concern on Capitol Hill in the recent period as the White House tendency to engage in agreements (or "national commitments") with other countries without legislative knowledge, scrutiny, or concurrence. As J. William Fulbright, chairman of the Senate Foreign Relations Committee, lamented:

> The Senate is asked to convene solemnly to approve by a two-thirds vote a treaty to preserve cultural artifacts in a friendly neighboring country. At the same time, the chief executive is moving military men and materiel around the globe like so many pawns in a chess game. [10]

Accordingly, Congress has been increasingly prone to insist that executive understandings — particularly those involving deployment of the armed forces abroad — take the form of "statutory agreements." Statutory agreements require that Congress be informed of their existence; that Congress be allowed to veto understandings with foreign countries to which it objects; or in some cases, that they either receive the approval of both houses of Congress, or be resubmitted to the Senate in the form of a treaty before they become operative. [11]

Appointment Power

Article II, Section 2 also provides that the president shall "nominate, and by and with the Advice and Consent of the Senate, shall appoint Ambassadors, other public Ministers, and Consuls." Subject to senatorial confirmation, the president chooses the nation's highest-ranking diplomatic officials. Traditionally, an ambassador serves as the *alter ego* of the head of state (or the president); foreign diplomats are accredited to him. It is, of course, expected that an incumbent president will appoint officials who share his conception of the nation's role in foreign affairs.

As with the treaty power, throughout American diplomatic history resourceful chief executives have discovered methods for circumventing limitations upon their appointment power. One such device is for the president to make an "interim appointment": the individual so appointed may hold office and perform important duties while the Senate is not in session. After the Senate reconvenes, the president has three choices: he may submit the name of the interim appointee for Senate confirmation; or the interim appointee's period of service will come to an end, and the president will nominate another individual (more acceptable to the Senate) for the position; or the president may decide not to fill the position at all.

The chief executive may also, and frequently does, use cabinet officers to undertake diplomatic assignments. In March 1979, President Carter relied upon Secretary of the Treasury Michael Blumenthal to arrive at certain understandings with the People's Republic of China before the United States opened an embassy in that country. [12] In the same period, Defense Secretary Harold Brown assured the government of Saudi Arabia and other Persian Gulf states that (in the light of the revolutionary upheaval in Iran) their security would be protected by the United States. [13]

The appointment of "personal representatives" is another device presidents have used to bypass senatorial confirmation of diplomatic officials. During World War II, President Franklin D. Roosevelt relied heavily upon his personal aide, Harry Hopkins, to conduct negotiations both with Great Britain and with the Soviet Union. President Dwight D. Eisenhower sent his brother Milton on an extensive "good will mission" to Latin America. The distinguished public servant W. Averell Harriman served as the personal representative of several presidents during and after World War II. [14] In recent years, chief executives have also used the vice president of the United States for such purposes; and from time to time, they have asked the first lady to represent the president in foreign countries.

Recognition of Foreign Governments

Article II, Section 3 of the Constitution confers upon the president another influential prerogative in the foreign policy field. It provides that the president "shall receive Ambassadors and other public Ministers [from foreign countries]." The power of the president to "recognize" other governments is derived from this constitutional provision.

In normal diplomatic relations between two nations, each formally recognizes the legitimacy of the other's government. The act is symbolized by the exchange of ambassadors (or ministers) between them and the establishment of an embassy within the other country. Foreign diplomats, it must be reiterated, are accredited to the president of the United States. Therefore, the prerogative as to whether to "receive" diplomatic representatives from other countries — and hence, whether to accord formal recognition to their governments — belongs solely to the president. In 1933, President Franklin D. Roosevelt decided (after the Communist regime had existed for more than 15 years) to accord formal diplomatic recognition to the Soviet Union. In 1979, President Carter made the same decision regarding the People's Republic of China, thereby ending a 30-year period of nonrecognition of its Marxist regime. Both decisions aroused widespread public and congressional controversy.

For many years, two theories have existed about the criteria that ought to be employed when the president recognizes another government. What might be called the "classical" international law conception holds that such recognition depends primarily upon whether the government in question is stable, has established its authority throughout the country, and is fulfilling its international obligations. If so, it should be recognized, irrespective of the nature of its government or ideological system. Applying this traditional standard, most governments throughout the world (except the United States) recognized Communist China between the end of the Chinese civil war in 1949 and the mid-1970s.

The other theory, the "Wilsonian" or distinctively American approach, holds that recognition is dependent upon the nature and character of the government in question. Specifically, it relies upon such criteria as whether the government enjoys popular support, whether it respects the rights of its citizens, and whether its conduct accords with international law. In 1913, President Wilson invoked such principles when he refused to recognize the new government of Mexico, headed by Victoriano Huerta (a regime Wilson called "a government of butchers"). Basically the same reasons dictated America's refusal for many years to recognize the Communist regime in Russia and Mao Tse-tung's regime in China.

Nonrecognition of Foreign Governments

If a president can recognize foreign governments, the president can also withdraw or withhold such recognition. In extreme cases, the president can dramatically sever diplomatic relations with another country, as Woodrow Wilson did with imperial Germany before America entered World War I. Another presidential option is to withhold American recognition for an indefinite period, until a country achieves internal political stability or perhaps modifies its behavior. The president can provide a warning to another country by calling the American ambassador home "for consultation," as President Carter did on January 2, 1980, when he recalled U.S. Ambassador to Moscow Thomas J. Watson in response to the Soviet Union's invasion of Afghanistan. And the president can require foreign diplomats in the United States to leave the country if their behavior becomes unacceptable to the White House.

INFORMAL TECHNIQUES OF LEADERSHIP

In addition to these constitutional powers, the chief executive possesses certain informal and extraconstitutional techniques for the management of foreign affairs. Five of these are especially important.

First, the president has unrivaled *access to information sources* required for effective decisionmaking. This information is available to the White House from many origins: departments and agencies within the executive branch; American embassies and other overseas posts; the "intelligence community" (which we shall discuss on p. 23); foreign governments; and from many other sources. The scope and nature of information available to the White House is usually not available to Congress or other rivals to the president's foreign policy role. Moreover, despite the tendency of some recent chief executives and their subordinates to abuse the concept, the confidentiality of this information is often protected by the principle of "executive privilege."

Second, one of the most noteworthy trends in the evolution of the presidency has been the chief executive's influential role *as a legislative leader.* Article II, Section 3 of the Constitution requires the president periodically to provide Congress with information on "the State of the Union." His annual "State of the Union" address, however, is merely one among literally hundreds of messages and recommendations sent from the White House to Capitol Hill. Even more important may be the president's "Budget Message" — normally a document of several hundred pages, containing budget recommendations in all spheres of domestic and foreign governmental activity. As a rule, Congress uses the budgetary recommendations submitted by the White House as a guide to its own deliberations. Although it may depart from presidential recommendations in certain respects, congressional action is massively influenced at all stages by the wishes of the president. After Congress has approved the budget, the president has wide discretion in the administration of the funds available to the executive branch. He may, for example, "re-allocate" funds from one budget category to another; and (although exercise of the power has proved legally controversial in recent years), modern presidents have also "impounded" (or refused to expend) funds provided by Congress for purposes which the White House did not approve.

Modern chief executives interpret their legislative role actively and dynamically. They are not content merely to "submit" their recommendations to Congress; they also recruit officials from almost every executive department and agency (and in some instances, private citizens' organizations) to lobby continuously on Capitol Hill on behalf of the president's program. [15] As we shall see more fully in Chapter 8, Congress has exhibited a mixed attitude toward White House lobbying activity. On the one hand, legislators frequently complain about intense "White House pressure" exerted on them to influence their votes and behavior. On the other hand — in view of the wide diffusion of power and responsibility within Congress itself, and its growing involvement in a broad range of internal and external issues — Congress expects the president to provide such leadership and would be hard pressed to function effectively without it.

The chief executive's unlimited access to information and his unique legislative role are only two of the informal techniques of presidential leadership. A third decisive instrument of executive leadership in foreign relations is *the president's ability to influence public opinion.* Even before the era of modern communications media, chief executives understood the potency of this instrument. President Theodore Roosevelt once observed:

People used to say to me that I was an astonishingly good politician and
divined what the people are going to think. . . . I did not "divine" how
the people were going to think; I simply made up my mind what they
ought to think, and then did my best to get them to think it. [16]

As a molder of public opinion, either in America or outside it, the
president of the United States has no peers. Routinely, the activities of
the chief executive are given maximum coverage by the news media.
Incumbent presidents have a visibility to countless millions of people at
home and abroad which no rival can match. When the White House believes it desirable, the president can pre-empt national TV and radio
coverage to acquaint the people with a crisis or development in foreign
affairs and inform them of the steps he proposes to take in response to it.
Almost invariably, the American people support the course of action favored by the White House. [17] According to an informed student of
American public opinion, once a president has made a decision in foreign affairs that becomes known to the public, he automatically receives
the support of at least 50 percent of the American people, irrespective of
the nature of the decision. [18]

At one time or another, every incumbent president since the 1930s
has been accused of "managing" the news to achieve his foreign policy
objectives. [19] President Franklin D. Roosevelt was a master of radio
communications; he used his "fireside chats" to the American people
with unchallenged effectiveness to rally public opinion behind his policies. During the Cuban missile crisis of 1962, President John F. Kennedy
made a dramatic national TV presentation informing the nation about
the erection of Soviet missile sites in Cuba and presenting his strategy
for responding to that danger. In 1978, President Carter staged a national telecast to inform the American people about the results of his
Camp David mediatory efforts to bring peace in the Arab-Israeli conflict. Although legislators and other citizens opposing the president's position sometimes are granted equal time by national news media to respond, such efforts seldom influence public opinion decisively.

In the fourth place, one of the oldest techniques of presidential leadership and an important instrument in the foreign policy field is *the
president's role as a political leader.* Normally, an incumbent president
is automatically the acknowledged leader of his political party. National
and local candidates value the endorsement of the president in their
political campaigns. While the number of patronage appointments
available to the White House has declined over the past 50 years, the
president still can make a limited number of appointments to federal office. Moreover, White House influence and entrée can be useful to legislators and citizens in dealing with the federal bureaucracy. Most
crucially perhaps, leaders and members of the president's own party are
constantly aware that the results of the next presidential election will
depend substantially upon the president's record in dealing with major
internal and external issues. An outstanding and popular record can be a

decisive force in achieving victory at the polls; a weak and unpopular record poses an obstacle to political victory that will be extremely difficult for the president's party to overcome.

Finally, one of the most decisive instruments of presidential leadership in foreign affairs was illustrated by President Theodore Roosevelt's diplomacy in building the Panama Canal. The first Roosevelt was committed to a policy of "making the dirt fly" in Panama — that is, he was determined to build the canal, despite the opposition of legislators and other critics. Toward that end, he authorized the construction of the canal even before the Senate had approved the Bunau-Varilla treaty (1904). Several years later, President Roosevelt observed:

> If I had followed traditional, conservative methods I would have submitted a dignified State paper . . . to Congress and the debates on it would have been going on yet; but I took the Canal Zone and let Congress debate; and while the debate goes on the Canal does also. [20]

Nearly a half-century later, during the Greek crisis of 1947, President Harry S. Truman committed the United States to a policy of "containment" toward expansive communism. Speaking to his colleagues in the Senate, Senator Arthur H. Vandenberg asserted:

> . . .the overriding fact is that the President has made a long-delayed statement regarding Communism on-the-march which must be supported [by Congress] if there is any hope of ever impressing Moscow with the necessity of paying any sort of peaceful attention to us. . . . [21]

Senator Vandenberg was alluding to *the president's power to commit the nation to a position or course of action in foreign affairs.* Once the chief executive had done so publicly, it was extremely difficult for Congress or public opinion to repudiate the president's policy. Failure to support the White House during the Greek crisis or comparable episodes could have highly inimical consequences for the security of the United States, for the nation's image abroad, for the credibility of its national commitments, and for many other dimensions of foreign affairs.

Towering above constitutional grants of authority to the president and various informal modes of executive leadership is this reality: the president of the United States is the head of state and acknowledged leader of the most powerful nation perhaps in the history of the world. The American people look to the White House for effective leadership in responding to internal and external crises and in protecting American interests abroad. When White House leadership in foreign affairs was characterized as "indecisive" and "irresolute" — as occurred in the Carter administration — the president's popularity was likely to drop sharply. When the chief executive provided clear and forceful direction to the nation's diplomacy, experience indicated that his actions would usually receive overwhelming public approval.[22] The graph on page 20 of President Carter's approval rating illustrates the correlation between the president's leadership in foreign affairs and his popularity.

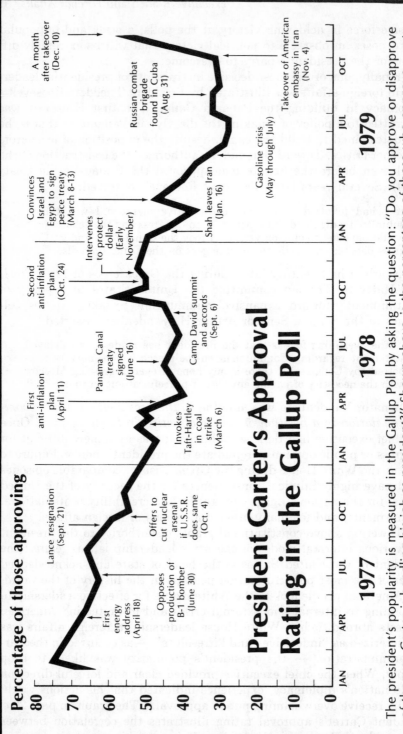

President Carter's Approval Rating in the Gallup Poll

Percentage of those approving

80
70
60
50
40
30
20
10

First energy address (April 18)

Opposes production of B-1 bomber (June 30)

Lance resignation (Sept. 21)

Offers to cut nuclear arsenal if U.S.S.R. does same (Oct. 4)

Invokes Taft-Hartley in coal strike (March 6)

First anti-inflation plan (April 11)

Panama Canal treaty signed (June 16)

Camp David summit and accords (Sept. 6)

Second anti-inflation plan (Oct. 24)

Intervenes to protect dollar (Early November)

Convinces Israel and Egypt to sign peace treaty (March 8-13)

Shah leaves Iran (Jan. 16)

Gasoline crisis (May through July)

Russian combat brigade found in Cuba (Aug. 31)

Takeover of American embassy in Iran (Nov. 4)

A month after takeover (Dec. 10)

JAN APR JUL OCT JAN APR JUL OCT JAN APR JUL OCT

1977   **1978**   **1979**

The president's popularity is measured in the Gallup Poll by asking the question: "Do you approve or disapprove of the way Carter is handling his job as president?" Shown above is the percentage of those who approve.

THE ROLE OF THE STATE DEPARTMENT

In the American system of government, the executive agency most directly concerned with foreign affairs is the Department of State, headed by the secretary of state, the highest ranking cabinet officer. The State Department is America's "foreign office"; under the authority of the president it supervises relations with over 150 independent nations around the world, with organizations like the United Nations, and with regional bodies like the Organization of American States (OAS). Yet from the perspective of its annual operating budget (about $1.4 billion in 1979) and its size (around 22,000 employees), the State Department ranks as one of the smallest executive departments. (The Department of Health, Education and Welfare, for example, has approximately five times as many employees.)

Traditionally, the State Department's primary concern has been political relations with foreign countries. Its five regional bureaus serve as the nucleus for communicating policy decisions to American embassies abroad and for receiving communications from them. Since World War II, there has also been a significant expansion in the department's "functional" bureaus — such as economic and business relations, international organizations' affairs, public affairs, and (one of the newest concerns) international environmental and scientific affairs.

Still another postwar development has been the department's recognition of a growing congressional role in foreign relations. An assistant secretary of state for congressional relations is assigned specific responsibility for maintaining constructive relations with Congress, and this function has become an increasingly important and time-consuming dimension of State Department activities. The Office of Congressional Relations collects and analyzes information on legislative attitudes toward foreign policy issues; it provides services requested by members of Congress, such as foreign travel arrangements; and, when required, it plays a prominent role in White House lobbying on Capitol Hill for the president's foreign policy program. State Department services to Congress sometimes take interesting forms. Former Secretary of State Dean Acheson recounted that for certain external programs (like foreign aid), legislators often felt compelled, for domestic political reasons, to oppose them. In one case, the State Department helped a legislator resolve that dilemma "by the promise of a powerful speech against the foreign aid bill when it came up for final vote in the House. We [the State Department] duly wrote it and all parties profited!" [23]

As we shall see more fully in Chapter 7, during the 1970s — and especially after the Carter administration took office in 1977 — protecting and promoting international human rights became a leading goal of American foreign policy. This new emphasis (or, more accurately, this intensified concern with an old theme in American diplomacy) was reflected in organizational changes within the State Department. Largely

at the instigation of Congress, the Office of Human Rights and Humanitarian Affairs, headed by an assistant secretary of state, was created
within the department. Its overall function was to keep human rights at
the forefront of American diplomatic concern; and, as required by law, it
supplied Congress with voluminous material on international human
rights questions.

Also under the direct supervision of the State Department is the
Agency for International Development (AID). Established in 1961, this
agency was given responsibility for administering American economic
and technical assistance programs to other countries. An indication of
America's declining involvement in foreign aid is provided by the reduction in AID's employees: from more than 15,000 in 1965 to just over 6,500
in 1979.

Routinely, newly elected presidents announce that they regard the
secretary of state as their chief foreign policy adviser and expect the secretary to provide overall direction to governmental activities in foreign
affairs. Yet in practice, the decline of the State Department's pre-eminence in the foreign policy field since World War II has been evident
to all careful observers. The department's image — with the White
House, with other executive agencies, with Congress, and often with
other governments — has been chronically poor. To the minds of some
presidents, the State Department has epitomized bureaucratic inertia,
devotion to traditionalism, and lack of imaginative leadership. [24] Ever
since the administration of President Franklin D. Roosevelt, presidents
have been prone to bypass the State Department; using one device or
another, they have ignored it and made crucial decisions without
consulting it. [25]

Almost every secretary of state for the past generation has left office
under a cloud of public and congressional criticism. Some (like John
Foster Dulles and Henry Kissinger) were repeatedly accused of making
decisions unilaterally and of ignoring their State Department subordinates. Others (like Dean Rusk and William Rogers) faced the complaint
that they were weak and not forceful enough in presenting State Department viewpoints to the president. Indicative of the State Department's
decline from its earlier position of primacy is the large number of studies
of its role. Since the early 1950s, more than 60 major studies have been
undertaken and many of these have been followed by reorganizations of
the department in the hope of restoring its once dominant role in the foreign policy process. [26]

The erosion of the State Department's position can be explained by
many factors and developments — some within the department and others extrinsic to it. Critics of the department have complained that it has
been slow to adapt its procedures and ideas to a rapidly changing world,
leaving the White House no choice but to look elsewhere for creative and
imaginative policy recommendations. Another trend — the growing involvement of a host of other executive agencies in foreign relations —

has diluted the State Department's authority and responsibility. Among all the departments and agencies of the national government, the State Department suffers from certain unique disabilities. As has often been said, the department has no "domestic constituency" to support its activities. Unlike the Labor or Agriculture departments, its programs are not usually supported by powerful domestic lobbies and citizens' groups. As often as not, the State Department has what might be called "negative constituents": those individuals and groups who vocally *oppose* American foreign policy toward Egypt, or Greece, or Cuba. (One of these — the pro-Israeli lobby in the United States — is discussed in Chapter 4.)

On Capitol Hill, the State Department is likely to be regarded as a "troublemaker" for legislators; it advocates costly foreign economic and military aid programs, which are frequently unpopular with the American people and are political liabilities for members of Congress. Alternatively, the State Department is often envisioned as the "Department of Bad News." Each year since World War II, the State Department has had to report to Congress and the American people on some actual or potential crisis in the Middle East, some ominous Soviet threat to American security, or discouraging information about the economic deterioration of countries throughout the Third World. Somehow, many Americans believe, if "the department operated more effectively," the United States would confront more favorable conditions abroad. [27] The frustration felt by members of Congress and their constituents on foreign policy issues are directed at the State Department — and this fact in turn adversely affects its morale and performance.

THE INTELLIGENCE COMMUNITY

Two other categories of executive agencies involved in the foreign policy process require brief examination. One of these is called the "intelligence community," consisting of those agencies and governmental bureaus (40 or more) which exercise intelligence functions within the American government. The principal members of the community were named in the formal definition of the intelligence community in Executive Order 12036, issued by President Jimmy Carter on January 24, 1978. These 11 agencies are:

The Central Intelligence Agency
The National Security Agency
The Defense Intelligence Agency
"The offices within the Department of Defense for the collection of specialized national foreign intelligence through reconnaissance programs"
The Bureau of Intelligence and Research of the Department of State
Army Intelligence

Navy Intelligence
Air Force Intelligence
The Federal Bureau of Investigation
The Department of the Treasury
The Department of Energy
The Drug Enforcement Administration

Intelligence is a minor part of the overall activities of some of these agencies in terms of money spent or people employed. Nonetheless, it is important in terms of national security and the total flow of information to the United States government. The function which makes the FBI part of the intelligence community is "counterintelligence" — that is, identifying covert foreign agents in the United States and frustrating foreign efforts at espionage and subversion. The role of the State Department's Bureau of Intelligence and Research is primarily analysis. The main contribution of the Treasury Department is to provide economic, financial, and monetary information. The function of the Department of Energy is to collect intelligence data concerning atomic energy and particularly to monitor atomic testing by other countries; but reporting on energy matters generally is of growing importance to national policymakers. The Drug Enforcement Administration has a wide network of agents concerned with intelligence about the trade in narcotics. [28]

As every reader of the daily headlines is aware, in recent years public controversy has surrounded the activities of members of the intelligence community — notably, the CIA — at home and overseas. Following the Watergate episode during the Nixon administration, for example, both executive and legislative officials investigated CIA's past operations and reassessed its purpose and missions. Sentiment emerged on Capitol Hill for bringing CIA and other intelligence activities more directly under the supervision of Congress. President Gerald R. Ford issued new executive guidelines governing intelligence operations. [29] Chapter 6 is devoted to a detailed description and analysis of recent efforts by Congress to investigate intelligence operations and to bring them under more stringent executive and legislative control. Two general observations about intelligence activities within the American democratic context are worth making here.

First, today, as in the past, the intelligence function continues to be recognized by officials on both ends of Pennsylvania Avenue, and by a majority of citizens, as an essential contribution to the preservation of national security and to the achievement of American diplomatic objectives. The Central Intelligence Agency was established in 1947 in large part because of vivid recollections by the American people and their leaders of the military disaster at Pearl Harbor (rightly or wrongly, viewed as an "intelligence failure" by the American government). Almost 40 years after Pearl Harbor, Americans were once more confronted with the adverse consequences of a crippled or inadequate intelligence community; in October 1979 the presence of a large Soviet military force in Cuba was belatedly discovered by the Carter administration. The collapse of the Iranian monarchy in 1979 also caught American officials (along with those in most other governments) by surprise.

Second, the dilemma created by the establishment of the CIA in the postwar era, and by the subsequent expansion of the intelligence community, largely remains unresolved today. It arises out of the conflict between two antithetical ideas: realization that failure to conduct effective intelligence operations can court national disaster (as at Pearl Harbor), versus a desire for open diplomacy, freedom of the press, freedom of access to governmental information, and public disclosure of actions of government officials — concepts deeply embedded in the American ethos. The tension in a democracy between these two ideas is real, continuing, and perhaps inescapable. If, as Chapter 6 suggests, congressional efforts to monitor and regulate intelligence operations have been less than completely satisfactory, the reason may be that the dilemma admits no simple or easy solution.

PROPAGANDA AND INFORMATIONAL PROGRAMS

The other executive agency playing a key role in foreign affairs is the International Communication Agency (ICA), formerly called the United States Information Agency (USIA). Although it is a separate administrative agency, ICA takes its policy guidance from the State Department. The agency's mission is to conduct propaganda and informational activities abroad in behalf of the American government. Perhaps its best known activity is the "Voice of America," the nation's worldwide radio network. In addition, ICA engages in a variety of other activities and programs — such as the production and distribution of films, the preparation of press releases, the sponsorship of cultural, scientific and other kinds of exhibits and lectures, and the operation of numerous overseas libraries containing books and other publications by Americans.

Ever since its creation in the early postwar period, controversy has surrounded the mission of America's propaganda establishment. ICA (and USIA before it) has had a stormy existence; during some periods, frequent turnover has occurred among officials engaged in propaganda activities. In a large part, this phenomenon can be explained by the conflict between two conceptions of the agency's proper mission. One view holds that it was intended to be primarily a *propaganda instrument* of the American government. As such, its dominant function ought to be portraying the internal and external policies of the United States in the most favorable light possible to foreign societies. The other conception is that ICA's principal mission is to engage in a "Campaign of Truth," as America's propaganda and informational program was designated by the Truman administration. This view would require the agency to be factual and objective in its depiction of the American society, with no attempt to gloss over its shortcomings and failures. (The underlying assumption of this approach is that objectivity is "the best propaganda" for a democratic nation.) The conflict between these two schools of thought has impeded the effectiveness of American propaganda and informational campaigns in the past and will likely continue to do so in the future. [30]

THE MILITARY ESTABLISHMENT AND FOREIGN AFFAIRS

Among national policymakers and informed citizens, World War II produced a realization that was not always present in earlier eras of American diplomacy: the military establishment plays a vital role in the foreign policy process. As late as that global conflict, both civilian and military officials tended to separate political and military questions sharply — as illustrated by President Franklin D. Roosevelt's view that the resolution of "political" questions arising during the war ought to await the outcome of military hostilities. [31] By the end of the war — after a new political-military conflict known as the Cold War had erupted among the Allies — American officials recognized the indissoluble link between these two aspects of national policy.

Following a prolonged study, a new Department of Defense was created in 1947 and other reforms of the American military establishment were undertaken. While the traditional American pattern of separate military services was preserved, they were brought under the jurisdiction of a single department, headed by a civilian secretary of defense. The Joint Chiefs of Staff (consisting of the commanders of each of the military branches and a chairman) was created to formulate unified military strategy.

Today, the Department of Defense has more than one million civilian employees, more than two million military personnel under its direction, and an annual budget at the end of the 1970s exceeding $139 billion. Some 733 American military bases overseas operated under the Pentagon's supervision. During this same period, around $50 billion was expended annually by DOD for goods and services required to maintain the military establishment. Operations of this magnitude inevitably generate public and congressional apprehension about excessive "military influence" over policymaking. While this fear was widely expressed during the Vietnam War, by the period of the Carter administration the opposite complaint was heard: that the military point of view on important external questions was being ignored by civilian officials in the Defense Department and the White House. [32]

Despite the experience of the Vietnam War and earlier conflicts, the principle of civilian supremacy continues to govern the role of the military establishment in the formulation and execution of national policy. Strategic assessments and calculations by military officials obviously must be considered in the stage of policy formulation; and the armed forces sometimes must be utilized to achieve national security and diplomatic objectives. Yet no military officials are members of the National Security Council. As has been true for more than two centuries, ultimate decisionmaking authority belongs to the president, who relies heavily upon civilian advisers. In the last analysis, presidential decisions (like White House budget recommendations to Congress) will largely determine the nature of the armed forces and their role in external policy.

OTHER EXECUTIVE AGENCIES AND FOREIGN AFFAIRS

A striking and highly significant development since World War II has been the increased interest and involvement in foreign relations by departments and agencies within the executive branch. The list of agency involvement is almost endless, and it becomes longer every year. The Agriculture, Commerce, Defense, Treasury, Interior, and Labor departments all have responsibility for problems having a foreign policy dimension. [33] For example, the Agriculture Department has played a pivotal role for many years in the "Food for Peace" program, which ships American food products to needy countries; it is also keenly interested in promoting agricultural exports to countries like Japan and other customers; and it has sent hundreds of experts abroad to assist less developed societies in raising their agricultural output. As has always been the case, the Commerce Department seeks to expand American business, investment, and trade opportunities abroad. The Treasury Department is actively concerned with fiscal and monetary issues, such as the soundness of the American dollar overseas. The Transportation Department seeks to formulate a national transportation policy, integrating both domestic and foreign resources. Even the Interior Department has responsibilities impinging upon foreign affairs (such as water reclamation projects involving the United States and Mexico).

A growing number of smaller and lesser known federal agencies has acquired responsibilities giving them a role in foreign relations. The National Aeronautics and Space Administration (NASA) sponsors space programs directly affecting the global balance of military power and America's ability to monitor the military progress of other countries. The Arms Control and Disarmament Agency is responsible for preparing reports and recommendations to the president on arms limitation proposals (such as SALT II). The Department of Energy is concerned about the proliferation of nuclear weapons abroad and about the safe disposal of nuclear waste products by all nations.

This proliferation of executive agencies involved in foreign affairs has had a parallel tendency within Congress, as we shall see more fully in Chapter 2. Today, there is hardly a legislative committee or sub-committee whose activities do not relate in some way to foreign affairs. The resulting linkage — the "connections" often established between an expanding number of executive agencies and the corresponding commit-tees of Congress — poses an increasingly difficult problem for the cre-ation and maintenance of unified governmental efforts abroad.

COORDINATING EXECUTIVE EFFORTS ABROAD

Threats to the unity of American foreign policy can arise from sev-eral sources, two of which are directly pertinent to our study: divisions and conflicts *within the executive branch* and disunity *between the White House and Congress* on foreign policy questions. At this stage, our interest is confined to the former problem. As Senator Vandenberg once bluntly informed the Truman administration: members of the Repub-lican Party wanted to cooperate with the White House in behalf of a "bi-partisan foreign policy," but they could only do so with one secretary of state at a time! The problem to which Vandenberg alluded has become more acute since the early postwar period. The Carter administration's response to the collapse of the Iranian monarchy in 1979, for example, in the words of one report, became

> the subject of fierce internal debate [within the executive branch], with many officials asserting that interagency disputes and bureaucratic compromises have hampered the efforts of Mr. Carter and his top advisers to fashion and carry out an overall strategy. [34]

The Carter administration's diplomatic efforts were impeded by "the creation of large, unwieldy committees" which — although designed to unify executive efforts in foreign affairs — had compounded the problem of "defining coherent policy goals and seeing them through." Another commentator found that the outstanding characteristic of executive policymaking in the late 1970s was "fragmentation," or the tendency of American policy to move "in a bewildering variety of directions," and to involve "a number of conflicting actors and centrifugal forces." [35]

These disabilities were in no sense unique with the Carter admin-istration, although they may have reached a new level of acuteness and public concern during that period. As successive executive departments and agencies have been drawn into the foreign policy process, incumbent presidents have relied upon various administrative devices to unify their activities. As we have already seen, the National Security Council was established early in the postwar period to provide such coordination on issues directly affecting national security. Interdepartmental commit-tees function at all levels of the national government with regard to spe-cific foreign policy issues involving more than one agency. Some chief executives, such as President Johnson, have relied upon special groups of advisers (called the "Tuesday group") to arrive at unified policy decisions. Under President Kennedy, the concept of the "country team" was introduced. In an effort to unify American governmental activities in foreign countries, all officials within a given country perform their duties under the supervision of the American ambassador (who, of course, receives instructions from the State Department, and ultimately from the president). Other presidents have designated the secretary of state as their principal foreign policy adviser and directed that the secretary assume responsibility for assuring unified executive efforts in foreign affairs.

Undoubtedly most of these techniques have been useful. Their value has often depended heavily upon the personality and operating style of the incumbent president. On some occasions, the executive branch has displayed extraordinary unity in dealing with a particular foreign policy issue (as in the Kennedy administration's handling of the Cuban missile crisis in 1962).[36] Yet the problem of fragmented and divided efforts within the executive branch continues to serve as an impediment to effective diplomacy by the United States.

To a significant degree, the problem reflects three facts about America's role in international relations. First, the United States is a *superpower*, with major and minor commitments in every region of a world gripped by rapid, and often revolutionary, change. As often as not, these commitments have been assumed as the result of insistent urging by other countries — which both elicit American assistance in solving their problems and are resistant to American "dictation" or guidance in doing so. By 1980, a case in point was Egyptian President Anwar al-Sadat's request for the United States and other countries to underwrite a multibillion-dollar "Carter Plan" to promote Egyptian economic progress and development. Yet for several years, Cairo had been highly resistant to outside suggestions directed toward Egyptian internal reforms, the elimination of corruption, and other steps required to make such aid effective.

Moreover, at home and abroad government has become *more involved in the lives of citizens and groups at all levels.* Efforts to solve the global "population problem," for example, require nothing less than successfully changing the traditional beliefs (in some instances the religious beliefs) and life styles of the Indian villagers, the peasants of the Nile Valley, and the slum dwellers of Mexico City. Such challenges have contributed to the "bureaucratization" of the foreign policy process; the growth of federal agencies competing for power, prestige, and jurisdiction; and the routine (and often successful) questioning of the State Department's once unchallenged position in foreign affairs.

Finally, the tendency toward uncoordinated executive activities in the foreign policy field reflects a fundamental change in the *nature of the international system* within the past two decades or so. What is sometimes called the "international agenda" — or those global and regional issues of dominant concern in Washington and other capitals —

has changed significantly since the early postwar period. As Secretary of State Henry Kissinger said in 1975:

> The problems of energy resources, environment, population, the uses of space and the seas, now rank with questions of military security, ideology, and territorial rivalry which have traditionally made up the diplomatic agenda. [37]

If executive agencies involved in the foreign policy process seem confused and disunified in their activities, the reason may be essentially that they *are* confused and uncertain about how the United States can effectively use its power to respond to a variety of novel and difficult problems that demand solution during the second half of the twentieth century. In turn, the disunity sometimes evident within the executive branch has greatly compounded the problem of achieving cooperative executive-legislative relations on major foreign policy issues.

NOTES

1. James B. Reston, "The Press, the President and Foreign Policy," *Foreign Affairs,* 44 (July 1966): 560.
2. Roger Hilsman, *The Politics of Policy Making in Defense and Foreign Affairs* (New York: Harper & Row, 1971), p. 18.
3. For more detailed discussion of the meaning and connotations of diplomacy, see Elmer Plischke, "The New Diplomacy: A Changing Process," *Virginia Quarterly Review,* 49 (Summer 1973): 321-345.
4. For fuller elaboration of this point, see the discussion on the "different worlds" which the State Department and Congress occupy, in Smith Simpson, *Anatomy of the State Department* (Boston: Houghton Mifflin Co., 1967), pp. 152-183.
5. For a succinct discussion of the intentions of the founders regarding the powers of the president and Congress in foreign affairs, see the report prepared by the Library of Congress for the House Foreign Affairs Committee, *Background Information on the Use of the United States Armed Forces in Foreign Countries,* 91st Cong., 2d sess., 1970. A more detailed treatment of individual constitutional provisions is provided in *The Constitution of the United States of America: Analysis and Interpretation* (Washington, D.C.: The Library of Congress, 1973).
6. A useful compendium of conflicting interpretations of the president's prerogatives over the armed forces is provided in the Senate Foreign Relations Committee, *Hearings on the War Powers Legislation,* 92d Cong., 1st sess. (March 8-October 6, 1971).
7. An informative discussion of the president's use of the armed forces to achieve diplomatic goals since World War II is Herbert K. Tillema, *Appeal to Force: American Military Intervention in the Era of Containment* (New York: Thomas Y. Crowell Co., 1973).
8. See *The New York Times,* December 20, 1978, dispatch by James Reston; and the editorial, "Unmaking a Treaty," on January 20, 1979. For summaries of the Supreme Court's decision in the case, see *The Washington Post,* December 14, 1979; and the Congressional Quarterly *Weekly Report* 37 (December 15, 1979): 2850.
9. Loch Johnson and James M. McCormick, "Foreign Policy by Executive Fiat," *Foreign Policy,* 28 (Fall 1977): 117. This article provides a com-

prehensive and illuminating discussion of White House reliance upon executive agreements since World War II and of Congress' response to that tendency.

10. Ibid., p. 118.
11. Ibid., pp. 118-124.
12. *The New York Times,* March 2, 1979.
13. *The New York Times,* February 13, 1979.
14. For more detailed discussion of the role and utility of presidential representatives see W. Averell Harriman and Elie Abel, *Special Envoy to Churchill and Stalin: 1941-1946* (New York: Random House, 1975).
15. For more detailed discussion of lobbying by governmental agencies, see *The Washington Lobby,* 3d ed. (Washington, D.C.: Congressional Quarterly, 1979).
16. Quoted in Sidney Warren, *The President as World Leader* (New York: McGraw-Hill Book Co., 1964), p. 23.
17. The president's crucial role in influencing public attitudes — and the flexibility which public opinion accords him in the management of foreign affairs — is a major theme of Bernard C. Cohen, *The Public's Impact on Foreign Policy* (Boston: Little, Brown & Co., 1973).
18. Daniel Yankelovich, "Farewell to 'President Knows Best,' " *Foreign Affairs,* 57 (1978): 670. The author concludes, however, that the "automatic support" factor for public approval of the president's foreign policy decisions is rapidly changing.
19. See, for example, the complaints expressed by several national news reporters about White House news "management," in David E. Haight and Larry D. Johnston, *The President: Roles and Powers* (Skokie, Ill.: Rand McNally, 1965), pp. 275-281.
20. Quoted in Thomas A. Bailey, *A Diplomatic History of the American People,* 8th ed. (New York: Appleton-Century-Crofts, 1969), p. 497.
21. Arthur H. Vandenberg, Jr., ed., *The Private Papers of Senator Vandenberg* (Boston: Houghton Mifflin Co., 1952), p. 344.
22. See the discussion of congressional perceptions of President Carter's diplomatic leadership in *The New York Times,* February 17, 1979.
23. Dean Acheson, *Present at the Creation: My Years in the State Department* (New York: W. W. Norton & Co., 1969), p. 93.
24. No modern president perhaps has been more prone to bypass the State Department than President Kennedy. For a discussion of Kennedy's views toward the department, see Theodore C. Sorensen, *Kennedy* (New York: Harper & Row, 1965), pp. 287-290. On one occasion, Soviet Premier Nikita Khrushchev complained to Kennedy about his own diplomatic officials, who "specialized in why something had not worked forty years ago," and he urged Kennedy to formulate his own views. See Sorensen, *Kennedy,* pp. 554-555.
25. A recent example was provided by the Carter administration's diplomacy during the "Iranian crisis" of 1979. According to one report the president sent a high-ranking American military officer attached to NATO to confer directly with Iranian military leaders; this official "was told by the White House to bypass the United States Embassy" in Tehran. Similarly, discussion between members of the White House staff and Iranian diplomatic officials left the American ambassador to Iran in ignorance about these communications. See *The New York Times,* January 12, 1979, dispatch by Richard Burt.
26. For a more detailed analysis of the State Department's postwar decline, see Robert Pringle, "Creeping Irrelevance at Foggy Bottom," *Foreign Policy,* 29 (Winter 1977-78): 128-140.

27. Robert A. Dahl, "Congress and Foreign Policy," in Sidney Wise and Richard F. Schier, eds., *Studies on Congress* (New York: Thomas Y. Crowell, 1969), pp. 207-208.

28. The evolution of the American intelligence system during and after World War II is discussed in Allen Dulles, *The Craft of Intelligence* (New York: New American Library, 1965). More detailed information on the agencies comprising the "intelligence community" may be found in Lyman B. Kirkpatrick, Jr., *The U.S. Intelligence Community: Foreign Policy and Domestic Activities* (New York: Hill & Wang, 1973); and in David Wise and Thomas B. Ross, *The Invisible Government: the CIA and U.S. Intelligence* (New York: Random House, 1974).

29. On February 18, 1976, President Ford issued Executive Order No. 11905, redefining the missions of the CIA and other intelligence agencies. On the same day, he called upon Congress to engage in more effective oversight of intelligence operations by creating a Joint Foreign Intelligence Committee. See *Weekly Compilation of Presidential Documents* (Washington, D.C.: General Services Administration), January 5, 1976, pp. 234-244.

30. The evolution of American propaganda and informational activities in foreign affairs is traced in John W. Henderson, *The United States Information Agency* (New York: Praeger Publishers, 1969). For a discussion of various theories and goals of American propaganda programs, see Terry L. Deibel and Walter R. Roberts, *Culture and Information: Two Foreign Policy Functions* (Beverly Hills, Calif.: Sage Publications, 1976). The reports by the director of the International Communication Agency to Congress on the agency's activities provide current information.

31. For a typical expression of this view during World War II by a high-ranking American military leader, see General Omar N. Bradley, *A Soldier's Story* (New York: Holt, Rinehart & Winston, 1951), p. 536. And for the Roosevelt administration's approach to political issues during the war, see Gaddis Smith, *American Diplomacy During the Second World War* (New York: John Wiley & Sons, 1966), pp. 12-16.

32. Detailed information on the scope and nature of Defense Department activities, along with problems which the agency is experiencing, are presented in "Shaking Up the Pentagon," *U.S. News & World Report,* 85 (July 17, 1978): 33-38.

33. A noteworthy tendency since World War II has been the active role taken by the labor movement in the United States with regard to foreign policy issues. For background on this development, see Ronald Radosch, *American Labor and United States Foreign Policy* (New York: Random House, 1969). American labor's more contemporary foreign policy activities and interests are discussed in Lane Kirkland, *et al.,* "Labor's International Role," *Foreign Policy,* 26 (Spring 1977): 204-248.

34. *The New York Times,* January 12, 1979, dispatch by Richard Burt.

35. Stanley Hoffmann, "A View from at Home: The Perils of Incoherence," *Foreign Affairs,* 57 (Winter 1978-79): 463.

36. For an interesting and informative discussion of successful executive efforts to coordinate foreign policy decisionmaking, see Robert F. Kennedy, *Thirteen Days: A Memoir of the Cuban Missile Crisis* (New York: New American Library, 1969).

37. Secretary Kissinger's views are quoted in Joseph S. Nye, Jr., "Independence and Interdependence," *Foreign Policy,* 22 (Spring 1976): 135.

2

Congress and Foreign Affairs: Its Traditional and Contemporary Roles

When the 96th Congress convened early in 1979, Frank Church, D-Idaho, became the new chairman of the Senate Foreign Relations Committee. Senator Church announced that under his direction the committee proposed to play an active and influential role in the foreign policy process. He was determined that the committee would achieve a role of "prominence in foreign affairs" and promised "the kind of leadership that will give it a common purpose and direction." When the committee's views differed from those of the White House on important diplomatic questions, then the committee "should become the main forum for opposing the White House and opening up public debate."[1]

Senator Church's conception of the role of the Senate Foreign Relations Committee reflected in microcosm the new assertiveness witnessed in recent years on Capitol Hill with regard to foreign affairs. In 1973, Senator Sam J. Ervin, D-N.C., called upon his legislative colleagues to challenge the prevailing idea that "American foreign relations are within the [exclusive] domain of the President"; Congress should reassert its "primary responsibility for the determination of substantive foreign policy."[2] For several years, Congress has been urged to exert its prerogatives more forcefully in the foreign policy field. Under the Carter administration, State Department officials called upon Congress to participate more fully with the executive branch in the conduct of foreign relations.[3]

CONGRESSIONAL ASSERTIVENESS: THE CHALLENGE AND THE PROBLEMS

All informed students of recent American foreign relations are aware that in the early postwar era the great milestones in the nation's diplomacy — establishment of the United Nations, the Greek-Turkish

Aid Program (1947), the Marshall Plan for European recovery (1948), NATO, and President Truman's "Point Four" program of aid to the developing countries (1949) — emerged as the result of collaboration between executive and legislative policymakers. Over the next 20 years, however, congressional influence in foreign relations declined, reaching its nadir during the period of the Vietnam War. During that period, the chairman of the Senate Foreign Relations Committee, Senator J. William Fulbright, D-Ark., lamented the decline in congressional influence in the foreign policy process — and he attributed the blame in no small measure to members of the committee who were unwilling to attend its meetings and to inform themselves adequately on important foreign policy issues.[4]

According to a student of the legislative process in the United States, Congress has "always been uncertain about its role in the field of foreign affairs."[5] Can Congress become a dynamic and effective force in foreign relations? Can it, as some proponents of a more influential legislative role advocate, emerge as a "partner" with the president in the foreign policy realm? A revitalization of legislative influence in external affairs faces numerous major and minor obstacles, most of which we shall discuss later.

At the outset, we need to be cognizant of the existence and consequences of a problem that has impeded effective legislative participation in the foreign policy process for more than two centuries and may be a more formidable obstacle today than at any stage in American history. In 1777, the Continental Congress established a five-member Committee for Foreign Affairs to conduct external relations. Yet, as one study found, "Partisanship and personalities, frequent changes in personnel and the use of special committees impaired the efficient functioning of the committee and made a coherent policy impossible." Congressional management of foreign relations was characterized by "fluctuation . . . delay and indecision"; and this was a primary reason why, despite their suspicion of executive power, the Founding Fathers strengthened the powers of the executive branch in the Constitution. As much as any other single factor, it was *the mismanagement of foreign affairs by Congress* under the Articles of Confederation that led to the calling of the Constitutional Convention in 1787.[6]

Evidence in the contemporary period indicates that the same conditions — the continuing diffusion of power and responsibility within Congress, and its inability to coordinate activities in the foreign policy field — are no less present today than in the late eighteenth century.[7] To illustrate the problem, let us examine the organization of the first session of the 95th Congress (1977). Of the 22 standing and special committees of the Senate, approximately half exercised major or minor jurisdiction over foreign affairs. Two of these — the Senate Armed Services and Foreign Relations committees — were directly and regularly concerned with national security and diplomatic questions.

The Foreign Relations Committee had nine subcommittees having jurisdiction over selected aspects of foreign relations (e.g., for African affairs, for European affairs, for foreign assistance). Since the mid-1950s, the United States has provided some $25 billion in food aid to foreign countries, much of it under Public Law 480 (the "Food for Peace" program). These and other agricultural programs came under the jurisdiction of the Senate Agriculture, Nutrition, and Forestry Committee.[8]

The Senate Appropriations Committee had three subcommittees dealing with national defense and foreign policy issues. The Senate Commerce, Science and Transportation Committee had four subcommittees (on aviation; on communications; on the Merchant Marine and tourism; and on science, technology and space exploration) whose jurisdictions impinged upon foreign affairs. A relatively new concern of Congress has been the energy crisis: three subcommittees of the Senate Energy and Natural Resources Committee dealt with international aspects of that problem. The Senate Finance Committee also had an energy subcommittee, along with one on international trade and another on "Tourism and Sugar." The Senate Governmental Affairs Committee had a subcommittee on Energy and Nuclear Proliferation; another of its subcommittees dealt with investigations (although all legislative committees can conduct investigations independently). Immigration into the United States was the province of the Senate Judiciary Committee. The Senate also had a Select Intelligence Committee, which had legislative and budgetary responsibility over the "intelligence community" within the executive branch.

A similar pattern can be found in the House of Representatives, where if anything the network of overlapping committee jurisdictions is even more complex and confusing. In 1977, approximately 56 House subcommittees were active in some dimension of foreign affairs!

A few examples from recent American diplomatic experience will highlight the problems created by this diffusion of responsibility in formulating and carrying out a unified national policy abroad. In 1962, in the face of outspoken White House opposition, the House Ways and Means Committee voted to deny trade concessions to Yugoslavia and Poland. Although this action was ultimately rejected by Congress, it threatened to reverse the policy of "building bridges" to Eastern Europe, to which the United States government was committed.[9] Several years later, within a two-year period, a bipartisan group of senators led a movement to reduce American military forces stationed in the NATO area (another step opposed by successive presidents); and the chairman of the Joint Congressional Committee on Atomic Energy called for greater European involvement in any decision to employ nuclear weapons in defense of the NATO area. The latter proposal encountered massive opposition both from the White House and from other legislators.[10]

During the same period, the Senate Foreign Relations Committee was investigating the Johnson administration's conduct of the Vietnam

War. After witnessing the factionalism present within the committee, one member said, "There are 19 men on it, and they represent 21-1/2 viewpoints." A pervasive feeling existed on Capitol Hill that the Senate Foreign Relations Committee was "rudderless and floundering," and that it was rapidly losing its influence as the Senate's spokesman on foreign policy issues.[11]

In 1977, President Jimmy Carter encountered strong congressional opposition to his policies towards South Korea, Southeast Asia, and southern Africa. More than at any time in recent memory, political leaders in the House and Senate were hard pressed to rally support on Capitol Hill for the president's foreign policy proposals.[12] Yet Congress was experiencing very little success in arriving at unified foreign policy positions of its own. On national security policy, for example, right-wing groups on Capitol Hill opposed further arms limitation (as in the SALT II accords with Moscow) and called for increased American defense spending; left-wing and liberal groups opposed increases in the national defense budget; and a third group demanded across-the-board reductions in all governmental spending.[13]

By the late 1970s, the House of Representatives sought to acquire greater influence in foreign policymaking. The effectiveness of the House in exerting its influence, however, was undercut by internal fragmentation.[14] The Senate finally approved, and the president signed, the new Panama Canal treaties. But the House Merchant Marine and Fisheries Committee was sharply critical of them; some members were determined to prevent the treaties from taking effect. Four other House committees were considering legislation needed to implement the treaties.[15]

The decentralization of authority and responsibility witnessed within Congress since World War II has also aggravated the problem of constructive executive-legislative relations in the foreign policy field. In the period following the Vietnam War — with both the American people and their leaders uncertain and confused about the basic principles that ought to guide the nation's diplomatic efforts — the challenge of producing unified governmental policies became extraordinarily difficult. More perhaps than at any time in its history, Congress appeared to be subject to centrifugal and decentralizing tendencies impairing its ability to arrive at coherent national policies and programs. As we noted in Chapter 1, disunified efforts have also increasingly characterized the foreign policy activities of the executive branch — and this fact in turn has contributed to Congress' rather fragmented and uncoordinated activities in the foreign policy field.[16]

Since World War II, executive and legislative officials alike have been mindful of the need for national unity and have endeavored (during some periods more than others) to build a bipartisan foundation under American foreign policy. One study, for example, found that in a typical year during the 1960s the secretary of defense and the secretary of state, in their attempt to justify American arms aid programs abroad, maintained close liaison with no less than 10 major committees on Capitol Hill. Foreign economic aid was normally reviewed by five major legislative committees; but executive officials might have to deal with as many as 30 committees and subcommittees of Congress on specific aspects of the foreign aid program.[17] During certain periods, the secretary of state perhaps devoted more time to congressional relations than to foreign affairs. Yet, ironically, almost every secretary of state since World War II has left office under severe criticism by Congress.

These examples illustrate the interplay between two contrary forces — the *determination* of Congress to play a more dynamic role in foreign affairs and, at the same time, the existence of *serious problems* inside and outside Congress that impede its capacity to do so.

CONGRESS' CONSTITUTIONAL PREROGATIVES

Like the executive branch, Congress has both formal constitutional and extraconstitutional prerogatives in foreign relations. Several general observations are needed to set these powers in perspective.

For the Founding Fathers, Congress was unquestionably viewed as the dynamic organ of the American system of government, as the "voice of the people," and as the depository of American democratic ideals. For a number of reasons — not least, their colonial experience — the founders of the republic were profoundly suspicious of executive power. Americans and their representatives at the Constitutional Convention believed that the abuse of power by executive officials, like King George III, the British prime minister, and the colonial governors, was largely responsible for the American Revolution. While the prerogatives of the president of the United States were less circumscribed than those of the state governors, it is noteworthy that the powers and responsibilities of Congress are listed first in the Constitution, and they are specified in much greater detail than those of the chief executive or the judicial branch.

Did the Founding Fathers expect Congress to play the leading role in foreign affairs, as well as in domestic affairs? Or, as the Supreme Court decided in 1936, did they understand that constitutionally these were different realms?[18] For 200 years, constitutional authorities have debated this question, and even today the answer is unclear.* Convinced

---

*Many commentators on American diplomacy draw a distinction between the roles of the executive and legislative branches in making and conducting foreign policy. Yet this traditional distinction is becoming increasingly difficult to draw and maintain in practice. The *conduct* of foreign policy — involving such questions as how foreign aid is actually administered, or the president's use of armed force to achieve a particular foreign policy objective — is not a matter that Congress today is willing to leave solely to the executive branch.

as they were that Congress uniquely embodied and reflected the people's will, the founders were also cognizant that throughout history the conduct of foreign affairs was an executive function. As Secretary of State Thomas Jefferson said, "The transaction of business with foreign nations is executive altogether."[19]

From their immediate experience — when the Continental Congress attempted to conduct the revolutionary war — the founders were also aware of innumerable practical problems that could arise if the foreign affairs of the new republic were entrusted to 26 senators and 65 representatives. The Washington administration's frustrating experience in trying to arrive at a unified position within the national government on the question of the Jay treaty with England in 1794 was an early case study in intragovernmental conflict on a major diplomatic issue. According to one historian, the treaty was only ratified after "stormy sessions" in both houses of Congress.[20]

Whatever their precise intentions regarding the role of Congress in foreign affairs, the founders gave the legislative branch important constitutional prerogatives in the foreign policy field. For convenience, we may divide these into four principal categories. Two prerogatives belong to the Senate alone, giving it a unique role in the foreign policy process — advice and consent to treaties and the confirmation of executive appointments. The Senate and the House of Representatives share two other powers specified in the Constitution — the power to appropriate funds and the power to declare war.

Advice and Consent Prerogative

Article II, Section 2 states that the president may make treaties, "by and with the Advice and Consent of the Senate . . . provided two thirds of the Senators present [when the vote is taken on it] concur. . . ."

Why did the framers of the Constitution require that agreements with other countries be approved by an extraordinary (two-thirds) majority of the Senate? The answer appears to be clear: as much as any other major constitutional provision, this one reflected the isolationist sentiments of the Founding Fathers and their determination that American involvement in international politics remain extremely limited. The provision reflected the American "congenital distrust of Europe."[21] And why was congressional participation in treaty-making limited to the Senate alone? From the experience under the Articles of Confederation, the drafters of the Constitution were painfully familiar with the consequences of foreign policy mismanagement by the entire Congress. The smaller, "indirectly" elected (until 1913), and more mature Senate — capable of withstanding the whims of public opinion — was expected to serve as a kind of "Council of State" to advise the president in foreign relations.

As we noted in Chapter 1, the ratification of international agreements by the United States involves a multistage process in which the

Senate plays a decisive role: it acts upon treaties submitted to it by the president. Despite a widespread popular misconception, the Senate does not "ratify treaties." It may give (or withhold) its "advice and consent" to them; but a treaty is ratified only when it has been approved by the Senate and signed by the president, who promulgates it as part of the "law of the land" (as treaties are designated in Article III, Section 2 of the Constitution).

Throughout the course of American diplomatic history, the vast majority of treaties has been approved by the Senate despite a few celebrated cases — as when, after World War I, the Senate so emasculated the Treaty of Versailles with amendments and reservations that it was unacceptable to President Woodrow Wilson.[22] In the postwar period, it has become common practice for the White House to invite senators to participate in the negotiations leading to major international agreements. This practice has come to be viewed as a method of imparting "bipartisanship" to foreign affairs and of enhancing the prospects for favorable senatorial action on a treaty.[23] Indeed, today the Senate probably expects to be included in important treaty negotiations. Legislators have even undertaken diplomatic negotiations on their own, sometimes in the face of expressed presidential opposition to their actions, as we shall see more fully in Chapter 8.

Since 1789, the Senate's unique prerogative in the treaty-making process has given the upper chamber a distinctive and prestigious position vis-à-vis the House of Representatives in foreign affairs. Until World War II, the voice of Congress on diplomatic issues was usually expressed *through the Senate*. It was Senate opposition that rejected American membership in the League of Nations after World War I; and during the interwar period, powerful voices in the Senate expressed the isolationist sentiment that actuated American foreign policy. During and after the war, influential senators — like Arthur H. Vandenberg, R-Mich., and Tom Connally, D-Texas — cooperated with the Roosevelt and Truman administrations to lay the foundations for the active internationalist role that the United States assumed after 1945.[24] By the mid-1960s, it was again the Senate (and, more specifically, the Senate Foreign Relations Committee) which took the lead in spearheading congressional opposition to America's role in the Vietnam War.

The House of Representatives was largely content to play a subordinate role in the foreign policy process; membership on the House Foreign Affairs Committee (for a period of several years called the International Relations Committee) was largely viewed as a symbolic assignment that few legislators coveted. As late as 1970, the chairman of the Foreign Affairs Committee regarded it as a junior partner in foreign policy decisionmaking; in his opinion the committee should normally support the executive branch's foreign policy positions.[25]

A noteworthy trend within Congress in recent years has been the extent to which the House of Representatives has sought to reverse its traditionally subordinate role in the foreign policy realm. If the House is assigned no formal constitutional responsibility in treaty-making, it can — and recent experience has shown that it will — use other prerogatives (like its predominant position in the appropriations process) to exert its influence in foreign relations. This viewpoint was illustrated by the remarks of one legislator early in 1979 in connection with the Panama Canal treaties:

> We in the House are tired of you people in the State Department going to your tea-sipping friends in the Senate. Now you good folks come up here and say you need legislation [to implement the Panama Canal treaties] after you ignored the House. If you expect me to vote for this travesty, you're sorely in error.[26]

Yet the Senate zealously preserves its prerogatives in the treaty-making process. Regarding House efforts to intrude upon its historic domain, the chairman of the Senate Foreign Relations Committee said, "Their nibbles end up being big bites, and we [are] being bitten to death."[27]

Confirmation Prerogative

The other (and much less influential) senatorial prerogative is the power to confirm executive appointments. In the minds of the Founding Fathers, these two unique senatorial powers — to approve treaties and to confirm diplomatic appointments — were interrelated. That is, the Senate should play a key role in the appointment of those officials who would engage in treaty negotiations; by doing so, the Senate would have a voice in framing the "instructions" given to these officials.[28] Within a relatively short time, however, this linkage broke down; the Senate no longer relied upon its confirmation power to influence the content of foreign policy. As a rule, presidential appointments in the diplomatic field are routinely confirmed by the Senate. During the 91st Congress, the Senate confirmed 2,744 appointments in foreign relations, and none of the president's nominees was rejected.[29]

Occasionally, the Senate relies upon its prerogative in order to express its view on foreign policy issues. At the beginning of the Eisenhower administration, for example, the Senate showed evident displeasure over the president's nomination of Charles E. Bohlen as ambassador to the Soviet Union. (Bohlen had been identified with what many legislators believed were the pro-Soviet policies of the Roosevelt administration during World War II.)[30] At the end of the 1970s, President Jimmy Carter's nomination of Leonard Woodcock as the first American ambassador to the People's Republic of China also encountered Senate opposition because of fear that the United States was "abandoning" Taiwan (called by the Taiwanese the Republic of China). Senatorial disaffection brought about certain concessions from the Carter administration to reaffirm America's defense ties with Taiwan.[31]

Power of the Purse

The remaining two powers conferred upon Congress by the Constitution to influence foreign relations are shared by the Senate and the House of Representatives. One of these — the prerogative relied upon most decisively by the British Parliament to establish its primacy over the monarchy — is what has historically been called "the power of the purse." In reality, this is two interrelated powers: congressional control over the *sources of revenue* available to the national government (such as taxation, tariff revenues, and loans); and — in accordance with the constitutional requirement (Article I, Section 9) that "No money shall be drawn from the Treasury, but in Consequence of Appropriations made by Law" — legislative approval for government *expenditures*.

Since all expenditures must be approved by Congress, it may increase funds for particular programs above White House recommendations; it may also refuse to grant funds for programs and policies in the foreign policy field; it may terminate programs already in existence; it may provide the required funds only when certain conditions have been met abroad; and it may exercise legislative oversight into administration of external programs, investigating such questions as whether they are achieving their objectives or whether their continuation is in the national interest. A few examples from congressional action in 1977 will illustrate the scope and importance of this power.

In authorizing the foreign military aid bill for fiscal year 1978, Congress appended some 16 "policy provisions" to the legislation. These included: a statement of legislative opposition to military aid to certain African states; a directive that the secretary of state review the Egyptian-American security program; a prohibition against aiding any country that was expanding its nuclear arsenal; and a requirement that the president report to Congress on the impact of American arms sales abroad.[32] In the foreign economic aid bill for 1978, Congress prohibited the use of American funds for assistance or reparations to North Vietnam, Laos, Cambodia, or Cuba.[33]

In authorizing funds for the Arms Control and Disarmament Agency, Congress required the agency, at the instigation of legislators who were suspicious of Soviet motivations in arms control, to report on the adequacy of American attempts to monitor Soviet compliance with existing arms limitations agreements.[34] In the bill authorizing funds for the operations of the State Department and related agencies, Congress specified that no American troops should be withdrawn from South Korea without consultation with Congress; that, in any negotiations with Cuba, the White House should take notice of Cuban military intervention in Africa; and that, in any new agreement with Panama, the "vital interests" of the United States should be protected.[35]

Authorization and Appropriations Process. Foreign policy programs requiring expenditures for their implementaion must be approved by Congress in two stages. As an example, take the annual foreign aid budget as proposed by the White House. Initially, Congress must *authorize* the foreign aid program — and the first major step in this process is for foreign assistance to be considered by the Senate Foreign Relations Committee and the House Foreign Affairs Committee. Theoretically, in the authorization phase, these committees are concerned with such questions as: Does foreign assistance promote the diplomatic interests of the United States? Can particular foreign aid projects (to Bolivia, or to Morocco, or to India) be justified? Is there a strong likelihood that the objectives of the foreign aid program can be achieved? Assuming that both committees eventually approve the foreign aid program, it must then be approved by the House and Senate; and both houses must ultimately agree upon a common authorization measure before this stage is completed.

Next, the foreign aid bill must go through the *appropriations stage*.[36] After the program has received legislative authorization, funds must be provided for its implementation. This is the province of the House and Senate Appropriations committees. Custom has established that the House of Representatives — through its spokesman, the House Appropriations Committee — plays the dominant role in the appropriations process.[37] In the postwar period, the House Appropriations Committee has had a decisive voice in influencing certain aspects of American foreign policy. Theoretically, neither the House nor the Senate Appropriations Committee is concerned with the merits of the foreign aid program, already authorized by Congress. The two appropriations committees are supposed to concentrate upon such questions as whether federal revenues are available to finance foreign aid (along with all other expenditures previously authorized). In practice, however, the lines between the jurisdictions and interests of the authorizing committees of Congress and the two appropriations committees have become indistinct and are seldom observed rigidly.

From 1955 to 1965, for example, the foreign aid program encountered its most formidable opposition on Capitol Hill from the Foreign Operations Subcommittee of the House Appropriations Committee. Headed by Representative Otto Passman, D-La. — an outspoken and determined opponent of foreign aid — the subcommittee subjected the foreign aid allocation to "Passmanization," in the course of which massive cuts were made in the program. Passman accused executive policymakers of attempting to "grab the check" to be paid by the American taxpayers for every social and economic need throughout the world.[38]

According to longstanding custom, the Senate Appropriations Committee functions as a "court of review" for the actions taken by its counterpart in the House. As a rule, most of the cuts made by the House in foreign aid (and other programs) are eventually restored by the Senate Appropriations Committee and by Congress as a whole.

Problems of Budgetary Procedures. For many years, students of the national legislative process, together with many members of the House and Senate, have recognized and deplored the fact that Congress' treatment of the budget is fragmentary, highly decentralized, and lacking in any real sense of priority among literally hundreds of budgetary categories. In an effort to remedy these longstanding defects, Congress enacted the Budget and Impoundment Control Act in 1974. The act created new Budget committees in the House and Senate whose responsibility it was to prepare a tentative — and later a final — budget for each chamber. This budget would presumably reflect each chamber's sense of spending priorities and would balance total budgetary outlays against anticipated governmental revenue. Without entering into a detailed analysis of recent budgetary procedures in Congress, our purpose is served by noting that this attempt at centralized budgetary control on Capitol Hill has not achieved its objectives thus far. The two new budgetary committees were superimposed upon the existing committee structure of Congress; and the locus of real power in dealing with expenditures has remained where it has been centered traditionally — in the authorizing and appropriations committees of Congress.[39]

Several further observations may be made about congressional reliance upon the "power of the purse" to influence the course of American diplomacy. Although one of Congress' most potent prerogatives, it has seldom been utilized to its fullest potential to affect foreign relations. In the preponderance of cases, Congress relies upon this power *to limit executive activities* in external affairs; the House and Senate tell the president what he *cannot do*, rather than what he can or must do abroad. Congressionally imposed limits upon American expenditures abroad frequently testify to the existence of genuine anxieties on Capitol Hill concerning particular foreign policy issues or developments, and they serve as forceful warnings to the White House of even deeper public skepticism and disaffection.[40] Occasional legislative efforts to provide more funds than requested by the White House for particular foreign policy programs risk the "impoundment" of such funds by the chief executive.[41]

Yet, as we shall see in our discussion of the Arab-Israeli conflict (Chapter 4) and of the problem of international human rights (Chapter 7), Congress has relied heavily in recent years upon its control over appropriations to achieve specific foreign policy goals enjoying high priority on Capitol Hill. As Chapter 7 illustrates, Congress can require that vast sums of money be expended for certain diplomatic purposes. It cannot, however, always guarantee that the funds will be expended wisely or that they will accomplish the goal Congress intended.

War Powers Prerogative

Four consecutive provisions of Article I, Section 8 collectively comprise the "war powers" of Congress. These confer upon Congress the power to "declare war"; to "raise and support Armies"; to "provide and maintain a Navy"; and to make rules for the regulation of the armed forces. These provisions have served as the basis for forceful assertions of legislative influence in external policy in the recent period. The Truman administration was widely criticized on Capitol Hill for ignoring legislative viewpoints and prerogatives when it involved the United States in the Korean War during the early 1950s. In time, the Johnson and Nixon administrations faced even more outspoken congressional disaffection for their escalation of the Vietnam War and for the invasion of Cambodia without the explicit approval of Congress. Two recent examples of legislative initiative in the foreign policy process — passage of the 1973 War Powers Resolution and efforts to limit the kinds of "national commitments" undertaken by the executive branch — indicate Congress' determination to exert its powers over the military establishment to influence the course of foreign relations.

Although the Constitution grants to Congress the power to declare war, several developments in modern international relations have combined to render this legislative prerogative largely a formality. In contrast to international practice for several centuries before the Constitution was drafted, today nations almost never declare war before engaging in hostilities. When Congress does issue a declaration of war (which has become rare), the declaration itself asserts that a condition of warfare actually exists; it is not an occasion for Congress to debate whether hostilities ought to exist.

More than a century ago, the Supreme Court held in a landmark case that the existence of a state of war depended upon prevailing conditions; the president was not required to await a declaration of war from Congress before responding to external threats.[42] Since the Vietnam conflict, chief executives have repeatedly referred to "functional equivalents" for a declaration of war, such as congressional approval of the national defense budget during the period of the Vietnam War; Congress' enactment of the draft; and passage of measures like the 1964 "Gulf of Tonkin Resolution," approving the president's use of armed force in responding to threats to American security interests.[43]

Only five (out of some 125) wars and violent encounters in which the United States has been engaged have been "declared" by Congress; most of them have involved major and minor conflicts, in which the president or a local U.S. official employed the armed forces for foreign policy ends. Neither of the two prolonged and costly postwar military engagements — the Korean War (called a "police action" by the Truman administration) and the Vietnam War — was formally "declared" by Congress, primarily because the incumbent president did not request Congress to do so.

The creation of a worldwide network of military alliances since World War II has also eroded the power of Congress to declare war. Article 5 of the NATO agreement, for example, provides that the parties shall regard an attack upon one signatory as an attack against them all — a provision which, according to many commentators, is tantamount to the threat of "automatic war" by the United States against an aggressor. Despite laments on Capitol Hill about the tendency of modern presidents to bypass Congress in decisions to employ the armed forces abroad, some legislators have said that a declaration of war in all cases involving military hostilities abroad would be inadvisable since it might turn a limited war into a global nuclear conflict (an inherent danger in the Vietnam conflict).[44]

At the Constitutional Convention, an early draft of the document gave Congress the right to "make war"; this language was later changed, granting Congress the power to "declare war." Suspicious as they were of executive authority, the founders recognized that the successful prosecution of a war requires *both executive and legislative participation;* one branch cannot conduct war alone. No one was more mindful of this fact than President George Washington, who had endured many frustrating experiences trying to get coordinated policy and effective support from the Continental Congress during the revolutionary war. Accordingly, the chief executive is also given important war powers: the president is designated commander in chief of the military establishment. As with other constitutional issues, the precise balance or allocation of the war powers between the two ends of Pennsylvania Avenue has been determined more by experience, precedents, and circumstances than by the intentions of the founders or by contending legal theories. On this front, the overall tendency has been for legislative prerogatives to be eclipsed by forceful assertions of executive initiative and leadership.

Included in the legislative war powers is the requirement that Congress "raise and support Armies" and that it "provide and maintain a Navy." Reflecting the American people's aversion to a "standing army," the Constitution prohibits Congress from making appropriations for the army for longer than two years. (No such limitation exists with regard to naval appropriations.) This requirement assured that the question of whether the nation needed a large military establishment — and the kinds of armed forces it required — would be subject to frequent legislative review.

Throughout modern history, however, Congress has seldom used this power to its fullest potential for the purpose of influencing American diplomacy. For a period of some 20 years until the late 1970s, the national defense budget was the largest item in overall federal expenditures. (By 1979, it had been surpassed by the budget of the Department of Health, Education and Welfare.) Particularly when the nation has been involved in external crises, the tendency of Congress has been to provide the kind of military establishment requested by the White House — and in some instances, it has increased expenditures for particular items in the Defense Department budget in the face of White House opposition. Even today, Congress does not want to be accused of taking a chance with the security of the nation or of depriving the president of the armed strength required to defend the nation's territory and interests (as in the years just before Pearl Harbor). It is noteworthy that following the Vietnam War, Congress was still reluctant to reduce American military expenditures drastically; and — as Senate debate over the SALT II arms control treaty in 1979 indicated — a significant number of senators and representatives believed that, if anything, American defense spending was too low.

Mounting legislative dissatisfaction with presidential use of the armed forces for foreign policy ends was forcefully demonstrated when the House and Senate passed the War Powers Resolution over President Nixon's veto in 1973.[45] As much as any other step taken by Congress in recent years, this measure symbolized legislative disenchantment with the "imperial presidency" and a determination to become an equal partner with the executive in the foreign policy process. The main provisions of the War Powers Resolution are more appropriately discussed in the case study dealing with the deployment of the armed forces (Chapter 5). At this stage, it suffices to make a few general observations about it.

In the language of the resolution, its purpose was to ensure that the "collective judgment of both the Congress and the President will apply to the introduction of United States Armed Forces into hostilities," or situations in which hostilities are believed to be "imminent," abroad. By this measure Congress insisted that its consent be obtained for the prolonged use of American troops in foreign conflicts; otherwise, the president would be required to withdraw American forces from actual or potential combat zones. In the relatively brief time that has elapsed since Congress passed the War Powers Resolution, it is difficult to assess its long-term impact upon the American foreign policy process. Advocates of a more influential congressional voice in foreign policy decisionmaking in general applauded the resolution, believing that it was a significant step towards that goal. Other commentators and informed citizens (including some legislators) were considerably less sanguine. Some questioned whether, in a context of foreign crisis, the resolution would really inhibit the president's reliance upon armed force to promote national security and diplomatic objectives. Other students of the American constitutional system believed that the resolution had in fact *strengthened* the position of the president as commander in chief of the armed forces, by according him wide latitude to deploy them with little effective hindrance by Congress.

Executive policymakers have given ambivalent answers regarding the resolution's meaning and implications. A succession of postwar presidents — Truman, Eisenhower, Kennedy, Johnson, and Nixon — took the position that their authority over the armed forces did not depend upon acts of Congress and could not, therefore, be limited by statutes or congressional resolutions.[46] Since the passage of the resolution, Presidents Ford and Carter have complained that it, along with other congressionally imposed restrictions upon the presidency, seriously impeded their ability to achieve diplomatic objectives. Yet in his response to the seizure of the American ship *Mayaguez* in May 1975, President Ford largely ignored the provisions of the War Powers Resolution — with little discernible protest from Congress.[47]

The War Powers Resolution contains ambiguous and imprecise language, leaving ample scope for differing executive and legislative interpretations of its requirements. Moreover, the constitutionality of the resolution has never been tested in the courts. Above all, it remains to be seen whether — and in what respects — the restrictions imposed by the resolution will survive a major external crisis involving national security. While the exact circumstances of such a crisis cannot be fully anticipated, it seems a safe prediction that the president — perhaps in response to overwhelming public sentiment — will take those steps required to protect the security of the United States, rather than jeopardize its security by strict adherence to the provisions of the resolution. Little reference was made to the War Powers Resolution by the American people or their legislative representatives late in 1979, for example, when citizens demanded that President Carter take strong steps to gain the removal of Soviet troops from Cuba and to protect American hostages and the nation's diplomatic interests in Iran.

Economic Powers

The Constitution also confers upon Congress certain general responsibilities that we may classify as comprising its *economic powers,* several of which have become increasingly important in the conduct of foreign relations. These include the power to levy and collect taxes; to impose tariffs upon imports; to borrow money; to regulate interstate and foreign commerce; and to coin money and regulate its value. Collectively, the economic powers of Congress are vast, affecting almost every sphere of national life.

Legislative assertiveness in the foreign policy field within recent years may be an inevitable result of the steady growth in the federal budget (approximately $564 billion in 1980). Each year, Congress is called upon to authorize and appropriate funds for literally hundreds of governmental programs, many of which impinge upon foreign relations. Congressional activities in the energy field, for example, directly affect American foreign policy toward the Middle East. Legislative measures to control inflation at home are a major factor determining the value of the dollar overseas; and they will also influence such intangible, but crucial developments, as the degree of confidence which foreign governments have in American leadership. The priority which Congress establishes between domestic and foreign spending is a major factor in determining the Soviet-American strategic balance, Washington's ability to fight "limited wars," or the capacity of the United States to respond to the economic needs of the Third World.

Since the late 1960s, legislative attitudes have tended to reflect an opinion that is pervasive throughout the American society as a whole: domestic needs should be given highest priority by national policymakers. In some measure, this frame of mind reflected a post-Vietnam neo-isolationist school of thought on Capitol Hill. Many believed that America's most effective contribution to international relations was to "set its own house in order" or successfully solve its own internal problems. (This idea — that America's example to the rest of the world was its most beneficial contribution to the international community — had also been a prominent theme in the traditional isolationist mentality.)[48]

Few of Congress' economic powers have more significant implications for foreign policy than its power to regulate commerce. The "trade wars" among the American states under the Articles of Confederation led to conditions of economic turmoil and instability — a primary reason why the Constitutional Convention was assembled. Congress, therefore, was given the exclusive power to regulate both trade among the states and between the United States and foreign countries.

Beginning with the Reciprocal Trade Program inaugurated by the Roosevelt administration, the United States has sought to maximize its foreign trade on the basis of reciprocal tariff concessions with other countries. Congress grants the president considerable discretion to negotiate trade agreements with other nations; and Congress periodically engages in major revisions of the trade laws — often at the instigation of domestic industries threatened by rising imports (as in the case of Japanese automobiles, textiles from Hong Kong, and fruits and vegetables from Mexico). In dealing with trade questions, Congress is continually subjected to pressure from domestic industries, business groups, labor unions, farmers, and others seeking to improve their competitive positions. In 1979, for example, the House Ways and Means Committee asserted — and the White House relayed the congressional warning to Tokyo — that the rising volume of Japanese imports was producing serious economic dislocations for the American economy.[49]

Incident to its power to regulate commerce, from time to time Congress investigates the behavior of American business firms overseas. In recent years, it has inquired into allegations that American corporations bribed officials in other countries to obtain preferential consideration. Political intervention in the affairs of Chile by the International Telephone and Telegraph Company has also been the subject of intensive legislative investigation.[50]

Today, there is hardly a foreign policy activity which lacks an economic dimension. For example, in four out of the five case studies which follow — beginning with Senate consideration of the new Panama Canal treaties, through legislative efforts to promote the cause of human rights abroad — economic considerations in some measure shaped congressional attitudes and behavior. Even with regard to ideological and ethical issues at the forefront of congressional concern — such as promoting human rights in the Soviet Union, or achieving racial equality in Africa — Congress has used economic instruments, like trade concessions and boycotts, to influence events abroad.[51] This may be merely one indication of a larger phenomenon in modern international relations: definition of a nation's power in *economic terms,* rather than according to purely military criteria.

The Oversight Function

Since the mid-nineteenth century, many students of the legislative process have agreed that "control of the government — the oversight function — is probably the most important task the legislature performs." As a result, "the bureaucracy lives under the heavy frown of congressional supervision all the time."[52] Although it is not specifically mentioned in the Constitution, the congressional power of investigation is a basic and influential legislative function — one which Congress has relied upon repeatedly in the modern period to influence foreign affairs. During the 1930s, for example, the investigation carried out by the "Nye Committee" into America's participation in the First World War had a momentous impact upon public opinion, strongly re-enforcing the existing isolationist mentality.[53] Conversely, during World War II, the "Truman Committee" (or Special Senate Committee Investigating the National Defense Program, headed by Senator Harry S. Truman, D-Mo.) investigated problems related to the war effort. This committee was widely cited as a model of constructive investigation by Congress.[54]

In the early postwar period, committees of the House and Senate examined political, social, and economic conditions in Europe; their reports played key roles in formulating the Greek-Turkish Aid Program (1947), the Marshall Plan (1948), and NATO (1949). Later congressional investigations focused upon why the United States "lost China" to communism. These inquiries yielded few positive results — and in the process, they impaired morale in the State Department and other executive agencies for many years to come.[55]

One of the most influential investigations in recent diplomatic experience was conducted by the Senate Foreign Relations Committee during the late 1960s on American participation in the Vietnam War. This well-publicized inquiry provided momentum for the emerging internal opposition to the war and was a major factor in the Nixon administration's decision to terminate it. The inquiry is a classic case of the use of Congress' investigative powers to bring maximum publicity to bear upon the behavior of the executive branch in foreign affairs.[56]

INFORMAL METHODS OF LEGISLATIVE INFLUENCE

In addition to its constitutional prerogatives, Congress has evolved certain informal — and sometimes extremely influential — methods for influencing the course of foreign relations. One of these is the ability of the House and Senate (or both) to pass resolutions expressing the opinions of legislators on diplomatic issues. Unlike statutes, such resolutions are not law and are not binding upon executive policymakers.* Nevertheless, expressions of congressional sentiment are not ignored or treated lightly by the White House or the news media. Ideally, every incumbent president desires to work constructively with Congress to achieve a maximum consensus on foreign policy questions, if for no other reason than that such unity is essential for diplomatic success.

Another informal power of Congress that has affected American diplomacy dramatically since World War II is foreign travel by senators, representatives, and their staffs. Before the war, such travel was exceptional. In the postwar period, however, it has become commonplace for legislators to visit foreign countries regularly. Reasons and pretexts for congressional trips are easily found: a particular legislative committee wants to investigate the defense posture of NATO; another one wishes to examine how American foreign aid to India is being administered; still another desires more information on communist movements throughout Latin America.[57] Individual legislators are also asked by the White House to undertake foreign assignments and, increasingly, legislators are invited to be the guests of foreign governments. As part of the Carter administration's effort to solidify support for the new Panama Canal treaties on Capitol Hill, the White House encouraged legislators to visit Panama.[58] In recent years, some legislators have traveled abroad for the avowed purpose of engaging in diplomatic discussions and negotiations with foreign governments.

More frequent and extensive foreign travel by legislators provides them with firsthand knowledge and alternative sources of information, lessening Congress' need to rely solely upon the executive branch. Some of these trips are undoubtedly "junkets" that add little to members' effectiveness, but others help to overcome provincialism on Capitol Hill, perhaps an inevitable outgrowth of legislative immersion in state and local issues and of growing involvement with constituency needs.[59]

Although the era of oratory on Capitol Hill (and elsewhere) may have ended, even today speeches by individual legislators can have a significant impact upon American foreign relations. Both within Congress and outside it, addresses and statements by senators, especially on foreign policy issues, are newsworthy and influence the attitudes of

---

*Resolutions expressing the opinions of one or both houses of Congress may take various forms. A "concurrent resolution" conveys the opinion of both houses on a particular question. It is not, however, law and thus does not require the president's signature. Similarly, a "sense of the House" or a "sense of the Senate" resolution may express the viewpoint of one chamber on a question. While executive policymakers are interested in congressional sentiment, they are not bound by such resolutions.

executive policymakers. During the 1940s and 1950s, for example, Senator Wayne Morse (initially a Republican, and later a Democrat from Oregon) was one of the earliest congressional critics of America's overinvolvement abroad and of its temptation to rely upon military force to solve external problems.[60] The chairman of the Senate Foreign Relations Committee during the late 1960s, J. William Fulbright, became perhaps the most outspoken opponent in Congress to White House policies toward Latin America, Southeast Asia, and other regions. In a widely publicized speech to the Senate on September 15, 1965, Fulbright denounced the Johnson administration's intervention in the Dominican Republic; his speech marked Fulbright's formal break with President Johnson's diplomacy, and it was extremely influential in solidifying liberal opposition to White House policies.[61] Early in 1979, Idaho Senator Frank Church, chairman of the Senate Foreign Relations Committee during the Carter administration, publicly criticized the government of Saudi Arabia for failing to support the administration's peacemaking efforts in the Middle East. Unless Saudi Arabia's position changed, Church believed, a "fundamental review" of American policy toward that country was necessary. Church's remarks (at variance with the administration's pro-Saudi Arabian stance) would also have an impact upon events in the Middle East.[62]

CONGRESS AND POSTWAR DIPLOMACY

Since the late 1960s, Congress has exhibited a new dynamism and militancy in exerting its prerogatives in external affairs. For the first 20 years after World War II, Congress was either largely content to leave the management of foreign relations to the executive branch — thereby providing impetus for the emergence of the "imperial presidency" — or, when it played a significant role in foreign relations, Congress normally supported those diplomatic policies and programs advocated by the White House. Recalling the decisive impact upon American diplomacy Congress had in earlier periods of American history and concerned about the steady accretion of executive power, many members of the House and Senate have advocated a return to a more influential role in the realm of external policy.

Congress' dynamic involvement in the foreign policy process must be viewed from the perspective of the diplomatic experience of the twentieth century. The post-Vietnam War era of legislative assertiveness in foreign relations, for example, may be regarded as another stage in the "democratization" of American diplomacy which began under President Woodrow Wilson. Although he was not always consistent with his own principle, Wilson believed in "open covenants, openly arrived at," in involving public opinion in the foreign policy process, and in other measures designed to make the conduct of diplomacy consonant with America's democratic values. As the branch of government most "representative" of the people (as many legislators believe), Congress can justify its diplomatic assertiveness by reference to such Wilsonian principles.[63] The perspective of history also reminds us that there have been many earlier periods of congressional activism in foreign relations — such as the era of the Spanish-American War and the decade of the 1930s. In the latter period, not even President Franklin D. Roosevelt — one of the nation's most skilled political leaders — was able to impose his will upon a Congress strongly attached to isolationism.

The Expanding Role of Government

The expanding role of government in all spheres of life, both at home and abroad, is another factor that has contributed to a growing congressional involvement in foreign affairs since the New Deal. In 1946, for example, total annual expenditures by the United States government were some $62 billion; by 1980, this total had increased some 809 percent. In one budget category — national defense spending — expenditures by the late 1970s exceeded the *total* federal spending 30 years earlier by some 50 percent. Nearly every important foreign (or closely related domestic) policy of the United States in the postwar period — from containing Soviet expansionism, to meeting the economic needs of societies throughout the Third World, to stabilizing world price levels for major commodities, to dealing with global environmental problems — provides an opportunity and an incentive for Congress to leave its imprint upon America's diplomatic record.

The emergence of the United States as a superpower after World War II — and its adoption of an "internationalist" foreign policy — were also crucial developments enhancing the role of Congress in foreign relations. Before the war — when isolationism was the American rule of foreign policy for over 150 years — congressional interest and participation in diplomatic issues was often minimal. During the isolationist period, the United States really had no "foreign policy," as the term was defined in Chapter 1. America was not then willing to commit its national resources to external goals.

After World War II, however, even leading proponents of that approach acknowledged that the isolationist era had ended.[64] Its demise was symbolized by President Harry S. Truman's historic address to Congress on March 12, 1947, inaugurating America's containment policy against expansive communism. In proposing the Greek-Turkish Aid Program, Truman put the choice squarely before Congress: either it would support those measures required to preserve peace and security abroad, or it would risk widespread global instability and the possible outbreak of World War III.[65] Painful as the choice was for many legislators, Congress faced the realities of the postwar era and supported those measures dictated by America's emergence as a superpower.

Domestic Implications of Foreign Policy

The growing interrelationship between domestic and foreign affairs since World War II also provides momentum for congressional assertiveness in external policy. This phenomenon is illustrated by the "Food for Peace" program, whereby American agricultural products are sold or donated to needy societies overseas. One study has called the program "a popular form of foreign aid on Capitol Hill because it benefits the donor economy more than the recipient." With considerable encouragement from Congress, the Department of Agriculture seeks to dispose of agricultural surpluses abroad, as a crucial step in maintaining the prosperity of American farmers.[66] Other examples of this interrelationship — such as the dependence of American prosperity upon access to, and the price of, Middle East oil — could be cited. Today, a State Department official has said, "no member of Congress can ignore foreign policy decisions and expect to be re-elected." Legislators can no longer say, "That's up to the president and Congress can't do anything about it."[67]

The Impact of the Vietnam War

A number of short-range (and possibly transitory) factors have also combined to inject Congress forcefully into the foreign policy process since the mid-1960s. An obvious one — the issue which perhaps more than any other ended congressional passivity in foreign policy decisionmaking — was the Vietnam War. This traumatic episode had innumerable consequences for the foreign policy of the United States, some of which would be felt for decades to come. The war served to crystallize emerging congressional disaffection with the course of American diplomacy; the "imperial presidency" was deemed responsible for the military and diplomatic debacle in Southeast Asia.

Legislative opposition to the war took diverse forms. Some members of the House and Senate believed that successive presidents had deceived or otherwise concealed from the American people the nature and scope of the nation's commitments in Southeast Asia. Critics of the war on Capitol Hill were also convinced that the White House had from time to time manipulated Congress into supporting presidential policies in the Vietnam conflict — a charge directed specifically at the Johnson administration's handling of the "Gulf of Tonkin" crisis in 1964, when Congress gave legislative sanction to the administration's retaliatory actions against North Vietnam.[68] The Nixon administration's invasion of Cambodia in 1970 was also widely denounced on Capitol Hill, since it lacked the approval of Congress.

Transcending all these specific complaints, however, was a fact which in time became evident to all informed Americans: *the United States was being defeated in the Vietnam War.* For Americans (who, as President Johnson stated repeatedly, were not accustomed to "losing wars"), this was a profoundly disturbing realization. The common denominator of the criticism directed by many legislators at the White House was the implicit idea that a more independent and forceful role *by Congress* in making decisions affecting Southeast Asia would have prevented this military and diplomatic failure. Alternatively, some legislators believed that if Congress had been at the helm of the ship of state, the United States would have achieved its goals in Southeast Asia. In either case, the results of more influential congressional involvement in the foreign policy process could hardly have been worse than those associated with several years of almost unrestrained executive power in the foreign policy field. Since the Vietnam War, legislators have concertedly echoed the demand which Senator Vandenberg directed at the Truman administration: legislators want to be in on the "take-offs," as well as the "crash landings" in foreign affairs.[69]

Changes within Congress

Internal changes within Congress itself — and within the broader context of American public opinion and the political system — have also encouraged and sustained its activism in foreign affairs. Three such tendencies within the legislative branch have been noteworthy. One of these is the fact that Congress is getting "younger": the average age of legislators has declined, and the viewpoints of many of its members today tend to reflect this change (as in the skepticism displayed by American youth toward the "establishment" and their demands for "participatory democracy"). Newly elected members of the House and Senate, for example, are no longer content to serve the expected "apprenticeship" before they express their viewpoints forcefully on public policy questions. (As we shall see in Chapter 3, one of the most crucial battles in the Senate over the new Panama Canal treaties was fought over an amendment offered by freshman Senator Dennis DeConcini.)

The second and related change within Congress has been the demand for procedural reforms. Traditional concepts — such as the seniority principle governing the selection of committee chairmen, and the often vast powers exercised by the chairmen of committees and subcommittees — have come under repeated attack. This trend toward democratization within the House and Senate have given individual legislators a more influential role in congressional deliberations and has accorded them new opportunities to express their ideas on major policy questions.[70]

A third significant change within Congress has been the rapid and dramatic growth in the legislative staff. In recent years, the congressional staff has grown more rapidly than the executive bureaucracy. A larger staff provides members of the House and Senate with more independent access to information and studies needed for sound decisionmaking — thereby enabling them to avoid the kind of crucial miscalculation made on the eve of World War II when isolationist senators confidently assured the Roosevelt administration that, according to their information, there would be no war on the European continent! Yet this expansion in the legislative staff also exacerbates the problem we identified in Chapter 1. It promotes a new diffusion of power and responsibility within the two chambers; it gives a growing number of congressional committees and subcommittees the resources for playing an active foreign policy role; and it compounds the difficulty of arriving at unified legislative efforts in the diplomatic field.[71]

Changes in Public Opinion

Mention must also be made of two forces in American public opinion that encourage Congress to exert its influence in foreign relations. One is the significant *increase in lobbying activities* directed at Congress (and the executive branch). This is highlighted by the case study on the Arab-Israeli conflict in Chapter 4. Pressure group activity has always been a conspicuous feature of the American political system. But most students of the American government would agree that both the intensity and the skill of lobbying campaigns have increased significantly since World War II. As future chapters will illustrate, a novel development in recent years has been the extent to which foreign governments (often in alliance with interest groups within the United States) have undertaken lobbying campaigns designed to influence the course of American foreign policy.[72]

The other salient characteristic of American public opinion that has provided Congress both an opportunity and an incentive to assert its prerogatives in foreign affairs is the evident *lack of a public consensus* on the nation's goals in international relations and on the best means for achieving them. This lack of consensus was perhaps an inevitable outcome of the Vietnam War and of certain other diplomatic setbacks experienced by the United States in the years which followed.[73]

At the risk of some oversimplification, we may divide the postwar history of American diplomacy into three stages. First, there was the period — from the early postwar era to the late 1960s — in which a durable national consensus existed in behalf of two ideas: Communist expansionism threatened the security of the United States and other independent nations; and it had to be resisted by the strategy of containment. There followed the period of disillusionment with American involvement in the Vietnam conflict and of ensuing diplomatic retrenchment which lasted until the late 1970s. In this period, millions of Americans and their leaders sometimes doubted America's ability to achieve *any* worthwhile foreign policy objective; and they were extremely cautious about the commitment of the nation's power overseas.[74] Then by the end of the 1970s, a new era of public and congressional disaffection with the limitations on America's influence and the nation's ability to protect its diplomatic and security interests emerged.

By 1980, the Carter administration encountered severe criticism inside and outside the United States for its failure or inability to use American power decisively in a number of foreign settings. The old anti-Communist consensus — which had sustained a foreign policy of wide interventionism throughout the international system — had disintegrated. On specific foreign policy issues, however — the military balance between the United States and the Soviet Union, or the presence of Soviet troops in Cuba, or attacks against the American Embassy in Iran and other countries — citizens called upon their leaders to safeguard American interests abroad.

What kind of balance should the United States maintain between indiscriminate interventionism and isolationism in foreign affairs? What principles should guide the nation in its role as a superpower in the years ahead? What diplomatic priorities should govern the application of American power in diverse foreign settings? Evolving the answers to these questions will prove a continuing challenge, engaging the attention of leaders and informed citizens for many years to come. One prediction, however, can be made with confidence: Congress is likely to express its views forcefully on these questions and to play an active part in the attempt to formulate a new national consensus on important foreign policy issues.

NOTES

1. For detailed presentation of Senator Church's views, see *The New York Times,* November 24, 1978, dispatch by James Reston.
2. See Senator Ervin's views, as quoted in *The New York Times,* October 12, 1973, dispatch by Linda Charleton.
3. Douglas J. Bennet, Jr., "Congress: Its Role in Foreign Policymaking," *Department of State Bulletin,* 78 (June 1978): 35-36.
4. See Senator Fulbright's views on the decline in the influence of the Senate Foreign Relations Committee in *The New York Times,* January 30, 1972, dispatch by John W. Finney.
5. Holbert N. Carroll, *The House of Representatives and Foreign Affairs* (Pittsburgh, Pa.: University of Pittsburgh Press, 1958), p. 3.
6. See the discussion of "Foreign Affairs and the Articles of Confederation," in Paul A. Varg, *Foreign Policies of the Founding Fathers* (East Lansing, Mich.: Michigan State University Press, 1963), pp. 46-66; and Albert C. V. Westphal, *The House Committee on Foreign Affairs* (New York: Columbia University Press, 1942), pp. 14-15.
7. For detailed examinations of the problems impeding Congress' role as an effective legislative body, see Richard Bolling, *House Out of Order* (New York: E. P. Dutton, 1965); the two studies by Joseph Clark, ed., *Congress: The Sapless Branch* (New York: Harper & Row, 1964) and *Congressional Reform: Problems and Prospects* (New York: Thomas Y. Crowell Co., 1965); Roger H. Davidson et al., *Congress in Crisis: Politics and Congressional Reform* (Belmont, Calif.: Wadsworth Publishing Co., 1966).
8. For more detailed discussion of agricultural dimensions of postwar American foreign policy, see "The Question of Changing U.S. Food Export Policy," *Congressional Digest,* 53 (December 1954): 289-314; and Donald F. Mc-

Henry and Kai Bird, "Food Bungle in Bangladesh," *Foreign Policy,* 27 (Summer 1977): 72-89.

9. *The New York Times,* June 17, 1962.

10. *The New York Times,* November 16, 1965, dispatch by John W. Finney; and February 26, 1967, dispatch by John W. Finney.

11. See Marvin Kalb, "Doves, Hawks and Flutters in the Foreign Relations Committee," *The New York Times Magazine,* November 19, 1967, pp. 56-57, 60-82.

12. *The New York Times,* June 22, 1977, dispatch by Graham Hovey.

13. *Congressional Quarterly Almanac: 1977,* 33 (Washington, D.C.: Congressional Quarterly, 1977), p. 319.

14. *The New York Times,* July 3, 1977, dispatch by Adam Clymer.

15. "House Opponents of Panama Canal Turnover Opposing Implementing Legislation," Congressional Quarterly *Weekly Report,* 37 (February 17, 1979): 306 and *The New York Times,* February 19, 1979.

16. For a detailed analysis of the problem under the Carter administration, see Tad Szulc, "Springtime for Carter," *Foreign Policy,* 27 (Summer 1977): 178-191.

17. Holbert N. Carroll, "The Congress and National Security Policy," in David B. Truman, ed., *The Congress and America's Future* (Englewood Cliffs, N.J.: Prentice-Hall, 1965), p. 152.

18. In *United States* v. *Curtiss-Wright Export Corp.,* 299 U.S. 304 (1936), the Supreme Court recognized a fundamental distinction between the powers of the national government in domestic and foreign affairs. In that case, the prerogatives of the chief executive to manage foreign relations were forcefully affirmed.

19. Jefferson's views on the role of the president in foreign affairs are quoted in Francis O. Wilox, *Congress, the Executive, and Foreign Policy* (New York: Harper & Row, 1971), p. 146.

20. Julius W. Pratt, *A History of United States Foreign Policy* (Englewood Cliffs, N.J.: Prentice-Hall, 1955), pp. 79-80.

21. Dexter Perkins, *The American Approach to Foreign Policy* (New York: Atheneum, 1968), p. 191.

22. For historical background on the Senate's actions with regard to treaties, see W. Stull Holt, *Treaties Defeated by the Senate* (Baltimore: Johns Hopkins University Press, 1933).

23. Cecil V. Crabb, Jr., *Bipartisan Foreign Policy: Myth or Reality?* (New York: Harper & Row, 1957), pp. 168-170.

24. The senatorial contribution during this period is highlighted in Arthur H. Vandenberg, Jr., ed., *The Private Papers of Senator Vandenberg* (Boston: Houghton Mifflin & Co., 1952).

25. See the views of Representative Thomas E. Morgan, chairman of the House Foreign Affairs Committee, as cited in Wilcox, *Congress, the Executive, and Foreign Policy,* p. 6.

26. See the views of Representative John D. Dingell in *U.S. News & World Report,* 86 (March 19, 1979): 46.

27. See the views of Senator Frank Church, as quoted in Loch Johnson and James M. McCormick, "Foreign Policy by Executive Fiat," *Foreign Policy,* 28 (Fall 1977): 133.

28. See the study prepared by the Library of Congress for the Senate Foreign Relations Committee, *The Senate Role in Foreign Affairs Appointments,* 92d Cong., 1st sess., 1971, pp. 3-10.

29. Ibid., p. 11.

30. See Dwight D. Eisenhower, *Mandate for Change: 1953-1956* (Garden City, N.Y.: Doubleday & Co., 1963), pp. 212-213.

31. See the views expressed at Senate hearings on the confirmation of Leonard Woodcock as ambassador to China, in the Congressional Quarterly *Weekly Report,* 37 (January 20, 1979): 97.

32. See the provisions of P.L. 95-92 and the *Congressional Quarterly Almanac: 1977,* 33, p. 365.

33. See P.L. 95-88 and the *Congressional Quarterly Almanac: 1977,* 33, p. 359.

34. See P.L. 95-108 and the *Congressional Quarterly Almanac: 1977,* 33, p. 345.

35. See P.L. 95-105 and the *Congressional Quarterly Almanac: 1977,* 33, p. 347.

36. For an illuminating analysis of the role of the House of Representatives in the appropriations process, see Richard F. Fenno, Jr., "The House Appropriations Committee as a Political System," *American Political Science Review,* 56 (June 1962): 310-324 and Jeffrey L. Pressman, *House vs. Senate: Conflict in the Appropriations Process* (New Haven, Conn.: Yale University Press, 1966).

37. See Jeffrey L. Pressman, "Focus on the Combatants: The Appropriations Committees," in Sidney Wise and Richard F. Schier, eds., *Studies on Congress* (New York: Thomas Y. Crowell Co., 1969), pp. 141-164.

38. The Baton Rouge *Morning Advocate,* March 3, 1979, dispatch by Peter Finney, Jr.; and Elizabeth B. Drew, "Mr. Passman Meets His Match," *The Reporter,* 31 (November 19, 1964): 40-43.

39. For the text of the Budget and Impoundment Control Act of 1974, see P.L. 93-344. An illuminating discussion of the problems encountered by Congress in the attempt to introduce more centralized decisionmaking on budgetary issues may be found in John W. Ellwood and James A. Thurber, "The New Congressional Budget Process: The Hows and Whys of House-Senate Differences," in Lawrence C. Dodd and Bruce Oppenheimer, eds., *Congress Reconsidered* (New York: Praeger Publishers, 1977), pp. 163-192.

40. A conspicuous example in recent years has been the effort by Congress to limit American contributions to the United Nations and its affiliated agencies. See "The Question of Reducing the U.S. Financial Role in the United Nations," *Congressional Digest,* 54 (March 1975): 65-96.

41. For examples during the Truman, Eisenhower, and Kennedy administrations, see "Controversy Over the Presidential Impoundment of Appropriated Funds," *Congressional Digest,* 52 (April 1973): 97-128.

42. See the *Prize Cases,* 5 Black 67 U.S. 635 (1863).

43. See President Lyndon B. Johnson's statement on the scope of his powers over the military establishment, as cited in Senate Foreign Relations Committee, *National Commitments,* S. Rept. 797, 90th Cong., 1st sess., 1967, p. 22.

44. Thus Senator Jacob Javits was convinced that it would have been most "unfortunate" if Congress had declared war in the Vietnam conflict; this act would have had "unforseeable consequences." See Jacob K. Javits, "The Congressional Presence in Foreign Relations," *Foreign Affairs,* 48 (January 1970): 226.

45. See P.L. 93-148, H.J. Res 542 (November 7, 1973).

46. See, for example, statements by recent presidents on their authority over the armed forces, as contained in Senate Foreign Relations Committee, *Hearings on War Powers Legislation,* 93d Cong., 1st sess., April 11-12, 1973, pp. 167-172.

47. *The New York Times,* March 8, 1976, dispatch by Bernard Gwertzman; May 26, 1978, dispatch by Terence Smith; and June 22, 1978, dispatch by Martin Tolchin. For a case study of congressionally imposed restrictions on the president's diplomatic powers, see N. C. Livingston and M. von Nordheim, "The United States Congress and the Angola Crisis," *Strategic Review,* 5 (Spring 1977): 34-44. Ex-President Gerald Ford's views on the War Powers

Resolution are contained in his memoirs, *A Time to Heal* (New York: Harper & Row, and the Reader's Digest Association, 1979), pp. 251-253, 279-283.

48. This point of view was exemplified in the approach of Senator J. William Fulbright to American foreign policy. Fulbright believed that the nation's diplomatic success depended "on the strength and character of our society, which in turn depend on our success in resolving the great social and economic issues of American life." See his *Old Myths and New Realities* (New York: Random House, 1964), pp. 109, 138. A more detailed analysis of recent neo-isolationist thought is provided in Cecil V. Crabb, Jr., *Policy-Makers and Critics: Conflicting Theories of American Foreign Policy* (New York: Praeger Publishers, 1976), pp. 214-299.

49. *The New York Times,* February 10, 1979, dispatch by Clyde H. Farnsworth.

50. See, for example, the investigations conducted by the Senate Foreign Relations Committee, *Multinational Corporations and United States Foreign Policy,* 93d Cong., 1st sess., March 20-April 2, 1973, Parts 1 and 2, focusing upon the activities of the International Telephone and Telegraph Company in Chile; and February 4-6, and May 4, 1976, Part 14, dealing with the overseas activities of the Lockheed Aircraft Corporation.

51. For an informative discussion of Congress' use of its economic powers to promote human rights abroad, see Richard H. Ullman, "Human Rights and Economic Power: the United States Versus Idi Amin," *Foreign Affairs,* 56 (April 1978): 528-543.

52. Ralph K. Huitt, "Congress, the Durable Partner," in Wise and Schier, eds., *Studies on Congress,* p. 45.

53. For a detailed study of this committee's influence, see Wayne S. Cole, *Senator Gerald P. Nye and American Foreign Relations* (Minneapolis, Minn.: University of Minnesota Press, 1962).

54. See Donald H. Riddle, *The Truman Committee: a Study in Congressional Responsibility* (New Brunswick, N.J.: Rutgers University Press, 1964); and Wilfred E. Binkley, *President and Congress* (New York: Alfred A. Knopf, 1947), pp. 268-269.

55. A useful source on congressional investigations is Arthur M. Schlesinger, Jr. and Roger Burns, eds., *Congress Investigates: A Documented History, 1792-1974,* 5 vols. (New York: Chelsea House Publishers, 1975). For a discussion and documentary materials on Congress' investigation of Communist influences on the State Department and other executive agencies during the early 1950s, see Vol. 5, pp. 3729-3923.

56. Beginning in the late 1960s, the Senate Foreign Relations Committee issued a number of reports and held several hearings on the Vietnam War. See *Stalemate in Vietnam,* 90th Cong., 2d sess., February 1968; and *Impact of the Vietnam War,* 92d Cong., 1st sess., 1971. Major hearings were entitled *Vietnam: Policy and Prospects, 1970,* 91st Cong., 2d sess., February 17-March 19, 1970; and *Vietnam Policy Proposals,* 91st Cong., 2d sess., February 2-March 16, 1970.

57. For an example of Congress' use of foreign travel to influence foreign policy, see Senate Foreign Relations Committee, *Congress and United States-Soviet Relations,* 94th Cong., 1st sess., 1975. This report summarizes a conference between members of the Senate and of the Supreme Soviet in which a variety of diplomatic issues were discussed.

58. I. M. Destler, "Treaty Troubles: Versailles in Reverse," *Foreign Policy,* 33 (Winter 1978-79): 50.

59. One of Congress' most severe critics in recent years has been Senator Joseph S. Clark who took note of the "endless series of demands" made upon legislators which had little to do with their constitutional responsibilities. See

Joseph S. Clark, "The Wonderful World of Congress," in Wise and Schier, eds., *Studies on Congress,* pp. 2, 7.

60. See Robert A. Smith, *The Tiger in the Senate: The Biography of Wayne Morse* (Garden City, N.Y.: Doubleday & Co., 1962).

61. For the text of Fulbright's speech, see the *Congressional Record,* September 15, 1965, Vol. 3, pp. S23855-S23865.

62. *The New York Times,* February 2, 1979, dispatch by Bernard Gwertzman.

63. For a detailed discussion of the impact of Wilsonianism upon the conduct of American foreign relations, see James L. McCamy, *Conduct of the New Diplomacy* (New York: Harper & Row, 1964), pp. 141-163.

64. Senator Taft's views are cited in Norman A. Graebner, "Isolationism," *International Encyclopedia of the Social Sciences* (New York: Crowell Collier and Macmillan, 1968), p. 219; and see Vandenberg, Jr., ed., *The Private Papers of Senator Vandenberg,* p. 1.

65. For the text of Truman's address see *Public Papers of the Presidents of the United States: Harry S. Truman, 1947* (Washington, D.C.: U.S. Government Printing Office, 1963), pp. 176-180.

66. McHenry and Bird, "Food Bungle in Bangladesh," pp. 83-85.

67. Douglas J. Bennet, Jr., "Congress in Foreign Policy: Who Needs It?" *Foreign Affairs,* 57 (Fall 1978): 43.

68. For a detailed discussion of the "Gulf of Tonkin Crisis," see Merlo J. Pusey, *The Way We Go to War* (Boston: Houghton Mifflin Co., 1971), pp. 115-149. An extremely critical account of the Johnson administration's relations with Congress during the crisis is provided in Senator J. William Fulbright, *The Arrogance of Power* (New York: Random House, 1966), pp. 50-53.

69. Senator Vandenberg's complaint was expressed with regard to the Truman administration's presentation of the Greek-Turkish Aid Program to Congress in 1947. See *The New York Times,* March 14, 1947, dispatch by James Reston.

70. See the views of Ross K. Baker on the decline of the seniority system in Congress and the tendency of legislators today to act as "a soloist who plays for his own fans in the audience rather than acting in concert with the other players," in *The New York Times,* November 13, 1979. See also Congressional Quarterly *Weekly Report,* 37 (January 27, 1979): 154.

71. At the end of the 1960s, the congressional staff numbered some 4,500 members. A decade later, it had grown to nearly 13,300 members. In the same period, the staff budget in the Senate was just over $30 million; a decade later it exceeded $100 million. In the House during this decade, staff expenses rose from $45 million to $168 million. See *The New York Times,* January 12, 1979, dispatch by James Reston. For background discussion, see Warren H. Butler, "Administering Congress: The Role of the Staff," *Public Administration Review,* 26 (March 1968): 3-13.

72. See Ross Y. Koen, *The China Lobby in American Politics* (New York: Harper & Row, 1974); and Stanley D. Bachrack, *The Committee of One Million: "China Lobby" Politics, 1953-1971* (New York: Columbia University Press, 1976).

73. Several diverse approaches to American foreign policy in the post-Vietnam War era are identified and discussed in Crabb, *Policy-Makers and Critics,* pp. 1-299. For a good discussion of the problem of arriving at a new foreign policy consensus, see James Chace, "Is a Foreign Policy Consensus Possible?" *Foreign Affairs,* 57 (Fall 1978): 1-17.

74. See Senator J. William Fulbright, *The Crippled Giant: American Foreign Policy and Its Domestic Consequences* (New York: Random House, 1972); and Stanley Hoffmann, *Gulliver's Troubles, or the Setting of American Foreign Policy* (New York: McGraw-Hill Book Co., 1968).

PART II

Congress Confronts the Issues

W e now turn our attention from the general pattern of interaction be- tween Congress and the president in the foreign policy process to five specific case studies or policy areas. The concrete issues selected for examination illustrate Congress' changing perceptions of its role in for- eign policymaking and how the executive branch and public opinion shape these perceptions.

Chapter 3 examines congressional action on the Panama Canal treaties approved by the Senate March 16 and April 18, 1978. This case study demonstrates how the Senate deals with the political dynamics of a highly controversial issue. It is a classic example of the Senate's participation in the treaty-making process and of its exercise of the con- stitutional advice and consent prerogative. Treaty provisions require fol- low-up legislation and appropriations, which involve the House in the treaty process as well. In the case of the Panama treaties especially, the House jealously guarded its own prerogatives.

In the Arab-Israeli conflict, the subject of Chapter 4, Congress has had a lively interest, but no direct constitutional role. It has resorted to one of the few direct levers available to it — the power of the purse — to influence policy formulation by the executive branch. The chapter also illustrates the role and activities of pressure groups in foreign policy.

Chapter 5, "The Armed Forces," recounts ways in which Congress has attempted to draw the line between the constitutional power of the president as commander in chief and the constitutional power of the Congress to declare war and "to make Rules for the Government and Regulation of the land and naval Forces." The chapter highlights the essential pragmatism of the congressional approach. When Congress has agreed with a president's use of the armed forces, it has acquiesced with- out asserting its constitutional prerogatives. When it has disagreed, it has attempted to oppose presidential policies.

In Chapter 6, we examine the legislative oversight role of Congress with particular reference to the intelligence community. Perhaps noth- ing better illustrates the changed attitudes in Congress toward its role in foreign policy than the change in its relationship to the intelligence community. The congressional approach went from almost total neglect following the creation of the Central Intelligence Agency in 1947 to line item scrutiny of the intelligence budget by committees in both the House and Senate in 1977.

Finally, in Chapter 7, congressional initiatives concerning human rights in American foreign policy are examined. Congressional dissatisfaction with the lack of attention given to human rights in foreign policymaking under the Nixon administration sharpened national focus on this hotly disputed issue. But Congress has continued to press human rights in American foreign policy beyond the desires, at times, of even the Carter administration. Chapter 7 also illustrates the limitations on the means available to Congress to implement human rights objectives.

3

The Panama Canal Treaties

Senate consideration of the Panama Canal treaties in 1977-78 is not only a classic example of the Senate's constitutional role in the treaty-making process. It not only marks a watershed in American foreign policy. It also provides an illuminating case study of the Senate as an institution and of how individual senators can maneuver through the political minefields of a highly controversial issue and turn it to their advantage. Finally, House action on the implementing legislation in 1979 illustrates the different views of the two bodies about how the treaty-making process ought to work. Specifically, it demonstrates the determination of the House to become a more influential body in dealing with major foreign policy issues. The story began years before the treaties reached the Senate.

BACKGROUND

"Strategic" is a word which is frequently misused to exaggerate the importance of an area, but it applies literally and forcefully to the 50-mile wide Isthmus of Panama joining the North and South American continents. Panama has lived off its geography from the time the first European, Vasco Núñez de Balboa, crossed the isthmus in 1513. In the sixteenth century, Spaniards used the isthmus to transship the gold and silver they took out of Peru and Bolivia. In the nineteenth century, Americans used it as the quickest route to the California gold fields, and American interests even built a railroad across it.

In the late nineteenth century, a French company undertook to dig a canal across the isthmus, a project ending in such dismal failure that the French began looking for a way to unload it and recoup at least some of their losses. The United States had been rather languidly interested in just such a project for a number of years, and this interest was now whetted not only by the French, but especially by the experience of the Spanish-American War in 1898 when it took more than two months to move warships from the Pacific to the Atlantic around the tip of South America.

At this time, Panama was a part of Colombia; and when the Colombian Senate, in August 1903, rejected a treaty giving the United States the right to build a canal across Panama, President Theodore Roosevelt and the French interests took matters into their own hands.

The result was a revolution in Panama on November 3, and the conclusion on November 18 of the Bunau-Varilla treaty between the United States and Panama. With unprecedented speed, the Senate approved the pact on February 23 by a vote of 66-14. The new treaty provided for American construction of a canal. Significantly, the Panamanian negotiator of this treaty was not Panamanian at all, but the Frenchman Philippe Jean Bunau-Varilla, the agent of the French canal company!

The new treaty was much more favorable to the United States than had been the treaty rejected by Colombia. It gave the United States control "in perpetuity" over a Canal Zone 10 miles wide and the authority to act "as if it were sovereign." The United States also got the right to use, occupy, and control any other lands or waters necessary or convenient for construction and maintenance of the canal, the right of eminent domain in the cities of Panama and Colon and adjoining areas, and the right to intervene for the general maintenance and protection of the canal. What Panama got was $10 million plus annual payments of $250,000 beginning in nine years. It also was given a United States guarantee of its independence, such as it was.[1] Roosevelt later bragged, "I took the canal zone."[2]

This set the stage for a clash of the national pride of both countries. For the United States, the canal became a symbol of American achievement in making a centuries-old, seemingly impossible dream come true. The United States overcame every imaginable kind of obstacle. Americans were proud of the smooth functioning of the locks and gates; after three-quarters of a century, the original engineering has not been improved on.

For Panamanians, the Canal — and more especially, the Canal Zone — became a symbol that Panama was something less than a whole country. The United States always recognized that the 1903 treaty left residual or titular sovereignty over the Zone in Panama. But since the United States had the right to act "as if it were sovereign" — even though it was not — this recognition had more importance as a legal theory than as a practical reality.

In response to Panamanian pressure, the United States renegotiated the 1903 treaty in 1936 and again in 1955. The annual payment was increased to reflect the devaluation of the dollar, and some concessions were made with respect to the Zone commissaries, U.S. exercise of eminent domain outside the Zone, and the right of intervention. But nothing fundamental was changed.

All this time, the Canal continued to operate smoothly and efficiently in the service of world commerce. It speeded the flow of supplies and the passage of the American navy through two world wars, the war in Korea, and the war in Vietnam. It was taken for granted as fundamental to American national security. Most Americans saw no reason to change something that was working so well.

Confrontation

Thus the stage was set for confrontation, and it was in the nature of things that trouble would erupt over the symbolic issue of the flag.

One of Panama's objectives in the 1955 negotiations for revision of the 1903 treaty was that ships transiting the Canal should fly both the Panamanian and the American flags in recognition of the maritime tradition that ships fly the flag of the country through whose territorial waters they are passing. The United States refused this demand.

There was also Panamanian agitation, sometimes riotous, to fly the flag in the Zone. This began to make an impression in the United States. Following particularly severe riots in Panama in November 1959, President Eisenhower announced in a December news conference that "we should have visual evidence that Panama does have titular sovereignty over the region."[3] Privately, he remarked that he had no objection to flying the Panamanian flag, but he was "goddamned if I'm going to do it with a gun at my head."[4]

At the same time, however, the hard-core resistance in the United States to any change was strengthened. On February 2, 1960, by a vote of 382-12, the House of Representatives passed a concurrent resolution declaring that "any variation in the traditional interpretation" of treaties with Panama, "with special reference to matters concerning territorial sovereignty, shall be made only pursuant to treaty"[5] — that is, with a two-thirds vote in the Senate.

The resolution did not obtain the concurrence of the Senate and therefore never took effect. This signaled the executive branch that the Senate was less determined to maintain the status quo than the House and might be willing to give it room to maneuver.

Bit by bit, the executive branch made concessions, leading to a 1963 agreement that the Panamanian flag would be flown together with the American flag wherever the latter was flown on land in the Canal Zone by civilian authorities. This new policy was disliked by the American residents of the Zone. When it was ordered that neither flag should be flown at Balboa High School, the students took matters into their own hands on January 7, 1964, and raised the American flag. They repeated this the next day.

On the afternoon of the following day, January 9, a group of approximately 200 Panamanian students from the National Institute in Panama City entered the Canal Zone with the intention of raising a Panamanian flag on the Balboa High School flagpole. They were confronted by twice as many American students, or more. Some scuffling ensued, and the Panamanians withdrew. Within a few hours, riots involving thousands of Panamanians and directed against the Zone erupted in Panama City and across the isthmus in Colon at the Atlantic terminus of the Canal. By the time order was restored on January 13, twenty-one people had been killed and 120 injured.

On January 10, while the riots were at their height, Panama took the drastic step of breaking diplomatic relations with the United States and made "complete revision" of the existing treaties a condition for resuming relations. After almost three months of tedious negotiations, both parties agreed "to seek the prompt elimination of the causes of conflict between the two countries, without limitations or preconditions of any kind" and to pursue the objective "of reaching a just and fair agreement which would be subject to the constitutional processes of each country."[6]

The Negotiations

There now began, with glacial speed, the tedious work of negotiation, which extended from the spring of 1964 to the summer of 1977. By 1967, the negotiators had reached agreement, subject to the approval of their governments, on a set of new treaties — one dealing with a new regime for the Canal, one dealing with possible construction of a sea level canal in the indeterminate future, and one dealing with American defense base rights. The texts leaked prematurely in Panama to the *Chicago Tribune,* and the resulting hue and cry in both countries, but especially in Panama, was so great that the Panamanian government felt compelled to repudiate the work of its negotiators.

In Panama, opponents of the draft treaties thought the United States had not made enough concessions; in the United States, opponents thought it had made too many. The negotiations began again with the problem in starker focus: to devise treaties which could be ratified in one country without being rejected in the other.

This proved to be an extremely difficult and time-consuming problem. Panamanian negotiators were subjected to intense pressures by nationalist elements at home, opposing any concessions to American demands. For their part, American negotiators had to carry on, in effect, two sets of negotiations — one with their own government and one with Panama. The first set of negotiations arose out of the diversity of American bureaucratic interests in Panama. The State Department, responsible for relations between the United States and the Republic of Panama and sensitive to world opinion, tended to argue for a more flexible U.S. position. The United States Army, which operated the Canal and governed the Zone, tended to reflect the views of the American residents of the Zone, views strongly in favor of maintaining the status quo. The Joint Chiefs of Staff, charged with the responsibility of defending the Canal and the Zone, were concerned principally with military base rights, with access, and with jurisdiction over American military personnel. Many of the delays in the negotiations were caused not only by the disarray of the Panamanians (who went through various changes of government during this period), but also by the time-consuming task of bringing the United States government itself to a unified position.

The Role of Congress. Each of the contending bureaucratic groups had its friends in Congress, generally corresponding to committee jurisdictions. The Senate Foreign Relations and House Foreign Affairs committees tended to be linked with the State Department; the Armed Services committees with the army and the Joint Chiefs of Staff; and the House Merchant Marine and Fisheries Committee (which, through a quirk in House rules, had jurisdiction over the Canal and Zone) with the Panama Canal Company and the Canal Zone government.

The Senate Foreign Relations Committee had the most direct interest because it would handle whatever treaty resulted. Some members of the committee privately advised the Johnson administration to begin the negotiations and to make some concessions. But generally the committee limited itself to keeping quietly informed while maintaining a low profile and leaving negotiations to the executive branch. Its members' political instincts told them that a treaty making significant concessions would be unpopular.

During most of the period of the negotiations, the chairman of the House Merchant Marine and Fisheries Committee (Leonor K. Sullivan, D-Mo.) and the chairman of its subcommittee on the Panama Canal (John M. Murphy, D-N.Y.) were among the most vocal opponents of change. Mainly through hearings and reports, the committee sought to lay the groundwork for the argument that American property in the Canal Zone could not be disposed of through a treaty, but only through legislation approved by both houses.

The basis for this argument lies in Article IV, Section 3 of the Constitution that gives Congress the "Power to dispose of and make all needful Rules and Regulations respecting the Territory or other Property belonging to the United States." There are, however, a number of precedents whereby territory has been disposed of by treaty, and there is also a question of whether the Canal Zone, where residual sovereignty remained in Panama, was ever American territory in the first place. The Department of Justice found a treaty to be a legal way to handle the matter. A number of members of Congress and the attorneys general of four states brought suit challenging the validity of the treaties under Article IV of the Constitution. All of these attempts failed in the Supreme Court, but the House may have had the last word, as we shall see, in the implementing legislation.

The first legislative involvement by Congress in the negotiations came in 1975, when it appeared that they might be drawing to a conclusion. Representative Gene Snyder of Kentucky, the ranking minority member of the Panama Canal Subcommittee, offered an amendment to the fiscal year 1976 State Department appropriation bill prohibiting the use of funds for negotiating "the surrender or relinquishment of any United States rights in the Panama Canal Zone." It passed the House by a vote of 246-164.

The Senate struck out the amendment, and the conferees agreed to a compromise that "any new Panama Canal treaty or agreement must protect the vital interests of the United States in the operation, maintenance, property and defense of the Panama Canal." In a startling demonstration of antitreaty sentiment, the House rejected this compromise by a 197-203 vote.

A second conference added a reference to protection of "vital interests . . . in the Canal Zone," and this was approved by the House by a shaky vote of 212-201.[7] Similar efforts by opponents of the still prospective treaties were made in 1976 and 1977, but these failed by larger margins.

The Treaties. Finally, in the summer of 1977, negotiations ended. The treaties were signed by President Carter and Brig. Gen. Omar Torrijos Herrera on September 7 in an unprecedented ceremony attended by representatives of 26 Western Hemisphere nations.

The two treaties in a single document were formally transmitted to the Senate September 16. One was called, simply, the Panama Canal Treaty. The other was called, more awkwardly, the Treaty Concerning the Permanent Neutrality and Operation of the Panama Canal (hereafter referred to as the Neutrality Treaty).

The Panama Canal Treaty terminated and superseded the treaty of 1903 and subsequent agreements. Thereby at one stroke it abolished the Canal Zone. The United States retained the right to manage, operate, and maintain the Canal and to provide for the movement of ships. This was to be done, however, not through the old Panama Canal Company, but through a new agency, the Panama Canal Commission, which was to have a board of nine members, four of whom would be Panamanians. After December 31, 1999, the Canal in its entirety would pass to Panamanian control.

Until that date, the United States retained military base rights, as well as the primary responsibility for defense of the Canal for the duration of the treaty. Panama was given a fixed payment of $10 million a year, plus 30 cents for each ton of shipping transiting the Canal, plus an additional sum of up to $10 million a year if there were a surplus of operating revenues over expenditures. Finally, there was a multitude of administrative provisions.

The Neutrality Treaty established a permanent regime of neutrality for the Canal "in order that both in time of peace and in time of war [the Canal] shall remain secure and open to peaceful transit by the vessels of all nations on terms of entire equality, so that there will be no discrimination against any nation, or its citizens or subjects, concerning the conditions or charges of transit, or for any other reason." The same regime of neutrality was to apply to any other canal that might be built in Panama. After termination of the Panama Canal Treaty in 1999, no nation other than Panama could operate the Canal or maintain military installations in Panamanian territory. Finally, the warships of the United States and Panama were to be entitled to transit the Canal "expeditiously."[8]

ADVICE AND CONSENT OF THE SENATE

With the treaties now formally before the Senate, the long preliminaries were over at last and the political process of Senate action could begin. The administration and the Democratic leadership in the Senate had already started to lay the groundwork. In April, the Senate Foreign Relations Committee had been informed that a breakthrough in the negotiations was imminent. The focus of executive-Senate contacts then shifted from the committee to the office of Majority Leader Robert C. Byrd. During the summer, Byrd arranged a series of quiet meetings with senators of differing viewpoints. These informal meetings marked a departure from what had been the customary leadership of Foreign Relations. Byrd was more assertive of his prerogatives as majority leader than had been any of his recent predecessors, with the exception of Lyndon Johnson. The Foreign Relations Committee was perceived to be less influential than it once had been. And, in any event, the White House and Byrd were not worried about how members of Foreign Relations would vote; they were worried about other senators.

The arithmetic was predetermined by the constitutional requirement that the treaties had to be approved by two-thirds of the senators present and voting. This meant that if all 100 senators voted (which they, in fact, did), supporters of the treaties needed 67 votes while opponents needed only 34. In November, a United Press International (UPI) poll showed 37 senators uncommitted, 36 either for or leaning for the treaties, and 27 either against or leaning against. The number shown uncommitted was almost surely exaggerated. Most senators who said they were undecided probably had a pretty good idea of how they would vote, but did not want to say so publicly at too early a stage.

A more realistic way of measuring senatorial opinion at this point would have been as follows:

- Those who passionately believed that the treaties were in the best interests of the United States and that rejecting them would be calamitous for the American position in the world;
- Those who were predisposed to support the president but not at the risk of their own political careers;
- Those who did not care very much one way or the other and approached the issue from the point of view of what they could get

out of it in terms of help in the Senate or from the administration on some other issue that they did care about;
- Those who did not like the treaties very much, but were reluctant to oppose the president;
- Those who passionately believed that the treaties were bad for the United States and would lead to disaster.

Except for the groups at each extreme, there were, of course, a multitude of shadings and gradations. Some senators voted solely on the basis of their mail and the polls. Although Senator Edward Zorinsky, D-Neb., personally favored the treaties, his constituents opposed them; in the end, Zorinsky opposed them, too. It is probably safe to say that most senators would have been grateful if they had not had to face the issue at all.

The competing strategies of the contending forces were dictated by these feelings and were essentially mirror images of each other. Supporters of the treaties had to make it politically safe for senators to vote yes, or failing this, at least to limit the political damage as much as possible. Opponents had to make the risk of voting yes politically unacceptable.

Each side pursued its strategy at several levels simultaneously. At one level, there was the battle for public opinion. At another, there were maneuvers to change the treaties. The objective of the opponents was simple: to change the treaties so much that even if they were approved by the Senate, they would be rejected by Panama. The objective of the supporters was more subtle: to reap the political benefit of something that could be presented as an improvement in the treaties without changing them so fundamentally as to lead to their rejection by Panama. At yet a third level, there was old-fashioned logrolling and vote-trading among senators and between senators and the White House. The question of the merits of the treaties themselves was the final debating point.

At this last level, the proponents of the treaties had to demonstrate to the satisfaction of reasonable but skeptical people that the treaties at a minimum protected, and at a maximum advanced, the national interests of the United States. The opponents had only to create doubts that this was true. If they could, in addition, demonstrate that the treaties raised the possibility of a threat to those interests, that was so much the better.

These strategies required time to work themselves out. The Foreign Relations Committee held 16 days of hearings on the treaties in September and October 1977 and January 1978. The published record comprises four volumes totaling 2,423 pages. The committee heard more than 90 witnesses on all sides of the issue, perhaps as impressive an array as has ever been assembled for a congressional hearing. They included not only the negotiators of the treaties, but also the secretaries of state, defense, and transportation, the attorney general, the chairman of the Joint Chiefs of Staff, and distinguished representatives of academia, business, and labor, as well as other groups. Former Secretaries of State Dean Rusk and Henry Kissinger testified, as did two former chairmen of the Joint Chiefs of Staff, Admiral Thomas Moorer and General Maxwell Taylor. During December and January, ten of the 16 members of the committee also visited Panama. Every aspect of the treaties was examined in exhaustive, repetitive detail. This was the indispensable foundation for the forthcoming Senate debate.

Following its hearings, the Foreign Relations Committee spent three days discussing the treaties, and on January 30 ordered them reported by a vote of 14-1. The dissenter was Senator Robert P. Griffin, R-Mich. He thought the treaties should be returned to the president for renegotiation.

Senate debate began February 6 and continued, to the virtual exclusion of all other business, until April 18 — the longest Senate debate on a treaty since the Treaty of Versailles ending World War I. The Senate gave its advice and consent to ratification of the Neutrality Treaty on March 16 by a vote of 68-32. The Panama Canal Treaty was approved April 18 by an identical vote. Democrats voted for the treaties 52-10; Republicans voted against them 16-22. Leading the opposition were Senators James B. Allen, D-Ala., and Paul D. Laxalt, R-Nev. The leaders of the protreaty forces, besides Majority Leader Byrd and Minority Leader Howard H. Baker, Jr., R-Tenn., were members of the Senate Foreign Relations Committee, Frank Church, D-Idaho (later to become chairman) and freshman Paul Sarbanes, D-Md.

The Battle for Public Opinion

Despite the outcry from conservative and veterans groups following disclosure of the 1967 draft treaties, many senators were astonished by the depth of the response which Ronald Reagan evoked in campaigning against concessions to Panama in 1976. The objective of opponents of the treaties was to convert this response into massive antitreaty mail to the Senate. Hundreds of thousands of letters and postcards poured in, at one point in ratios as great as 300-1 against the treaties. Some of them were nasty. One received by Senator Thomas J. McIntyre, D-N.H., said the writer and 200 million other Americans hoped that McIntyre and all the rest were assassinated if the treaties were ratified.[9]

The opposition strategy was based on a principle of congressional political behavior: one gets elected not so much by pleasing people as by not offending them. This principle has become more important with the growth of single-issue politics — that is, the growing numbers of people who judge candidates not on their overall record or platform, but on their stand with respect to a single issue such as abortion or gun control. The Conservative Caucus, one of the most active opposition groups, had a voter pledge program with the goal of getting commitments from 10,000 voters in each state that they would "never vote for any person who votes for the treaties."

Although the proponents, whose efforts were coordinated in the White House, did not neglect the public at large, their campaign was directed specifically to individuals who could mold public opinion. To counter the perception of the treaties as a sellout or a giveaway, the White House secured endorsements from broadly representative, respected community or national leaders whose prestige, it was hoped, would make it respectable to support the treaties. To this end, a series of intimate briefings was organized to take place in the White House itself with appearances by the president, his national security adviser Zbigniew Brzezinski, the secretary of state, the secretary of defense, and one or more members of the Joint Chiefs of Staff. Candidates for invitations to these meetings were frequently suggested by senators who wanted to vote for the treaties and needed outside help in convincing important constituents.

Twenty-four senators who voted on the treaties sought re-election in 1978. Of those who voted for the treaties, seven were re-elected and eight defeated. Of those who voted against the treaties, eight were re-elected and one was defeated. There is no way to determine with any precision the weight that should be assigned to the controversy over the treaties in assessing these results; but it seems safe to say that, other things remaining equal, the result of a Senate vote on the treaties might well have been different in 1979 than in 1978.

Changing the Treaties

The administration's effort to bring public opinion around was a necessary, but not a sufficient, condition for Senate approval of the treaties. It was also necessary that senators be in a position to take credit for improving the treaties in one way or another.

Senators by and large react negatively when confronted with a take-it-or-leave-it proposition, and changing the treaties was a way to avoid looking like a rubber stamp for the president. It was also a way to allow a senator to have something with his name on it written into the treaties. This was not only important to senatorial egos; it also tended to make a senator view the treaties (with his handiwork in them) more sympathetically. Furthermore, proposals to change the treaties gave the leadership a potent weapon. It is always easier for a senator to get an amendment adopted if it is accepted by the leadership, and in many cases the leadership decides whether or not to accept an amendment on the basis of how the senator will vote on final passage. Finally, changing the treaties contributed — or so senators thought — to a public perception that although the treaties might have been defective as they had been negotiated, the Senate had changed them to remedy those defects and protect the national interest. This provided an opportunity for senators to begin by criticizing the treaties and to end by supporting them.

The amendment process is one of the ways the Senate skirts an issue rather than meeting it head on. It is one way of defusing single-issue politics. In this case, it enabled a senator to avoid coming out foursquare for the treaties as negotiated. He might win this argument on the basis of logic and the facts, but not in political terms. The alternative was to argue, not in favor of the treaties as signed, but in favor of the treaties as they had been changed by the Senate, preferably by adoption of an amendment or reservation proposed by the senator making the argument.

The real issue in the Senate became the degree of change. Supporters of the treaties had to limit the changes to what would be acceptable to Panama; opponents had to push them beyond those limits.

The lengths to which both sides went in pursuing these tactics are to be seen in the numbers of changes proposed. In all, senators offered 145 amendments, 26 reservations, 18 understandings, and three declarations — a grand total of 192 changes of one kind or another. Some of these got incorporated in the resolutions of ratification as "conditions" — a new terminology for Senate action on treaties, perhaps important to somebody semantically, but not legally. (The murky distinctions between amendments, reservations, understandings, declarations, and conditions are explained in Chapter 1.)

A large number of the proposed changes duplicated in some way or superseded others. In the course of the Senate debate, 88 were actually voted on. All the approved changes were acceptable to the leadership. The most important concerned the neutrality and defense of the Canal and transit rights for the American navy.

Neutrality and Expeditious Transit. The provision regarding neutrality of the Canal, Secretary of State Cyrus R. Vance told the Foreign Relations Committee, "means that there is no limit under the treaty on the freedom of the United States to assure permanently the canal's neutrality."[10] And in response to a question from Senator Clifford P. Case, R-N.J., he was even more specific: "I think our right [to intervene] is clear, and there can be no question about it."[11]

Panamanians, of course, had a different view. Even before the treaties had been signed, chief negotiator Romulo Escobar Bethancourt said, "We are not giving the United States a right of intervention. What we are giving is an assurance that the Canal will be permanently neutral."[12]

The matter was enlivened a bit more when Senator Robert Dole, R-Kan., made public a confidential telegram from the American embassy in Panama to the State Department reporting a conversation with negotiator Carlos López Guevara. López had told an embassy officer: "Panama cannot agree to the right of the U.S. to intervene."[13]

Naturally. No Latin American government can agree to such a right and expect to survive. But the treaties' opponents now had an issue that cast doubt on the right of the United States to defend the Canal's neutrality in the indefinite future. From this, it did not take much imagination to conjure up a situation in which the Canal could conceivably be seized by forces hostile to the United States and then closed to American shipping.

With respect to the right of U.S. and Panamanian naval vessels to "transit the Canal expeditiously," Vance said this meant "our ships can go to the head of the line." Escobar and López said that the U.S. Navy would not be given "preferential rights," that such language had been proposed and rejected during the negotiations. Although it seemed reasonable to suppose that the right to transit the Canal "expeditiously" meant the right to do so without waiting in line, there was enough confusion about the matter to allow for the specter of the American navy waiting on one side of Panama while the world was in flames on the other side.

In a letter to the Senate Foreign Relations Committee October 5, the State Department sought to deal with the problem of ensuring the Canal's neutrality, but succeeded only in muddying the waters further:

> Panama and the United States each will have the right to take any appropriate measures to defend the Canal against any threat to the regime of neutrality established in the Treaty.
> The Treaty does not give the United States any right to intervene in the internal affairs of Panama, nor has it been our intention to seek or to exercise such a right.[14]

The State Department did not say the United States had the right to take "any measure" — only "any appropriate measures." Nor did the department deal with what would happen if a threat to the Canal arose from an internal situation in Panama.

The uproar over the ambiguities concerning the Canal's neutrality and the transit of the United States Navy alarmed both governments and appeared to be a genuine threat to the treaties in the Senate. General Torrijos at this time was in Europe on a tour (which also included Israel) designed to drum up international support for the treaties. On his way home, he stopped for a day in Washington to see President Carter. From this meeting there emerged a "statement of understanding" which said, with respect to neutrality:

> The correct interpretation of this principle is that each of the two countries shall, in accordance with their respective constitutional processes, defend the Canal against any threat to the regime of neutrality, and consequently shall have the right to act against any aggression or threat directed against the Canal or against the peaceful transit of vessels through the Canal.
> This does not mean, nor shall it be interpreted as, a right of intervention of the United States in the internal affairs of Panama. Any United States action will be directed at insuring that the Canal will remain open, secure and accessible, and it shall never be directed against the territorial integrity or political independence of Panama.

With respect to the passage of American and Panamanian warships, the statement of understanding stated:

This is intended, and it shall so be interpreted, to assure the transit
of such vessels through the Canal as quickly as possible, without any
impediment, with expedited treatment, and in the case of need or
emergency, to go to the head of the line of vessels in order to transit the
Canal rapidly.[15]

This statement of understanding calmed the uproar, but it did not
wholly eliminate the problem, which was enmeshed in the larger strategies of the contending forces. Nobody understood the delicacy of the
situation better or maneuvered more skillfully to win passage of the treaties than Senate Minority Leader Howard Baker. From the beginning of
Senate consideration of the treaties, Baker kept his own counsel and
studiously presented an open mind to the public. At the opening of hearings in September, Baker announced, "For the time being I have decided not to decide what I think about the treaties."[16]

On a tour of Latin America in January, Baker spent five days in
Panama. It is indicative of the importance the White House attached to
Baker's trip that he was accompanied by Frank Moore, the president's
chief congressional liaison officer. While in Panama, Baker and his
group, which also included Senators Jake Garn, R-Utah, and John H.
Chaffee, R-R.I., spent one day and part of another with General
Torrijos. In the course of these conversations, Baker negotiated with
Torrijos some changes in the treaties. As the group's report explains:

> . . .the delegation advised General Torrijos that the treaties as submit-
> ted to the Senate had no chance of obtaining the Senate's consent to
> ratification. He was further advised that there might be enough flexibil-
> ity in the Senate to secure consent to ratification were guarantees of
> United States rights more clearly spelled out in the treaties by way of
> amendment. In particular, reference was made to the need to incor-
> porate the language of the Statement of Understanding previously is-
> sued by General Torrijos and President Carter into the text of the trea-
> ties with regard to the United States' right to defend the Canal after the
> year 2000 and to secure priority passage in time of emergency. Torrijos
> indicated that he was open-minded with regard to modification of the
> treaties and that it was his belief that no additional plebiscite would be
> necessary under the Panamanian Constitution if modifications of the
> treaties were limited to the incorporation of the Statement of Under-
> standing, as that statement had been fully explained to the Pana-
> manian people prior to their October plebiscite.[17]

Amendments were drafted to incorporate in the treaties the text of
the statement of understanding. With Byrd as the principal sponsor and
Baker as the driving force, the provision on neutrality was adopted by a
vote of 84-5 and the provision on expeditious transit by a vote of 85-3. If
this did not set at rest all doubts, it at least went far enough to give a
large measure of protection to senators voting for the treaties.

Pursuing the strategy of giving senators the maximum opportunity
to associate themselves with changes in the treaties, within limits
acceptable to Panama, Byrd urged the Foreign Relations Committee not
to incorporate changes of its own but rather only to recommend changes

to the Senate. This would give senators a way to cosponsor amendments in the Senate and thereby have their names identified with specific changes. It was also a sharp departure from the usual practice in which a Senate committee actually makes the changes it desires and sends a finished product to the Senate. This finished product is, of course, subject to amendment; but if a senator agrees with the changes made by a committee, the only way he can identify himself with them is by making a speech. He cannot get his name in the record as having been one of those suggesting the change.

Some members of the Foreign Relations Committee, including its chairman, John Sparkman of Alabama, did not like Byrd's suggested procedure very much. Nevertheless, in the interests of advancing the treaties, they cooperated.

Defense of the Canal. On March 15, freshman Senator Dennis DeConcini, D-Ariz., met with President Carter and received his support for an amendment (which became a "condition") allowing the United States "to use military force in Panama" or to take such other steps as it deemed necessary to keep the Canal open after the year 2000.[18] With administration support, this was adopted in the Senate, with respect to the Neutrality Treaty, on March 16 by a vote of 75-23.

The Panamanians, as should have been foreseen, took strong exception. With a vote nearing on the second treaty, this development threw the administration and the Senate leadership into consternation. There was nothing to be done about the Neutrality Treaty; the Senate had already completed action. Unless a way was found to modify this action in the Panama Canal Treaty, however, the clear likelihood existed that the whole painstakingly put together package would be rejected by Panama. But if the condition were modified so much as to cause the defection of DeConcini on the second vote, the package might well be defeated in the Senate.

Frantic negotiations ensued — within the Senate, between the Senate and the administration, between the Senate and Panamanians, and between the administration and Panamanians. William D. Rogers, a Washington lawyer and former assistant secretary of state for inter-American affairs, was brought in as an unofficial catalyst and go-between. (Rogers is not to be confused with William P. Rogers, the former secretary of state and also a Washington lawyer.)

Well-known for his expertise with respect to both Latin America and the ways of Washington, Rogers was approached by the Panamanian government to represent it in the affair in an attorney-client relationship. He consulted the State Department, which advocated his involvement, and the Justice Department, which warned of a possible conflict of interest stemming from his previous service as assistant secretary. This problem was resolved by Rogers using only his good offices — an arrangement, as he ruefully pointed out, which meant that he could not be paid. The condition he laid down was accepted by both governments: he would be the sole channel of communication between them. This meant not only that he could be sure of being fully informed, but also that he would be in a position to advise each government with respect to the substance of the communications. It was a position he could not have been in if he had been representing the government of Panama as an attorney. It was also, he said later, a condition he would not have accepted if it had been proposed by an outside party while he was in the State Department.

In the end — on Sunday morning, April 16, preceding the final Senate vote on Tuesday the 18th — the matter was resolved in a meeting in Frank Church's Capitol hideaway office among Church; Byrd; Paul S. Sarbanes, the chairman of the Foreign Relations Committee's Latin American subcommittee; Rogers; Panamanian Ambassador Gabriel Lewis; and Deputy Secretary of State Warren Christopher.

The compromise text was in the form of a new condition omitting the reference to the use of force and stating that any action the United States might take to keep the Canal open "shall not have as its purpose nor be interpreted as a right of intervention" in Panama nor of "interference with its political independence or sovereign integrity."[19]

Ambassador Lewis checked this new condition with his government. Panama approved it later that day; Senator DeConcini approved it the following day. The Senate leadership had successfully extricated itself from the dilemma brought about by Carter's agreement to the DeConcini amendment in the first place. This agreement is explicable only in terms of the president's anxiety to nail down at any price an additional vote for the treaty. Carter did get the additional vote, but he almost lost the treaty.

The effort to vitiate the effect of the DeConcini amendment without appearing to do so brought to a high point another facet of Senate consideration of the Panama treaties, an aspect which was unprecedented in the long history of the Senate's role in the treaty-making process. This was the degree of involvement of senators in direct negotiations with foreign officials about a treaty after the treaty had been negotiated and signed by the executive branch.

During the period between the signing of the treaties in September and the opening of Senate debate in February, almost half the Senate visited Panama and talked to General Torrijos and other Panamanian officials. For most of these senators, it was a fact-finding and orientation trip. Some went because they were genuinely interested in obtaining on-the-scene impressions, some because they felt their political future required it. But some of them — Senator Baker, for example — discussed with Torrijos and others prospective amendments to the treaties, at least in general terms. This process culminated in the frantic negotiations over the DeConcini amendment when the Panamanian ambassador personally took part.

With respect to a wide range of matters, senators have always had a variety of social and other informal contacts with the Washington diplomatic corps and with foreign officials. Frequently, senators have been members of American delegations to international meetings. But the extent to which senators became directly involved with Panamanian officials raised a new question for foreign governments: Are they dealing with one United States government or with two — or with even more, in view of the fact that the Senate rarely takes a unified approach? In making a treaty, do they have to go through a process of multiple negotiations — one with the executive branch and a second (or third or fourth) with the Senate? And if it is a multiple negotiating process, how much reliance can foreigners put on the first stage? The question recurred in connection with the SALT II agreement with the Soviet Union.

Quid Pro Quos: The Politics of the Senate

As the time for the final vote on the first treaty approached, the administration increased its pressure on uncommitted senators — pressure which was by no means wholly unwelcome and which no doubt explained why some senators had remained uncommitted as long as they did. It gave them more bargaining power with the administration.

After the Democratic senators from Georgia, Herman Talmadge and Sam Nunn, announced their support on March 14, Washington abounded with so many reports of quid pro quos that Talmadge felt compelled to deny that the administration had agreed to support his farm bill.

The administration did, however, support a Nunn-Talmadge reservation the same day. The Georgia senators started out wanting a reservation that gave the United States the right to keep military forces in Panama beyond the expiration of the Panama Canal Treaty in 1999, arguing that this might be necessary to defend the Canal under the permanent Neutrality Treaty. They ended accepting one which merely stated the obvious — that nothing in the Neutrality Treaty precluded the U.S. and Panama from reaching a further agreement or arrangement to station American forces in Panama.

Senator Richard S. Schweiker, R-Pa., (who voted against the treaties) remarked that "if you want a bridge or road or other federal project, it [being uncommitted] might help, but I don't think you should decide this issue on what you can get for your state." And Douglas J. Bennet, the assistant secretary of state for congressional relations, declared, "I don't know of a single vote which has been decided by non-germane considerations."[20]

Perhaps not, but there are plenty of cynics around the Senate office buildings who are convinced that a part of the price of the Panama Canal treaties will still be tucked away in the federal budget (probably under public works) in the fiscal year 1983. Some of these cynics are senators who announced their support of the treaties early and thereby, as they see it, lost bargaining power with the president.

Whether or not these kinds of explicit quid pro quos existed, there were many other, more subtle ones, such as seeing to it that senators were kept informed about administrative actions affecting their states. Failure to do this on the part of the Carter administration was a source of great irritation to some senators, particularly those who had no enthusiasm for the treaties anyway and felt they were running a political risk in voting for them. "They keep expecting us to fall on our swords," said Senator James R. Sasser, D-Tenn., "but there's been very little reciprocity."[21]

In other cases, the administration cooperated with senators' efforts to protect their political flanks in connection with policies indirectly related (if at all) to Panama. In response to a complaint by Senator Richard Stone, D-Fla., about "retreat in our hemisphere," the president promised to "oppose any efforts, direct or indirect, by the Soviet Union to establish military bases" in the hemisphere and to "maintain our bases in the Caribbean necessary to the defense of the Panama Canal and the security of the United States." Given the careful qualifications in this statement, it is difficult to imagine any president doing anything else, but Stone seized on it as an important policy clarification that would permit him to vote for the treaty.[22]

Two cracks appeared in the tenuous protreaty coalition in the days preceding the final vote. They were due in no small part to the administration's own desperation. As senators saw, or thought they saw, increasing concessions being made to those who held out the longest, some who had already committed themselves began to waver, thereby seeking to re-establish their bargaining power.

On April 13, Senator James Abourezk, D-S.D., linked his support of the treaty to the administration's energy policy. In October 1977, Abourezk, a quixotic liberal, had led an unsuccessful Senate filibuster against deregulation of natural gas prices. He lost in the Senate, but antideregulation forces had won in the House, and the matter had to be resolved in a conference committee which had been deadlocked for months. In an effort to find a way out of the impasse, some of the conferees had been holding private meetings which Abourezk took as a violation of the spirit, if not the letter, of a recent requirement that conference committee meetings be held in public. Now he threatened to withhold his support of the treaty if the private meetings continued, and if the president agreed to deregulation of natural gas. Under pressure from fellow liberals in the Senate, Abourezk finally relented. The last to speak before the final vote, he salvaged what he could by announcing he had "learned" from the White House "that they intend to try to encourage an open democratic process" in the energy conference.

On April 14, the day after Abourezk had linked the treaty to energy policy, Senator S. I. Hayakawa, R-Calif., linked it to the American po-

sition in the world generally. This is what treaty supporters had been doing all along. They argued that rejection of the treaty would damage
America's world position, but Hayakawa put a new twist on the matter.
During his campaign for the Senate in 1976, Hayakawa said he favored
keeping the Canal, because "we stole it fair and square" — one of the
year's memorable quotations. Hayakawa voted for the Neutrality Treaty
in March, but in April he announced he was "reconsidering" his support. The president's decision not to build the neutron bomb and the
U.S. negotiating position on SALT, among other things, made the
United States "look like a weak nation," he said.

The freshman senator's change of heart won him a private meeting
with the president and a chance to issue a previously prepared press release immediately after the final vote, in which he stated that Carter
had offered to meet with him regularly to discuss important foreign
policy and defense issues before he made final decisions on them.

IMPLEMENTING LEGISLATION

Legislation was now required to implement the treaties. Sup-
posedly, this involved no more than housekeeping details — providing
for the administration of the new Panama Canal Commission, the setting of tolls, the payment of claims, adjustments in laws pertaining to
employees and courts in the Canal Zone, and generally disentangling the
United States after 75 years of acting "as if it were sovereign." But
carrying out these actions involved the House in the treaty process; opposition to the treaties had always been stronger there than in the
Senate.

Action in the House

Jurisdiction over the implementing legislation in the House was
shared by four committees — Foreign Affairs, Merchant Marine and
Fisheries, Post Office and Civil Service, and Judiciary. Primary jurisdiction belonged to Merchant Marine and Fisheries, whose chairman, Representative John M. Murphy of New York, had long been a vocal and
adamant opponent of a new treaty relationship with Panama. The
adminstration wanted the implementing legislation to be flexible and to
operate automatically; Murphy's inclination was to require further
congressional consideration of successive steps.

The administration, for example, wanted the Canal Commission to
be a government corporation (like the old Panama Canal Company),
which would pay its expenses out of the tolls it collected. Representative
Murphy wanted it to be a government agency, with tolls deposited in the
Treasury and expenses paid out of appropriations, so that an annual opportunity would exist to fight over the treaty-mandated payments to
Panama.

The administration wanted property transferred to Panama automatically as provided in the treaties; Murphy wanted each transfer subject to congressional approval — another opportunity for obstruction.

In determining whether Canal revenues were sufficient to permit the $10 million annual payment to Panama provided by the treaty in years of surplus, the administration wanted to count only the normal expenses of operating and maintaining the Canal. Murphy wanted to include interest on the American investment in the Panama Canal Company with the result that Panama probably would not get the money.

In April 1979, the House Merchant Marine and Fisheries Committee reported a bill generally reflecting Murphy's views. Bad as it was from the administration's point of view, there arose an even worse alternative in a bill sponsored by Representative George Hansen, R-Idaho. Hansen wanted to require that Panama pay the costs of implementing the treaties; in addition, the United States would be reimbursed for the entire net investment cost of construction of the Canal. He estimated the total of these charges at $4 to $5 billion. Hansen's bill picked up 180 cosponsors, much to the administration's dismay.

Ironically, the administration abandoned its own bill and settled on the Murphy bill as its chosen instrument in the House. This was a little like a chicken seeking refuge in a fox's den to escape a lion.

On May 17, the House agreed to consider the legislation by the narrow margin of 200-198. This so alarmed the House leadership that it postponed further votes until a campaign could be mounted to solidify the administration's position.

In the meantime, House opponents of the treaties took advantage of unrelated events in Central America and the Caribbean. The civil war in Nicaragua in July led to the downfall of President Anastasio Somoza, thereby ending a family dynasty of more than 40 years over two generations. Representative Murphy had gone to school with Somoza and had maintained a close personal friendship with him over the years.

Two weeks before the House voted on the implementing legislation, the Panama Canal Subcommittee of Murphy's Merchant Marine and Fisheries Committee held hearings on allegations of Panamanian gun-smuggling to Somoza opponents. Lt. Gen. Gordon Sumner, who had resigned in May as chairman of the Inter-American Defense Board because of his differences with the Carter administration over Central American policy, charged that Torrijos was under the influence of "Communists-Marxists" and that Panama was "an unreliable and indeed dangerous partner."[23] Witnesses included Luis Pallais, the vice president of the Nicaraguan Congress. (It is exceedingly rare for a congressional committee formally to take testimony from a foreign official. Historically, this has been considered bad diplomatic practice, because it impinges on the separation of powers: only the executive branch is supposed to have *formal* communications with foreign governments. It also means that Congress opens itself to demands to be heard from contending foreign political factions, and this takes it down the slippery slope of intervention in foreign politics.)

The House took its crucial votes on June 20 and 21. On the first day, Hansen offered the gist of his bill as an amendment to the Murphy bill. Murphy countered with a substitute amendment, which for practical purposes restated the provisions of his bill as reported by the Merchant Marine and Fisheries Committee. The Murphy substitute prevailed, 220-200. The next day, a motion to recommit the bill with instructions to include the Hansen amendment was rejected by the even closer vote of 210-216; then the bill was passed, 224-202.

Action in the Senate

After biting the bullet of passing the treaties in 1978, the Senate approached the implementing legislation with all the enthusiasm of a man playing Russian roulette for the second time. In contrast to the House, where four committees shared jurisdiction, in the Senate the problem was all dumped into the lap of the Armed Services Committee. This came as a vast relief to the Foreign Relations Committee, which had borne the brunt of the battle the year before and whose new chairman, Frank Church, was threatened with conservative opposition in the 1980 election in Idaho, coincidentally the home state of Representative Hansen.

In the Senate Armed Services Committee, nine of the 10 Democratic members exercised the prerogatives of seniority to avoid handling the bill, leaving that task to the most junior member, Carl Levin of Michigan. (Levin was the only senatorial candidate in 1978 to defeat an incumbent who had voted against the treaties.)

Hearings were held by the committee the week after the House passed its bill, and on July 17 the bill was ordered reported by a favorable vote of 9-8. The committee accepted the administration proposal to make the Canal Commission a government corporation, and it rejected House provisions putting the commission under the Defense Department, setting conditions on the $10 million annual contingency payment to Panama, giving the U.S. military control of the Canal in wartime, and requiring congressional approval of property transfers. The committee report called the provisions of the House bill "inconsistent with the treaty."[24] President Aristides Royo of Panama also complained that the House bill would violate the treaty.

On July 26 by a 64-30 vote, the Senate passed the bill in substantially the form recommended by the Armed Services Committee after rejecting several amendments which would have brought the bill closer to the House version.

The Conference Report

Adjusting the differences between the House and Senate versions in conference committee was not easy. In agreeing to send the bill to conference, the House had voted 308-98 to instruct its conferees to insist on the House provisions relating to the Canal Commission, transfers of property, conditions on the payments to Panama, and Defense Department control. The conferees perforce settled on an agreement that generally followed the House bill with only minor changes.

This still did not satisfy the hard-core opponents in the House who used the additional argument of the presumed threat posed by the newly discovered presence of a Soviet combat brigade in Cuba. On September 20, the House rejected the conference report, 192-203. (The Senate had passed it a few hours earlier, 60-35.)

Now, with time growing short, the exercise of trying to reach House-Senate agreement had to be repeated. New conferees were appointed, and on September 24 they reached a new agreement. It contained a few new concessions to the House, mainly in the form of nonbinding language in the statement by the conferees. This provided that the president could put the Canal under military control if foreign combat troops deemed to be a threat to the Canal were stationed in Panama. The second conference report was agreed to in the Senate, 63-32, on September 26; the House approved it the following day, 232-188. One of the main arguments used in the House was that, no matter what happened to the implementing legislation, the treaties were going into effect October 1. In voting to approve the legislation, the House avoided taking the extreme position of the opponents to make implementation as difficult as possible. But it gave the opponents many other days in court.

POSTSCRIPT

As noted earlier, the administration's posture throughout this case was one of making steady, incremental concessions, not only with respect to the substantive provisions of the treaties and the implementing legislation, but also with respect to unrelated matters of political importance to individual members of Congress. One of the last victims of this process might have been the snail darter, the small fish threatened with extinction by construction of the Tellico Dam in Tennessee. Two nights before the House vote on the second conference report on Panama, Carter signed the energy and water appropriations bill for fiscal 1980 which contained a provision, opposed by the administration, ordering completion of the dam. Carter had vetoed a bill with a similar provision the year before and had been sustained. Now, he said, "I believe that avoiding a divisive veto battle will help focus congressional efforts on priority concerns."[25] One of these priority concerns was reported to be the Panama implementing legislation and the desire to avoid retaliation by representatives favoring the dam.

As a case study illustrating Congress' new assertiveness in the foreign policy field, the Panama Canal treaties call attention to several significant tendencies. First, they highlight the growing decentralization of the House and Senate, and of Congress collectively. As we have seen, several influential congressional committees played leading roles in the process of treaty ratification and of providing the implementing legislation needed to make the new agreements effective. Second, the case study provides an excellent example of the determination of the House of Representatives to become an equal partner with the Senate in congressional action on major foreign policy issues. Third, the intrusion of legislators into the realm of diplomatic negotiations — once a province reserved solely for the president or those acting under his authority — is dramatically illustrated.

Finally, no episode from recent American diplomatic experience perhaps more forcefully communicates Congress' determination to appear as the "defender" of the nation's diplomatic and security interests than this case. Owing to changes made in the new Panama Canal treaties on Capitol Hill, they were successfully presented to the American people as consonant with the security demands of the United States. Without that assurance it is doubtful the new treaties could have been ratified.

NOTES

1. Isthmian Canal Convention, popularly known as the Hay-Bunau-Varilla Treaty, was signed in Washington November 18, 1903, and entered into force February 26, 1904. (33 Stat. 2234. Treaty Series 431) The text, as well as a wealth of other documentary material, is included in *Background Documents Relating to the Panama Canal,* Senate Foreign Relations Committee (Washington, D.C.: U.S. Government Printing Office, 1977). Hereafter cited as *Background Documents.*
2. *The New York Times,* March 24, 1911, quoted in Henry F. Pringle, *Theodore Roosevelt: A Biography* (New York: Harcourt, Brace & Co., 1931), p. 330.
3. *Background Documents,* p. 1047.
4. As quoted to the author in a personal conversation with a senator.
5. U.S., Congress, House, H. Con. Res. 459, 86th Cong., 2d sess., 1960.
6. *Background Documents,* p. 1093.
7. Ibid., p. 1499.
8. *Panama Canal Treaties,* Executive N, 95th Cong., 1st sess.
9. Ward Sinclair, "The Closing of the Senate Club," *The Washington Post Magazine,* April 23, 1978.
10. U.S., Congress, Senate, Foreign Relations Committee, *Hearings on Panama Canal Treaties,* 95th Cong., 2d sess., Part 1, p. 12. Hereafter cited as *Hearings.*
11. *Hearings,* Part 1, p. 30.
12. *Statement to National Assembly of Panama,* August 19, 1977, quoted in *Hearings,* Part 1, p. 77.
13. *Hearings,* Part 2, p. 214.
14. Ibid., Part 1, p. 488.
15. Ibid., Part 1, p. 454.
16. Ibid., Part 1, p. 7.

17. U.S., Congress, Senate, *Report of Delegation Studying the Panama Canal Treaties and Other Matters of Interest to the U.S. in Latin America,* S. Doc. 80, 95th Cong., 2d sess., pp. 5-6.

18. U.S., Congress, Senate, Foreign Relations Committee, *Senate Debate on the Panama Canal Treaties: A Compendium of Major Statements, Documents, Record Votes and Relevant Events* (Washington, D.C.: U.S. Government Printing Office, 1979), p. 404. This volume is an encyclopedic collection of the official records. Hereafter cited as *Senate Debate.*

19. *Senate Debate,* p. 485.

20. Congressional Quarterly *Weekly Report,* 36 (March 18, 1978): 675.

21. For an illuminating account of Sasser-White House relations, see "The Sasser Disaffection: How Not to Win Friends," *The Washington Post,* April 19, 1978.

22. *Hearings,* Part 5, pp. 57, 100-102. See also "The Realpolitic of the Panama Canal Treaties," *The Washington Post,* February 2, 1978.

23. *The Washington Post,* September 26, 1978.

24. U.S., Congress, Senate, Armed Services Committee, *Implementing the Panama Canal Treaty of 1977 and Related Agreements,* S. Rept. 255, 96th Cong., 1st sess., pp. 5, 9.

25. *The Washington Post,* September 26, 1979.

4

The Arab-Israeli Conflict

One of the most intractable problems of the post-World War II era has been the Arab-Israeli conflict. It has been particularly difficult for the United States because of contradictory interests — on the one hand, a deep commitment to the idea and the reality of a Jewish state; on the other, the importance of the Arab states because of their geography, their leadership of the Moslem world, and especially their oil reserves.

The problem has been complicated by arguments over American policy concerned more with nuances and shades of emphasis than with fundamentals. Although President Harry S. Truman's policy supporting the establishment of the state of Israel was opposed by high officials of the State Department, for 30 years there has been no serious question that the bedrock of American policy was support of the Israeli right to exist behind secure and recognized boundaries. The arguments have been over how best to implement this policy and bring about a just and enduring settlement of the Israeli conflict with the Arabs. In terms of concrete issues, these arguments have generally come over how much pressure, and what kind, to bring to bear on the parties.

The interest of Congress has been continuing and generally supportive of the Israeli position. The discussion presented in our case study will show that:

● Appropriations for Israel have been increased over what a succession of presidents asked;

● Appropriations for the Arab states have sometimes been reduced; more often they have been hedged with conditions which were not made applicable to Israel;

● Terms of loans and of military sales to Israel have been softened;

● Military sales to the Arab states have been approved grudgingly and sometimes with humiliating conditions;

● U.S. contributions to the United Nations Educational, Scientific and Cultural Organization were cut off because of what was perceived to be an anti-Israeli resolution passed by that organization;

● Legislation was passed regulating the ways in which American companies do business with the Arab countries;

• Legislation was passed by Congress making a trade agreement with the Soviet Union contingent on Jewish emigration, as discussed in Chapter 7;

• Actions have been taken against racial, religious, or sexist discrimination and general violations of human rights in Arab countries, but reports of mistreatment of Arabs in Israel or in Israeli-occupied territories have generated less interest;

• There is a widespread, but unconfirmed, suspicion that members of Congress or their staffs pass on to the Israeli embassy information they receive in confidence from the executive branch;

• Terrorist attacks on Israelis by Palestinians are condemned, but little attention has been devoted to Israeli attacks on Lebanon.

To those primarily concerned with American interests in the Arab world, such disparities in Congress' behavior have looked like interference with executive initiatives and efforts at evenhandedness in dealing with the parties to the Arab-Israeli conflict. To those committed to the idea of a Jewish state, congressional sympathy for Israel has looked like the first line of defense against perceived pro-Arab sentiment by the executive branch.

The situation in the Middle East changed dramatically with Egyptian President Anwar Sadat's visit to Jerusalem in 1977; and, in the period that followed, American attitudes subtly and gradually began to change. Again, the changes had more to do with nuances than with fundamentals.

By the fall of 1979, the negotiations to implement the Israeli-Egyptian peace treaty had made good progress in disposing of the easy issues, such as return of the Sinai Peninsula to Egypt. This progress highlighted the more difficult issues remaining, such as the status of the West Bank of the Jordan River, which Israel had occupied since the Six Days War in 1967. And this came at precisely the time that the Israeli government of Prime Minister Menachem Begin was following a policy, controversial within its own country, of expanding Israeli settlements on the West Bank, settlements which were viewed as illegal by both the United States and the United Nations. More sentiment critical of Israel, as expressed privately anyway, was heard in Congress than had previously been the case.

BACKGROUND

The state of Israel is the fulfillment of Zionism or the doctrine of a Jewish state. Zionism as a political idea was developed and elaborated by Theodor Herzl at the end of the nineteenth century. For Herzl, a native of Hungary who spent most of his life in Austria and France, Zionism was the answer to the anti-Semitism which was so pervasive in nineteenth century Europe as, in his view, to make assimilation of Jews impossible.

The World Zionist Organization, with Herzl as its president, was established by a conference he organized in Switzerland in 1897. Herzl entered into unsuccessful negotiations with the Turkish government for lands in Palestine and with the British for lands in the Sinai Peninsula. Britain offered, instead, some territory in Uganda which Herzl favored accepting, but which the Zionist Congress of 1903 turned down.

World War I edged Zionism forward, and World War II gave it fulfillment. In 1917, Lord Balfour, the British foreign minister, issued the now famous Balfour Declaration:

> His Majesty's Government view with favour the establishment in Palestine of a national home for the Jewish people, and will use their best endeavors to facilitate the achievement of this object, it being clearly understood that nothing shall be done which may prejudice the civil and religious rights of existing non-Jewish communities in Palestine, or the rights and political status enjoyed by Jews in any other country.

A similar statement was adopted by the United States Congress as a joint resolution in 1922. Two points are to be noted. First, the reference is to a "national home for the Jewish people" — which is not necessarily the same thing as a Jewish state. Second, there was a proviso against prejudicing the rights of the Arabs in Palestine.

The Balfour Declaration was also incorporated into the British mandate for Palestine under the League of Nations. Resistance from the Arab population of Palestine (which had previously been part of the Ottoman Empire) was almost immediate, and the British government soon got involved in an argument, which continued until Israel was established in 1948, over the levels of Jewish immigration that would be permitted.

This question became acute in the aftermath of World War II. Pressure mounted not only for the survivors of the holocaust — Nazi Germany's campaign to exterminate the Jews — to immigrate to Palestine, but also to establish a Jewish state there. On November 29, 1947, the United Nations General Assembly voted for a plan to partition an independent Palestine into separate Jewish and Arab states, tied together in an economic union, with the city of Jerusalem under direct U.N. trusteeship.

The United Nations plan satisfied neither Arabs nor Zionists, each of whom wanted all of Palestine. On December 3, 1947, the British announced that they would consider their mandate from the League of Nations terminated on May 15, 1948, and both Jews and Arabs prepared for a war which, in fact, did not wait until May. The state of Israel was proclaimed in Palestine at midnight May 14. Truman recognized it 11 minutes later.

Throughout this period, Truman acted largely on his own, although he received encouragement from many legislators. Truman gave increasing Jewish immigration to Palestine priority over establishing a Jewish state, but he was a Zionist from personal conviction. The State Department advised against his policy. Dean Acheson, undersecretary of state at the time, frankly states in his memoirs, "I did not share the President's views on the Palestine solution."[1] Pro-Zionist pressures were coming from Capitol Hill, notably from Senator Robert F. Wagner and Representative Emanuel Celler, both prominent New York Democrats. Secretary of Defense James V. Forrestal, concerned even then over access to Arab oil, supported the State Department. Postmaster General Robert Hannegan, charged with arranging Truman's re-election, supported the Zionists who were themselves extraordinarily active. "I do not think I ever had as much pressure and propaganda aimed at the White House as I had in this instance," Truman wrote later.[2]

For whatever reason or mixture of reasons, the state of Israel was created. There then began the continuing effort by the United States to balance its diverse interests in the Middle East.

THE ACTORS

Israel

In many respects, it is remarkable that the state of Israel even exists and even more remarkable that it came into being only half a century after Herzl articulated modern Zionism. For many Israelis and other Jews as well, however, it is the fulfillment of a more ancient dream going back to biblical times.

The dream has been made a reality only after a long and torturous history culminating in the horror of Hitler's holocaust and in four wars against the Arabs — the War of Independence (1948-49), the Suez War (1956), the Six Days War (1967) and the Yom Kippur War (1973). Throughout its short existence, Israel has been surrounded by hostile neighbors. On a map of the Middle East, it is a tiny blip; until it occupied the West Bank of the Jordan River in the 1967 war, it was only eight miles wide at its narrowest point. After a generation of immigration, it still had a population of only 3.7 million; there are more than 125 million Arabs, 54 million of them in countries bordering Israel. Furthermore, Israel is a country almost totally lacking in natural resources. In view of these facts, private and official American aid has been vital to Israel's survival.

Israel's defense strategy, which has paid off in the four wars against the Arabs, has been based on a high state of readiness, mobility, and superiority of weapons and training to offset Arab superiority in numbers. Notwithstanding that it has by far the strongest military establishment in the area, Israel feels insecure. Its preoccupation with security shows itself in many ways: insistence on maintaining its own strong, largely foreign-equipped military forces; nervousness over foreign weapons available to the Arabs; reluctance until the late 1970s to make any concessions as part of a negotiating process; sensitivity to any indication, however slight, of wavering American support; insensitivity to the problems of the Arabs, particularly those refugees who fled Palestine as a consequence of the establishment and expansion of Israel.

All of this is complicated by a formidable array of economic problems, despite a high standard of living. The land is mostly desert, with few mineral resources. A massive deficit exists in foreign trade, supported only by foreign subsidies. Inflation is endemic, spiralling in 1979 to a rate of 100 percent. Israel's taxes are also among the highest in the world. Israel's need for continuing economic support from the United States has limited the options available to Congress in formulating U.S.-Israeli foreign policy.

The Arabs

While the Israelis, despite their insecurity, are brimming with pride over their accomplishments, the Arabs have long felt a sense of humiliation, outrage, and injustice. First, they saw forcefully taken from them lands in Palestine which they viewed as rightfully theirs, driving the inhabitants into a wretched existence as refugees. Secondly, despite their overwhelming numbers, they suffered four crushing military defeats.

On top of all this, there has been a feeling of hopelessness. In the Arab view, Israel has had the unflinching, unquestioning support of the United States for whatever it wanted. As Arabs saw it, the Israeli government, through the pro-Israeli lobby in the United States, controlled American foreign policy in the Middle East. A new element was injected into this picture, however, with the Arab embargo of oil exports to the United States at the time of the Yom Kippur War in 1973. The demonstration of the dependence of the United States, Western Europe, and Japan on Arab oil (and of their inability to do much about it) has considerably brightened the Arabs' view of their long-term prospects.

Beyond this, however, it is unwise to generalize about the Arabs. Nine different countries are considered Arab — Egypt, Syria, Jordan, Lebanon, Iraq, Saudi Arabia, South Yemen, North Yemen, and Kuwait — as well as a series of tiny sheikdoms along the Persian Gulf and four North African states known collectively as the Mahgreb — Algeria, Morocco, Tunisia, and Libya. There are many other distinctions to be made — between rich (those who have oil) and poor (those who do not); between those who are adjacent to Israel and those who are not; and among conservative, moderate, and radical regimes. The Arabs do, of course, share a common religion (Islam) and a common language (Arabic), but this common ground has resulted in no more unity than have Catholicism and Spanish in Latin America. Divisions within the Islamic faith itself were never more apparent than in November 1979 when Moslem fanatics took over the Grand Mosque in Mecca.

Throughout most of the period since 1948, Israel has been the principal unifying force throughout the Middle East, to the extent that there has been unity at all. Yet differences have also existed — ranging from intransigent radicalism to cautious moderation — even with respect to Israel. Indeed, the most serious split in the Arab world since 1948 came about in 1979 when the other Arabs joined to ostracize Egypt because it signed a peace treaty with Israel.

The poorer Arab countries, including the confrontation states of Egypt, Jordan, Syria, and Lebanon, suffer from all of Israel's economic problems compounded. Their people are less skilled. Egypt, in particular, has an unmanageable population growth. All of them have more acute social problems and much greater maldistribution of wealth and income than has Israel.

Finally, in contrast to Israeli democracy, the Arab states have varying degrees of authoritarian government. This has been an important factor in American perceptions.

The United States

In American government, three major groups of policymakers with three different points of view on the Arab-Israeli conflict have emerged. The bureaucracy of the executive branch, represented in this case principally by the State and Defense departments, has tended to favor either a pro-Arab or an evenhanded approach. State Department specialists in the Middle East tend to view the area in terms of international, rather than domestic, politics. They see many more Arabs than Israelis, with the Arabs much more politically turbulent, much more susceptible to anti-American (sometimes Soviet) influence, and — with their huge oil reserves and strategic geography — essential to the survival of industrial economies in the United States, Europe, and Japan. The Defense Department, and particularly the officers of the uniformed services, have tended to support this assessment, but with even more emphasis on oil and strategic considerations.

The White House, as the elected part of the executive branch, has been more sensitive to domestic political considerations, though it has by no means ignored the global factors which weigh so heavily on the bureaucracy. Increasingly, the president and his aides have become aware of American diplomatic and security interests throughout the Middle East.

Congress has been the most pro-Israeli actor of all in the American foreign policy process. This is partly a reflection of the strength of the pro-Israeli lobby in the United States; partly a reflection of the deep feelings and sincere convictions of influential legislators; and partly a reflection of American public sentiment. Public opinion polls have repeatedly shown that the American people as a whole are sympathetic to Israel.

It is a mistake, of course, to assume that all Jews are Zionists or that all Zionists are Jews. It must be remembered that Zionism is essentially a *political* movement; its dominant goal has been the creation and protection of a Jewish state. Zionism draws supporters from people of many religious faiths (or none at all). Nevertheless, the basic strength of the pro-Israeli lobby rests in the American Jewish community. This community's political influence is greatly disproportionate to its numbers. The Census Bureau reports that there are a little more than six million members of Jewish religious congregations in the United States, or possibly three percent of the total population. An additional number of persons calling themselves Jews (who are not members of congregations) are also intensely concerned with Israel. The pro-Israeli lobby gets its strength not so much from its numbers, as from its money, from the depth of its feelings, from the local prominence of some of its leading members, and from its broad base of support in public opinion.

A once prominent pro-Israeli senator used to say privately that Israel's most valuable territory was upper Park Avenue, the residents of which have distributed campaign contributions throughout the country. Logically, this particular source of the lobby's strength would decline if there is ever public financing of congressional political campaigns. A possible decline in their influence explains why so many pressure groups are opposed to public financing.

But money only partly explains the power of the pro-Israeli lobby in Congress. Morris Amitay, executive director of the American Israeli Public Affairs Committee and principal spokesman for the lobby, puts it this way:

> A lot of these [uncommitted] Senators are from the Midwest, West, down South, and these [Jews] are some of the elite types of people that these Senators like to be with and talk to, besides the pull of actual contributions. I do not think anyone ever likes to be approached on the very gut political level. You look around at who the Jewish constituents are from sparsely inhabited states. They are teachers, they are doctors, they have invariably been involved some way in politics. They are usually respected people in the community, so you do not have to pitch it at the level of, 'I contributed ten thousand dollars to your campaign — unless you do this you will make me unhappy and I will contribute to your opponent next time.' At most it's implicit, and it is not even implicit a large percentage of the time.[3]

Other factors explain the pro-Israeli lobby's influence. Its strength is an extreme example of two broad aspects of American politics.

One of these is the principle, discussed in Chapter 3, that politicians generally get elected and re-elected less by pleasing people than by not offending them. From this it follows that a vocal, passionate minority has more influence than an apathetic or indifferent majority. This is explicitly recognized in Congress with respect to the pro-Israeli lobby. Said one senator, in explaining the number of cosponsors of the Jackson amendment to the Trade Act of 1974 relative to Jewish emigration from the Soviet Union, "[T]here is no political advantage in not signing. If you do sign, you don't offend anyone. If you don't sign, you might offend some Jews in your state."[4]

The other factor is ethnic politics. In pressing for support of Israel over other American foreign policy considerations, the Jewish community in America is taking the same approach that the American Polish community has done with respect to American policy toward Poland; that the American Greek community has done with respect to the Greek-Turkish dispute over Cyprus; that substantial portions of the black community have taken with respect to Africa; and that the growing Hispanic community has taken with respect to Latin America in general and Mexico in particular. Sometimes the demands of these special interest groups and the broader national interest coincide; sometimes they do not.

The pro-Israeli lobby, powerful as it is, is only a part of the reason why sentiment in Congress has been so sympathetic to Israel. If Congress voted in secret, there would possibly be fewer pro-Israeli votes. Yet it is by no means certain that the outcome in the House and Senate would be reversed. The late Senator Hubert H. Humphrey, D-Minn., and former Senator Clifford P. Case, R-N.J., were two members of Congress who were not Jewish but were — from personal conviction — pro-Israel. Cynics may argue that Humphrey's many national campaigns left him indebted to Jewish contributors and that Case represented the state with the second highest Jewish population. But Humphrey was passionately devoted to the Israeli cause before he burst on the national scene, and Case would have been if New Jersey were six percent Arab instead of six percent Jewish. Case, as a matter of fact, went beyond belief in Zionism, to express his support of Israel in geopolitical terms:

> The existence of Israel, its strength to defend itself, is essential to the preservation of the West, to the preservation of NATO, and inevitably, in the end, to the preservation of the United States. More than that, it is essential to the preservation of the moderate Arab regimes.[5]

Historically, American policymaking with respect to the Arab-Israeli conflict has followed a general pattern in which the White House has initially overruled the bureaucracy; then Congress has overruled the White House and pushed it, under a sucession of presidents, to do more for Israel than executive officials were inclined to do, or prevented them from putting pressure on Israel. This pattern has produced a situation that has hampered the executive branch in its negotiations with the Israeli government. Israeli officials have known that if they could not get what they wanted from the State or Defense departments or the White House, they could often go to their supporters in the United States — or directly to Congress, for that matter — and get it there.

In 1974, the late General George S. Brown, chairman of the Joint Chiefs of Staff, described the process this way:

> We have Israelis coming to us for equipment. . . . They say don't worry about Congress. We will take care of the Congress. This is somebody from another country, and they can do it.[6]

This legislative behavior pattern has extended not only to what is done by the United States for Israel, but also to what is done for the Arabs. Israeli and Zionist sensitivities are so great that American overtures to Arab states are likely to be looked on askance. Just the prospect of congressional opposition has killed many initiatives favorable to the Arabs in the executive branch.

The Israeli government, through its embassy in Washington as well as directly from Jerusalem, maintains close contacts with Congress and with pro-Israeli lobbying groups, principally the American-Israeli Public Affairs Committee (AIPAC) and an umbrella organization called the Conference of Presidents of Major American Jewish Organizations (Conference of Presidents, for short). Israeli prime ministers, foreign ministers, and defense ministers visit Washington frequently, and Capitol Hill is a routine stop on their rounds for informal meetings with key committees or with the House and Senate membership in general. More senators would turn out to have their pictures taken with Golda Meir when she was prime minister of Israel than would show up for an important Senate debate.

These visiting officials almost always confer, as well, with the Conference of Presidents and with other prominent American Jewish leaders. During a particularly tense period in the negotiations for the Israeli-Egyptian peace treaty, Prime Minister Begin met with 2,000 Jewish leaders in New York on his way back to Jerusalem from Washington. He drew cheers with the charge that Carter had asked him to sign a "sham" treaty. Begin then said to his audience, "You have great influence. Do not hesitate to use that influence."[7]

Two conditions within the American society have provided the pro-Israeli lobby a highly favorable milieu in which to achieve its goals. One of these is the pro-Israeli orientation of a majority of the American people, making citizens and their leaders often highly receptive to the lobby's position on major policy issues. Students of political persuasion have long recognized that their most effective efforts occur when they motivate a group to believe or to act in accordance with its pre-existing inclination or orientation.

By that standard, pro-Israeli lobbying activities in the United States have many advantages not enjoyed by their adversaries. American society is a product of the Judeo-Christian tradition. (There is no comparable Islamic-Christian tradition.) Israel is a stable and functioning democracy vis-à-vis conditions of anarchy and of authoritarian rule Americans perceive in other Middle Eastern states. Many of the settlers and the political elite of Israel have come from the West. (One of its recent prime ministers, Mrs. Golda Meir, came to the United States when she was eight years old and lived there for 15 years.) Israel has made successful use of the billions of dollars in external assistance it has received since its establishment (versus the frequent waste and misuse of foreign aid by other countries in the region). In addition, countless numbers of Americans have traveled to Israel during the past generation and witnessed firsthand its accomplishments, whereas a much smaller number has visited the Arab states of the Middle East (in part because of travel restrictions often imposed by Arab governments). Such factors have combined to provide the pro-Israeli lobby in the United States a highly positive environment within which to influence the American public and national leaders.

A second advantage enjoyed by the lobby is the fact that no strong countervailing force to it exists in the United States. There are, for example, only about 1.5 million Arab-Americans. Most of them are Lebanese, a group that — until the agony of the Lebanese civil war began in the mid-1970s — was the least passionate of the contending forces in the Middle East. However, the National Association of Arab Americans, founded in 1972, had gradually become sophisticated and more influential in its lobbying activities. By mid-1979, representatives of Arab nations had also become more active in their efforts to influence legislators. A potential pro-Arab force is the oil industry, but it has generally been circumspect in dealing directly with Arab-Israeli questions.

A recent arrival on the scene of lobbies interested in the Middle East is organized blacks. Many blacks were outraged by what they perceived to be the forced resignation of Andrew Young as ambassador to the United Nations in August 1979 for holding a conversation with the U.N. representative of the Palestine Liberation Organization. United States policy, like Israeli policy, was to have nothing to do with the PLO until it disavowed terrorism and recognized Israel's right to exist. After his resignation, Young made clear his opinion that a prohibition on talking to the PLO carried this policy too far and ignored a political reality in the Middle East. Many leaders of the black community agreed with him. Walter Fauntroy, the District of Columbia's nonvoting delegate in the House, and the Reverend Joseph Lowery, president of the Southern Christian Leadership Conference, went to Lebanon to meet Yasser Arafat, head of the PLO. They cancelled a planned visit to Israel when Begin refused to receive them.

CONGRESSIONAL ACTIONS

The issue that perhaps most clearly illuminates the congressional position in the Arab-Israeli conflict concerns foreign aid and military sales.

From its establishment in 1948 through September 30, 1978, Israel received a total of $11,914,000,000 in United States economic and military assistance of one kind or another, and more than half a billion dollars in loans from the U.S. Export-Import Bank. The sum total is roughly five percent of all the foreign aid funds and Export-Import loans distributed globally by the United States since the end of World War II.

It is more than $3,200 per capita, based on the 1978 population estimate of 3.7 million — and during most of its history, Israel had fewer people. In addition, Israel has received as much as $7 billion more from private sources in the United States, principally from people who buy Israeli bonds or contribute to the Jewish Agency, the international body concerned with immigration to Israel.[8]

The Arab confrontation states have not done badly as recipients of American foreign aid; through September 1978, Egypt, Jordan, Syria, and Lebanon had received $7 billion.

Congress has always been dubious about the foreign aid program and in dealing with most countries it has often put conditions on foreign aid designed to induce particular behavior by recipients — with the exception of Israel. With respect to foreign aid in general, the administration usually sends proposals to Congress, which haggles over them for months, reduces them, and grudgingly approves what is left. With respect to foreign aid for Israel, the pattern not infrequently has been the reverse: the administration has been pressed to ask for more aid and sometimes even that has been increased. There have been years when the foreign aid bill would have been defeated if not for the large sums for Israel.

With respect to other countries, Congress has frequently used the foreign aid program as leverage to achieve other foreign policy objectives. With respect to Israel, Congress has brought pressure to bear on the executive branch to prevent it from doing the same thing.

In many respects, the congressional approach to aiding the Arabs has been the mirror image of the approach to aiding Israel. While Congress has urged the executive branch to do more for Israel, it has haggled over less aid for the Arabs. While it has inhibited the executive branch from using leverage on Israel, it has tried its own leverage on the Arabs and in the process has reduced the leverage which might otherwise been available to the executive branch. When the executive branch favored the carrot in dealing with the Arabs, Congress used the stick. When the executive branch wanted to use the stick in dealing with Israel, Congress responded with carrots. The result was that neither the carrot nor the stick worked very well.

Beginning in the mid-1970s, with the Egyptian break with the Soviet Union and increasing with the Israeli-Egyptian rapprochement, Congress has been generous to both Israel and Egypt. Economic aid to Egypt has been approaching $1 billion a year, compared to $800 million for Israel. (But Israel has been getting $1 billion in arms.)

Israeli Withdrawal from Sinai

Following the Suez War of 1956, the United Nations called on Israel to withdraw its troops from Egyptian territory. Israel refused to comply. President Eisenhower indicated he would uphold any economic sanctions imposed on Israel by the U.N. in an effort to force compliance, and this brought an immediate outcry from Capitol Hill. Seventy Democratic members of Congress told Secretary of State John Foster Dulles they understood Israel's reluctance to withdraw. House Majority Leader John McCormack said that Israel's refusal was "justified." Senate Minority Leader William Knowland said that sanctions against Israel would be "immoral" and "insupportable" without sanctions against the Soviet Union for its occupation of Hungary. Lyndon B. Johnson, then the Senate majority leader, told Dulles that sanctions would be "a most unwise move." The Senate Democratic Policy Committee unanimously opposed sanctions.[9] Sanctions were not imposed, and Israeli troops withdrew in March, four months after the U.N. resolution.

The question of Israeli withdrawal from the Sinai arose almost 20 years later, following the Yom Kippur War of 1973. This time the withdrawal was a much more prolonged and complicated process. The first step, in the form of a modest disengagement of Israeli and Egyptian forces, was taken in January 1974.

In March 1975, Secretary of State Henry Kissinger began a new round of shuttle diplomacy aimed at a further disengagement. It did not go well, and after a couple of weeks Kissinger called it off. On March 24, President Ford announced a "reassessment" of American policy in the Middle East and said, "If they [the Israelis] had been a bit more flexible . . . I think in the longer run it would have been the best insurance for peace."[10]

Matters continued in suspense for weeks while the policy "reassessment" by the executive branch was in progress. During this time, the administration delayed submitting to Congress its foreign aid request for Israel. On May 21, a letter to Ford signed by 76 senators was released. The letter expressed the senators' hope that the request would be "responsive to Israel's urgent military and economic needs" and declared that peace in the Middle East required that Israel "obtain a level of military and economic support adequate to deter a renewal of war by Israel's neighbors."

"We believe," the letter continued, "that a strong Israel constitutes a most reliable barrier to domination of the area by outside parties," and "We urge you to make it clear, as we do, that the United States acting in its own national interests stands firmly with Israel in the search for peace in future negotiations, and that this premise is the basis of the current reassessment of U.S. policy in the Middle East."[11]

A few days later the *New York Times* reported from Jerusalem:

> The letter, in the view of the Israeli leadership, demonstrates that there is a limit to the political leverage the Ford administration can apply against Israel in the course of its current reassessment of Middle East policy. Israeli officials were delighted by the timing and content of the letter, which they have happily taken to calling 'the spirit of the 76.'[12]

In June, Israeli Prime Minister Yitzhak Rabin came to Washington for talks with Ford, Kissinger, and the usual visit to Capitol Hill. In

August, Kissinger resumed his shuttle diplomacy in the Middle East, and the second Sinai disengagement agreement was signed in September.

During consideration of a measure authorizing American personnel to monitor the agreement, the Senate killed, by a vote of 54-28, an amendment by Ernest F. Hollings, D-S.C. His amendment reaffirmed the American policy of continuing to seek a Middle East settlement in accordance with the provisions of U.N. Security Council Resolution 242 of 1967 (which, among other things, called for Israeli withdrawal from territories occupied in the 1967 war).

The Israeli-Egyptian peace treaty, signed in March 1979, provided for withdrawal in three years from the exchange of ratifications. Throughout this controversy over the Israeli presence in the Sinai, the administration eventually got what it wanted — but not without difficulty.

Egyptian Closure of the Suez Canal

Frustrated by the continued closure of the Suez Canal to Israeli shipping, Congress in 1959 tried to bring economic pressure to bear on Egypt through the multilateral development agencies and the bilateral American aid program. In December 1959, a group of 66 members of the House unsuccessfully urged the World Bank to disapprove a $56 million loan to Egypt for development of the Canal. The issue came up again in 1960 in the House Banking and Currency Committee in connection with a bill authorizing United States participation in the International Development Association (IDA), which gives low-cost credits to the Bank's poorest member countries. Several members wanted to prohibit IDA loans to countries impeding free navigation through international waterways. In return for not pressing the amendment, they obtained assurances from Secretary of the Treasury Robert Anderson that American representatives in IDA would act and vote in accordance with the objectives of freedom of navigation.

Congress added a provision to the Mutual Security Act of 1960 requiring that foreign aid be administered "to give effect" to the principle that the United States favors freedom of navigation in international waterways. Specific application of the principle was left to the determination of the president, who was required to report to Congress on what he had done about it.

This rather loose language was opposed by the Eisenhower administration, which argued, as it had done in 1957 in the case of Israeli withdrawal from the Sinai, that the objectives could best be met through the United Nations. Senator J. William Fulbright, then chairman of the Foreign Relations Committee, charged that the provision would use the Mutual Security Act as a "club" and that it was offered "because of the existence of a pressure group in the United States which seeks to inject the Arab-Israeli dispute into domestic politics."

Senator Francis Case, R-S.D., accused the Senate of converting the Mutual Security Act into a "weapon of unilateral economic sanctions as a substitute for concerted international action by the United Nations." He found the demonstration of "such a theory of dollar diplomacy" unfortunate. Senator Wayne Morse, D-Ore., felt instead that the time had come "to make perfectly clear to the Arab countries that we are not going to be blackmailed by them any longer."

The issue of freedom of navigation arose again in a different context on June 8, 1967, while the Six Days War was at its height. Israeli planes and naval vessels attacked the U.S.S. *Liberty,* an American navy communications ship standing 15 miles off the Gaza Strip. Thirty-four American sailors were killed and 75 were wounded. A navy court of inquiry determined that the Israeli aircraft "had ample opportunity" to identify the ship before what the court called the "unprovoked" attack. Very little was said about the *Liberty* in Congress.

Military Sales to Israel

The United States has been selling to Israel about $1 billion worth of arms each year, but Congress regularly provides that Israel is to be forgiven repayment of half of the amount of the sale. (An exception was made with respect to the $2.2 billion in arms sales authorized as part of the Egyptian peace treaty aid package; total repayment is expected.)

France, more sensitive than most western countries to its interests in the Arab world, cancelled delivery of Mirage aircraft to Israel in 1967. Israel then turned to the United States with a request for F-4 Phantoms. President Johnson stalled, hoping for leverage to persuade the Israelis to withdraw from the territories they had occupied in the Six Days War or perhaps to sign the Nuclear Non-Proliferation Treaty. (Intelligence reports indicated that Israel either had, or was on the verge of having, nuclear weapons.) But the pressure began to mount.

The 1968 foreign aid authorization bill expressed the sense of Congress that the president should take steps to negotiate with Israel for the sale of as many supersonic planes as might be necessary to provide a deterrent force capable of "preventing future Arab aggression." The supersonic planes were to offset the sophisticated weapons received by the Arab states from the Soviet Union and to replace those lost by Israel in the Six Days War. Congress gave final approval to the bill October 8, and on October 9 Johnson issued instructions for negotiations for the sale of the F-4s to begin. In December, the president approved the sale of 50 planes.

In December 1969, a report that France had agreed to a $400 million arms sale to Libya of 50 Mirage jet fighters and 200 heavy tanks triggered an Israeli request for more F-4s and other arms, including A-4 Skyhawk jets. This request came at a time of increasing tension in the Middle East caused by Arab terrorist attacks in Israel and Israeli reprisals, mainly against Palestinian bases in Lebanon, but including one air attack on a factory near Cairo. It was also a time when the United States was trying to reach an agreement, tacit or otherwise, with the Soviet Union to limit arms shipments to the Middle East.

President Nixon told a press conference in January that a decision on the Israeli request would be made in 30 days. In March, Secretary of State William P. Rogers told a press conference that the United States had decided to "hold in abeyance" the Israeli request because "Israel's air capacity is sufficient to meet its needs for the time being."

On March 28, the U.N. Human Rights Commission condemned Israel for its actions against Arabs in the territories it had occupied in the 1967 war. The vote was 12-0, with 16 abstentions (including the United States). On May 12, Israel attacked Palestinian installations in Lebanon, and the U.N. Security Council unanimously called for Israeli withdrawal. A week later, the Security Council condemned Israel for its "premeditated military action" against Lebanon. The vote was 11-0, with four abstentions (again including the United States).

While in Washington May 20-22, Israeli Foreign Minister Abba Eban pushed his request for the planes. On June 1, 73 senators signed a letter to Secretary Rogers urging prompt agreement. On June 7, Rogers said that the decision on aircraft sales to Israel would be announced soon, and that the sales would be made in a "balanced and measured way so that we don't signal to the Arabs that we are so behind Israel that we'll support them no matter what they do."

Meanwhile, a number of resolutions had been introduced in Congress calling on the administration to sell planes to Israel. The House Foreign Affairs Committee urged the president to request supplemental appropriations if necessary.

The foreign military sales bill, debated in the Senate in June, expressed the sense of Congress that the president should negotiate with the Soviet Union and other powers a limitation on arms shipments to the Middle East. Paradoxically, the bill stated that the president should be supported in his position that arms would be made available and credits provided to Israel and other friendly states to meet the threat to their security. An amendment by Senator John Williams, R-Del., to eliminate this provision was rejected by the Senate by a vote of 1-59.

Williams also offered an amendment to strike out the specific dollar figures, arguing that Congress should approve each sale. Senator Frank Church, D-Idaho, argued in opposition that the amendment would lead to an unlimited authorization. The main opposition, however, was based on apprehension that the amendment would jeopardize the sale to Israel. Senator Claiborne Pell, D-R.I., who had signed the June 1 letter, contended that "Israel, a country for which we have great sympathy, is being used as the vehicle to carry the load of military credit sales to many countries to which I feel such credit sales should not be made."[13] The Williams amendment was rejected by a 6-56 vote.

On July 30, 71 senators signed a letter to President Nixon urging it be made clear that the United States intended "to protect and defend its interests" in the Middle East and southern Europe.[14] On August 13, the executive branch announced plans to send arms to Israel "so that the arms balance does not tip against Israel."

In November 1971, Senator Henry Jackson, D-Wash., offered an amendment to the defense appropriations bill to provide a $500 million credit to Israel for arms sales, something which the administration had not requested. Senator Fulbright, chairman of the Foreign Relations Committee, opposed the amendment:

> Everyone knows the critical question now is whether Israel is to re-tain the territory which she conquered in that [1967] war. Apparently, Israel has made up her mind that it is going to retain it, which auto-matically, I think, prevents the possibility of a negotiated settle-ment. . . . I think Congress is interfering with the efforts of the Admin-istration to bring about a negotiated settlement in the Middle East.[15]

And Republican Senator Henry Bellmon of Oklahoma also voiced his objections:

> President Sadat has taken a great many steps and has made many moves that seemed impossible a few months ago. . . . He simply cannot be expected to go on forever taking the kinds of action he has taken un-less the United States or the government of Israel . . . can give some evi-dence that these actions are beginning to produce some results.[16]

A point of order that the funds had not been authorized was re-jected, 14-81, and the amendment was agreed to, 82-14.

During the Yom Kippur War in October 1973, Israel bought $1 bil-lion in military equipment from the United States on a cash basis with payment due in 120 days. On October 19, while the fighting was still go-ing on, President Nixon asked Congress for $2.2 billion in emergency assistance to Israel. Congress complied, although some members won-dered whether the aid might be linked to the peace negotiations sched-uled to begin in Geneva on December 21. In the House debate on the au-thorization bill, Chairman of the Foreign Affairs Subcommittee on the Near East Lee H. Hamilton, D-Ind., declared:

> The $2.2 billion request is so large, so poorly justified, so militantly defended by some that it frankly makes it very difficult to vote for the request even if members, like myself, want to support Israel and assure its deterrent strength. The administration and Israel's strongest supporters should try to appreciate that most members of Congress are committed to and want to support the reasonable defense budget of Is-rael, but that performances like those surrounding this request may po-larize positions and produce undesirable and undeserving opposition.[17]

Attempts to link the bill to negotiations or to cut it, however, were defeated. Representative Paul Findley, R-Ill., offered an amendment in the House stating that the aid was intended to support implementation of the 1967 and 1973 U.N. resolutions. These resolutions called for Israeli withdrawal from occupied Arab territory; they also called for acknowledgement of the sovereignty, territorial integrity, and political independence of every state in the area and for guarantees of freedom of navigation. Findley argued:

> This bill is silent on nonmilitary solutions and Arab interests. It is advanced as necessary to "maintain the balance of power" in the Middle East, but Arab states could understandably interpret it as a bill to help maintain only the occupation of Arab lands.[18]

Findley's amendment was rejected, 82-334.

In the Senate, Fulbright offered an amendment to prohibit the use of more than $1.2 billion until the president determined that Israel was taking appropriate steps to comply with the U.N. resolutions. Fulbright's amendment was tabled, 62-12.

Military Sales to Arabs

In 1975, Congress amended the law to strengthen its control over foreign military sales, which had mushroomed to $8 or $10 billion a year and gave every prospect of growing even more. Any sale amounting to $25 million or more was required to be reported to Congress, which then had a period of 20 calendar days to disapprove the sale by concurrent resolution (thereby avoiding a presidential veto). The law was further amended in 1976 to extend the period for congressional action to 30 days and to make it applicable to any sale of "major defense equipment" amounting to $7 million or more. The principal force behind enactment of these provisions was growing concern over the increase in military sales by the United States, particularly of sophisticated items to less developed countries. A secondary consideration was to provide a means for Congress to veto sales to the Arabs. Although Congress has received hundreds, perhaps thousands, of notifications under this provision, it has only once made a serious objection about an arms sale to any non-Arab country (a $1.2 billion sale of airborne warning and control system planes to Iran).

Hawk Missiles to Jordan. Jordan had long been among the more moderate of the Arab states, despite the loss of its territory west of the Jordan River in the Six Days War. Its ruler, King Hussein, was a regular and popular visitor to Washington where he left an impression of beleaguered reasonableness. This was all the more remarkable in view of the fact that by 1970 approximately 40 percent of Jordan's population consisted of Palestinian refugees from Israel. A canny politician, Hussein had managed to survive on his shaky throne with the help of large subsidies from abroad ($2 billion from the United States alone through 1978). Of this total, $800 million was in the form of military assistance or credits. Most of this military aid was used to support the Arab Legion, which principally occupied itself with fighting Palestinian terrorists and thus did not alarm the Israelis.

It was another matter, however, when Hussein asked for Hawk ground-to-air missiles in 1975, because these advanced weapons were perceived to threaten the widely acknowledged superiority of the Israeli Air Force. Indeed, one reason Hussein wanted the Hawks was that he had felt so defenseless in the wars of both 1967 and 1973. Strengthening his air defense capabilities became an obsession with the king.

On July 10, 1975, the Defense Department notified Congress of its intention to sell to Jordan 14 batteries of Hawk missiles valued at $260 million, eight batteries of Vulcan antiaircraft guns valued at $90 million, and $4 million worth of Redeye shoulder-fired missiles. Objections were immediately heard from Israel's supporters in Congress. Resolutions of disapproval were introduced in the Senate by Clifford P. Case, R-N.J., and in the House by Representative Jonathan Bingham, D-N.Y.

Extensive hearings were held on the issue. Proponents based their case mainly on political grounds — the weapons were essentially defensive and Hussein felt defenseless; if the sale were disapproved, Hussein would be driven to look elsewhere for help and would come under increasing pressure from his army to pursue a more radical policy. Opponents, on the other hand, were preoccupied with the capabilities of the weapons. Testimony was taken from U.S. Air Force generals about the losses that might be suffered in neutralizing a Hawk battery. The delicate question was raised as to whether the U.S.-supplied planes of the Israeli Air Force were capable of electronic countermeasures against Hawks, or whether they could be made so.

The deadline for action by both houses of Congress to block the sale was July 30, just about the time Congress was scheduled to adjourn for its summer recess. The House International Relations Committee, as it was then called, reported Bingham's resolution of disapproval July 24. Although the law provided for expedited consideration of such resolutions in both houses, time was growing short and the outcome of a vote, particularly in the Senate, was by no means clear. In these circumstances, opponents of the sale brought pressure on the administration to withdraw the notification and submit it again, perhaps in a modified form, in September when Congress could consider the matter at greater leisure (though under the law, it would have no more time to do so in September than it had had in July). This was done. The letter of intent was withdrawn July 28 and resubmitted in September.

The main concern of the opponents by this time had been reduced to the mobility of the Hawks. A Hawk battery, consisting of several missiles and associated fire control equipment, is a cumbersome thing; and it seemed unlikely that, once in place, it could readily be moved. It was, however, designed to be mobile as used by the United States. Opponents conjured up the possibility that the Hawks could be moved behind advancing Jordanian troops to provide them with constant antiaircraft protection. This, in the opponents' view, meant that the Hawks could be used offensively as well as defensively.

The State Department in this situation had to conduct a dual negotiation — on the one hand, with congressional opponents of the sale and on the other, with Hussein, whose pride had become involved. Some members of the Senate Foreign Relations Committee were corresponding with Hussein directly on the matter through the Jordanian embassy in Washington. The committee at one point even considered sending a delegation of its members to Amman to meet with Hussein personally, but it thought better of this.

In the end, on September 17, President Ford gave assurances that the Hawks would be deployed solely as "defensive and non-mobile anti-aircraft weapons" and that they would not be accompanied by either the equipment or the training to provide mobility. The sale would also be conditioned, he said, on their not becoming part of any binational or multinational force. (The pro-Israeli group had been alarmed over tentative negotiations for a joint Jordanian-Syrian military command.) On September 18, Hussein publicly said that these limitations were "insulting," but the next day he gave private assurances to the American embassy in Amman that he would accept them. Congress then let the matter drop, and the sale went forward under the new conditions.

C-130 Transports to Egypt. On March 25, 1976, the executive branch notified Congress of its intention to sell Egypt six C-130 transport aircraft (including spare parts and training) valued at $65 million. Although this was a much more modest proposal than the Hawk missiles to Jordan, it aroused the same kind of reaction in Congress. The price of approval of the sale was a promise by Secretary of State Kissinger that no additional sales to Egypt would be proposed in 1976. Perhaps none would have been proposed anyway, but by extracting this promise from Kissinger, for the price of six transport planes the Israeli bloc was able to ensure that for at least nine months Egypt could not update or replace (at least from the United States) any of its aging Soviet equipment.

Sales to Saudi Arabia. Sales of missiles were made to Saudi Arabia in 1976 and of advanced jet aircraft in 1978. In the first case, the threat of congressional disapproval led to a reduction in the number of missiles. In the second, it led to conditions imposed on the equipment carried by the planes and on their use by the Saudis.

The sales were made by the executive branch in the context of overall American policies toward Saudi Arabia. Saudi Arabia is a large, thinly populated country occupying most of the territory between the Persian Gulf and the Red Sea. It possesses the world's largest oil reserves, and its conservative government generally exerts a moderating influence in the Organization of Petroleum Exporting Countries (OPEC). The sales were considered by Congress in the context of the Arab-Israeli conflict. Even with the number of missiles scaled back, administration forces had to resort to an unprecedented and questionable parliamentary maneuver to block Senate consideration of a resolution disapproving the sale.

On September 1, 1976, the executive branch notified Congress of its intention to sell 1,000 Sidewinder air-to-air missiles and 1,500 Maverick air-to-ground missiles, valued at $702 million, to Saudi Arabia. The matter was complicated by the fact that it was submitted simultaneously with letters of intent to make a large number of other arms sales. This raised two separate but related issues: arms sales to less developed countries in general, and arms sales that might threaten Israel.

Resolutions were promptly introduced in the Senate to disapprove each of the sales, but attention focused on the sale to Saudi Arabia. In a public hearing September 21, the Senate Foreign Relations Committee heard contentions that the Saudi sale would threaten the security of Israel. During this same period, negotiations were going on between Kissinger and the pro-Israeli bloc on the committee, represented by Hubert Humphrey, Clifford Case, and Jacob Javits. As a part of these negotiations, Kissinger agreed to reduce the sale to 850 Sidewinders and 650 Mavericks.

Notwithstanding this reduction, on September 24 the committee voted 8-6 to report a resolution disapproving the sale. The resolution was duly reported to the Senate where, under the law, it took a privileged position on the calendar. On September 27, before there had been any further action, the committee was dumbfounded to learn that the Senate had acceded to a unanimous consent request by the committee chairman, Senator John Sparkman, to recommit the resolution, thereby vitiating the action of the committee in reporting it. Sparkman had made his request on the Senate floor early in the morning; only a few senators were present. It is unheard of for a chairman to make a request to recommit without the agreement of his committee. As it developed later, Sparkman made the request on his own, on the basis of a personal appeal from Vice President Nelson Rockefeller and without consultation with any other member of the committee or notice to the committee staff.

Case asked unanimous consent that the recommittal action be vacated. Abourezk objected and the action stood, with time running out on the period for congressional action. Shaking with rage, Case called Sparkman's behavior an "inexcusable breach of courtesy." Sparkman later apologized, but the sale went through.

On April 28, 1978, the executive branch formally notified Congress of its intention to make the following major sales of military jet planes:

• Fifteen F-15s worth $431 million and 75 F-16s worth $1.5 billion (including support equipment and spare parts) to Israel;

• Fifty F-5s worth $590 million (including spare parts, associated munitions, and training) to Egypt;

• Sixty F-15s worth $2.5 billion (including spare parts, support equipment, munitions, and training) to Saudi Arabia.

Congressional approval of the arms sales to Israel was not in doubt. Circumstances were also favorable for the sale to Egypt: the world still basked in the afterglow of Sadat's visit to Jerusalem, and the F-5 is not a high performance aircraft. But the sale to Saudi Arabia of the F-15, one of the most advanced planes in the U.S. inventory, was another matter. The sale had been pending since 1974, and the Carter administration had agreed to it only reluctantly in January 1978 when the Saudis bluntly told the president during his visit to Riyadh that they regarded it as a test of their relationship to the United States.

As consideration of the matter proceeded in the Senate Foreign Relations Committee, the administration promised that Israel would get more F-15s in 1983-84 and that Saudi Arabia's planes would be delivered without multiple ejection racks so that they could not carry a big bomb load. Secretary of Defense Harold Brown also passed on to the committee assurances from Saudi Arabia that the U.S. would have the right to suspend or cancel deliveries, that the planes would not be based at Tabuk (the nearest Saudi air base to Jerusalem — 250 miles), and that Saudi Arabia would not acquire additional combat aircraft during the F-15 delivery period.

At least equally important in the deliberations, however, was Saudi oil. The Senate debate over this sale of planes was the first time that oil gave the Arabs any significant counterweight to Israeli influence in Congress. As such, it might be a portent for the future.

On May 11, the Senate Foreign Relations Committee voted 8-8 on the resolution disapproving the sales. This ordinarily would have been the end of it, but in order to keep control of the parliamentary situation in the Senate and to prevent somebody else from bringing it up, the committee then voted unanimously to report without recommendation the resolution it had just defeated on a tie vote.

The Senate debated the matter on May 15 and defeated the resolution of disapproval by a vote of 44-54. Senator Mike Gravel, D-Alaska, summed up the difficulty in which members found themselves, "This vote, if it is not done properly, kisses away in the future all kinds of financial support that would inure to a candidate for office."[19] Gravel voted against the resolution and for the sales.

Consideration of this group of sales was accompanied by the suspension of a member of the staff of the Senate Foreign Relations Committee while the FBI investigated an allegation that he had passed on to the Israelis classified information he had received from the Defense Department about Saudi air bases. Although the investigation dragged on for months, nothing came of it, and the employee was reinstated.

CONCLUSION

For roughly a quarter of a century following the establishment of Israel, Congress was a bastion of pro-Israeli sentiment in the United

States government. As we have already observed, legislative opinion in this respect mirrored the predominantly pro-Israeli sentiments of the American people; and during certain periods, the president and some of his advisers clearly supported Israeli goals. As time passed, however, executive policymakers became more sympathetic to Arab viewpoints and less prone to accept Israel's point of view on issues engendering conflict in the Middle East. This transition was highlighted by the diplomacy of the Carter administration. The change in official American thinking toward the Arab-Israeli conflict occurred much more slowly in the legislative branch, where support still remained strong for Israel's position. Yet as our case study has shown, in time many legislators acknowledged the necessity for a more balanced approach to problems in the Middle East.

Several developments during the 1970s had the collective effect of calling into question the longstanding assumption of automatic support on Capitol Hill for Israel's policies. The first of these was the use by the Arabs of oil as an economic and political weapon beginning with the Yom Kippur War in 1973. After this fourth round in the Arab-Israeli conflict, to a degree unprecedented in its history, the United States found itself vulnerable to an embargo of oil shipments from the Middle East. In the years which followed, the energy crisis underscored for millions of Americans the crucial importance of the region for American prosperity and economic well-being.

The second development affecting congressional attitudes was the election in 1977 of the conservative government of Prime Minister Menachem Begin's Likud Party. This government followed ideologically based, unyielding policies with respect to the Arab territories occupied by Israel in the 1967 Six Days War and their Palestinian inhabitants. "The idea that Palestinian Arabs would have a right to self-determination," said Foreign Minister Moshe Dayan, "is absolutely unacceptable to us."[20] The Begin government also expanded Israeli settlements on the West Bank and became more aggressive in its attacks on presumed bases of Palestinian terrorists in Lebanon. These policies were controversial in Israel, a controversy which was reflected among American supporters of Israel.

The third development was the Israeli-Egyptian peace process, in which the Carter administration played a leading role.[21] After President Anwar Sadat expelled the Soviets from Egypt in 1972, Cairo began to develop more cordial relations with the United States. Sadat's expressed interest in a peace settlement with Israel — dramatized by prolonged Israeli-Egyptian-American discussions at Camp David late in 1978 — was applauded by both executive and legislative officials in Washington. By contrast, the Israeli-Egyptian peace negotiations often highlighted Israeli rigidity on the Palestine question. (Even some Jewish groups in the United States, for example, questioned the Begin government's uncompromising position on the political future of the West Bank of the Jordan River.)

As a consequence of signing the peace treaty with Israel, Egypt became isolated in the Arab world to a degree not anticipated in either Cairo or Washington. This drew Egypt and the United States closer together. Washington had to use its influence with other Arab governments (notably Jordan and Saudi Arabia) to attempt to counteract the activities of the Arab "rejectionist front" and to promote regional stability.

Finally, there were changing attitudes in the United States toward the Palestine Liberation Organization (PLO). For years, American (and Israeli) policy had been to have nothing to do with the PLO until it recognized Israel's right to exist and abandoned terrorism. The resignation of U.N. Ambassador Andrew Young in 1979 because of his unauthorized discussions with representatives of the PLO caused some Americans to ask whether it was not going too far for the United States even to refuse to talk to the PLO — the group recognized by many Palestinians and their Arab supporters as the most vocal advocate of their rights.

As American diplomacy entered the decade of the 1980s, several members of Congress were privately counseling the Israelis to become more diplomatically flexible — a change that might open the way for greater freedom of action by the executive branch in confronting the thorny problems of the Middle East.

NOTES

1. Dean Acheson, *Present at the Creation: My Years in the State Department* (New York: W. W. Norton & Co., 1969), p. 169.
2. Harry S. Truman, *Memoirs*, vol. 2, *Years of Trial and Hope* (Garden City: Doubleday & Co., 1956), p. 158.
3. Quoted in Stephen D. Isaacs, *Jews and American Politics* (Garden City: Doubleday & Co., 1974), pp. 264-265.
4. *The New York Times,* April 6, 1973.
5. U.S., Congress, Senate, *Congressional Record* (daily edition), 95th Cong., 2d sess., May 15, 1978, p. S7378.
6. Quoted in Russell Warren Howe and Sarah Hays Trott, *The Power Peddlers: How Lobbyists Mold America's Foreign Policy* (Garden City, N.Y.: Doubleday & Co., 1977), p. 278.
7. Marquis Childs, "Stirrings Against Carter," *The Washington Post,* March 13, 1979.
8. Howe and Trott, *The Power Peddlers,* p. 347.
9. *The New York Times,* February 21, 1957.
10. *The New York Times,* May 25, 1975.
11. *The New York Times,* May 22, 1975.
12. *The New York Times,* May 27, 1975.
13. U.S., Congress, Senate, *Congressional Record,* 91st Cong., 2d sess., June 12, 1970, 116:19621.
14. *The New York Times,* July 31, 1970.
15. U.S., Congress, Senate, *Congressional Record*, 92d Cong., 1st sess., November 23, 1971, 117:42884.
16. Ibid.
17. U.S., Congress, House, *Congressional Record*, 93d Cong., 1st sess., December 11, 1973, 119:40821.

18. Ibid., p. 40837.
19. U.S., Congress, Senate, *Congressional Record* (daily edition), 95th Cong., 2d sess., May 15, 1978, p. S7396.
20. *The Christian Science Monitor,* September 12, 1979.
21. The role of the Carter administration in promoting Israeli-Egyptian peace negotiations is described more fully in *The Middle East: U.S. Policy, Israel, Oil and the Arabs,* 4th ed. (Washington, D.C.: Congressional Quarterly, 1979), pp. 3-15.

5

The Armed Forces

Where to draw the line between the power of Congress to declare war (Article 1, Section 8) and the power of the president as commander in chief (Article 2, Section 2) is one of the most controversial issues in the Constitution. How far may the president go in ordering troops into combat or into situations where combat is likely, in the absence of a declaration of war by Congress? How far may Congress go in restraining the president? How far may, or should, Congress go in determining where the armed forces are to be deployed, even in nonhostile environments? What is the proper role for Congress in dealing with the foreign policy consequences of such deployments in the form of quid pro quos for the rights to foreign bases?

These important questions have been the subject of scholarly exegesis, and it is not our purpose to review that voluminous literature here. Nor shall we review the long history of dispute over these questions, during which the pendulum has swung between the two ends of Pennsylvania Avenue. Rather, we shall look at examples of the use of armed forces since World War II and examine some of the problems that have arisen.

What becomes clear from the post-World War II practice is that Congress pays much less attention to constitutional niceties or consistency than it does to pragmatic considerations. When Congress has agreed with the general thrust of a presidential policy, it has acquiesced in the use or even the enlargement of presidential power. When it has disagreed, it has asserted its own prerogatives.

KOREA

Korea is a good illustration of how Congress' attitudes towards its own powers change over time. In 1950, Congress was content to let the president act on his own authority in sending American troops to Korea. In 1977, Congress insisted on having a voice in deciding whether to bring them home.

Getting In

Korea emerged from World War II a divided country. Installed by the Soviet Union, a Communist regime (the Democratic People's Republic of Korea or North Korea) governed north of the 38th parallel. Below that line, the Republic of Korea (or South Korea) developed close ties with the United States. Growing tension characterized relations between the two countries. Ever since World War II, an avowed goal of American foreign policy has been the reunification of Korea on the basis of free and democratic elections — an objective repeatedly blocked by North Korea's refusal to participate in them.

On Sunday, June 25, 1950, North Korean troops crossed the 38th parallel in an evident attempt to overrun South Korea. In the week of frantic American decisionmaking which followed, Congress played no significant role, nor gave much indication of wanting to. In major part, this was due to the fact that most members of Congress supported, initially anyway, the adminstration's response to this crisis. Such disagreement as developed was over whether Congress should formally bestow its blessing on the administration's Korea policy and whether such a blessing was constitutionally necessary or politically desirable.

The first American response to the North Korean invasion was to call for an emergency meeting of the United Nations Security Council. On Sunday, with the Soviets absent, the Security Council voted 9-0 to order North Korea to cease the invasion and withdraw.

That night, following a meeting with executive officials, President Truman ordered General Douglas MacArthur, the American commander in the Far East with headquarters in Tokyo, to evacuate Americans from Korea and to get ammunition and other supplies to South Korea, by airdrop if necessary. MacArthur was authorized to use air and naval power, but was cautioned to keep south of the 38th parallel. This precaution becomes more significant in the light of later events.

As the meeting broke up, Truman directed that the State Department prepare a statement for him to make on Tuesday, perhaps to Congress, although that was left undecided. He emphasized that no other statement was to be made in the meantime, not even by Secretary of State Dean Acheson or Secretary of Defense Louis Johnson, both of whom had previously been scheduled to appear the next day before the Senate Appropriations Committee in connection with the mutual defense assistance program.

Truman's injunction of silence reflected a typical and traditional executive branch attitude — namely, to arrive at a finished policy before involving Congress in the decisionmaking process. The extent to which Congress was willing to acquiesce in this procedure is shown by Acheson's remark that the Appropriations Committee hearing, which was held in executive session, "went off without too much trouble."[1]

On Monday, June 26, Truman himself talked to the chairman of the Senate Foreign Relations Committee, Tom Connally, D-Texas. The president inquired whether the senator thought a declaration of war would be necessary "if I decide to send American forces into Korea." Connally replied:

> If a burglar breaks into your house, you can shoot at him without going down to the police station and getting permission. You might run into a long debate by Congress, which would tie your hands completely. You have the right to do it as commander in chief and under the U.N. Charter.[2]

On Monday night, Truman authorized MacArthur to use air and naval power in direct support of South Korea and again cautioned him to stay south of the 38th parallel. On Tuesday, June 27, the U.N. Security Council met again and called on all members of the United Nations to give assistance to the Republic of Korea. This was later used to give an added color of legitimacy to American actions.

The morning of that same day, Truman met with a bipartisan group of 14 members of Congress from both houses. Acheson summarized the situation in Korea. Truman read a press release (the statement he had asked on Sunday night to have prepared), announcing American air and naval support for South Korea. The president then asked for the views of the congressional leaders; Truman later reported in his memoirs that they "approved of my action."[3] According to Acheson, "Senator [Alexander] Wiley seemed to express the consensus by saying that it was enough for him to know that we were in there with force and that the President thought the force adequate."[4] (It was not.) Connally recalls that he and others stressed the importance of the U.N. action and that "a few wondered if Congress should approve."[5]

Republican Senator Robert A. Taft of Ohio, who was not in the group invited to the White House, did not wonder; he was convinced. In a speech in the Senate on Wednesday, June 28, Taft noted that the congressional leaders had no opportunity to change the president's statement and that "there has been no pretense of consulting the Congress." There was, he said, no legal authority for what the president had done, yet he added that "if a joint resolution were introduced asking for approval of the use of our Armed Forces already sent to Korea and full support of them in their present venture, I would vote for it."[6]

On Thursday, June 29, Truman expanded the involvement of United States' air and naval forces to include military targets in North Korea, but not beyond. He also authorized the use of ground forces to secure the port, airfield, and communications facilities at Pusan on the southeast coast. On the morning of Friday, June 30, Truman gave MacArthur authority to use the ground forces under his command. The United States was then fully committed to the conflict.

That same day, a second White House meeting was held with members of Congress. Perhaps twice as many were present as on Tuesday. Truman reported to the legislators the orders he had issued about ground troops. There was, says Acheson, "a general chorus of approval," and Republican Representative Dewey Short of Missouri declared that "Congress was practically unanimous in its appreciation of the President's leadership."[7] But Senate Republican leader Kenneth Wherry questioned the president's legal authority. Republican Senator Alexander Smith suggested a resolution approving the action. The president said he would consider this and asked Acheson to prepare a recommendation.

Acheson recommended against the resolution at a meeting with the president July 3, by which time Congress, incredibly, had recessed for a week over the Fourth of July. Senate Majority Leader Scott Lucas was the only member of Congress present at the meeting, and he agreed with Acheson. Lucas argued that the vast majority of Congress was satisfied and the minority could not be won over but could keep debating and delaying a resolution so as to dilute much of its public effect.[8]

Getting In Deeper

During July and August, the North Koreans swept down the peninsula and the U.N. forces, principally Americans, were hard pressed to hold a beachhead around Pusan. Then in September, MacArthur made a surprise amphibious landing at Inchon on the northwest coast, cutting off the bulk of the North Korean forces to the south and rapidly driving the remainder north of the 38th parallel. This totally changed the military situation and led to a rethinking, both in Washington and in the United Nations, of American and U.N. objectives. (The United States, we need to recall, had long advocated the political reunification of Korea under a democratic system.)

As a consequence, what had started in June as a defensive operation aimed at restoring the status quo ante became in September and October an offensive operation aimed at achieving a united, independent, and democratic Korea. In June, MacArthur had been instructed not to cross the 38th parallel; now he was authorized to do so. The U.N. General Assembly went further on October 7 in a resolution that looked ahead to the possibility of U.N.-sponsored elections in a unified Korea.

This was a radical change in American and U.N. policy, a change that led to disastrous consequences, but Congress had almost nothing to do with it. Two members of the Senate Foreign Relations Committee — Henry Cabot Lodge, Jr. of Massachusetts and John Sparkman of Alabama — were serving as delegates to the General Assembly that year. Sparkman later confessed to doubts about the wisdom of the offensive operation; but if he expressed those doubts at the time, he certainly did so quietly.

That the doubts were well-founded became apparent in late November when massive Chinese forces poured across the Yalu River boundary between China and Korea and drove the U.N. troops southward. In the course of the bitter winter of retreat, a long-simmering dispute erupted between MacArthur on the one hand and the Joint Chiefs of Staff, the president, and the State Department on the other. In brief, MacArthur wanted to widen the war by air attacks on China; the government in Washington, fearful of possible Soviet intervention and of becoming inextricably entangled on the mainland of China, wanted to fight a limited war in Korea.

MacArthur steadily became more strident in his criticism of the administration's policy, and on April 10, 1951, Truman relieved him of all his commands. This led Congress to inject itself into the Korean conflict for the first time in a major way.

Two separate but related issues were involved: civilian control of the military (one of the bedrock principles of the American government) and the conduct of the war itself or, more broadly, the grand design of America's global strategy.

As has repeatedly occurred in connection with other cases, Congress involved itself in the controversy over MacArthur's dismissal on pragmatic grounds of policy — not on grounds of constitutional principle or procedure. Nobody questioned Truman's authority as president and commander in chief to relieve a general, but many people questioned his wisdom in doing so. At the bottom of this dispute was a fundamental difference over a defensive or an offensive global strategy — over whether to contain the Communist world or whether to put unrelenting pressure on it at all available points. This difference was epitomized in Korea. On one side, General MacArthur and his supporters wanted to expand the war by carrying it to China. On the other side, President Truman, his principal advisers, and their supporters wanted to confine hostilities to Korea.

In the context of the recall of MacArthur, the debate over this broader issue took the form of a series of narrow, essentially tactical questions, such as whether to bomb north of the Yalu River. It was a classic example of the problem of where to draw the line between the day-to-day *conduct* of the war (which was the prerogative of the president as commander in chief), and the long-range *policy* of the war itself (in the determination of which Congress had a major role). The problem would arise again two decades later in connection with the bombing of Hanoi during the Vietnam War.

The outcry that followed the firing of MacArthur was immense, both in Congress and in the public at large. The general returned to the United States, for the first time in 14 years, more as a hero than as an officer disgraced for insubordination. He was met everywhere by wildly enthusiastic crowds. Congress took the astonishing step of inviting him to address a joint session and greeted him with an emotional ovation.

Pursuant to action by the Senate, the Armed Services and Foreign Relations committees made a meticulous and exhaustive inquiry into MacArthur's dismissal under the general heading "Military Situation in the Far East." For 43 days, beginning May 3 and ending June 27, 1951, the two committees took testimony from 14 witnesses, including

General MacArthur, Secretary of State Acheson, Secretary of Defense George Marshall, and all the members of the Joint Chiefs of Staff. The record of the proceedings covers 3,691 pages. In the end, no report was issued and no further action taken, although different members of the committees voiced different conclusions.

The hearing served the purpose — which was intended by the Democratic leadership of the two committees — of defusing the Truman-MacArthur controversy by talking it to death. In large part because of the prolonged public airing which the controversy received in Congress, popular and legislative support for General MacArthur's position declined significantly. The result was that the conduct of the Korean War was left where the Democratic leaders of Congress wanted it: in the hands of the president.

Following lengthy negotiations, an armistice in the Korean War was finally signed on July 27, 1953. No peace treaty between the belligerents was ever concluded, however; and relations between the two countries remained hostile throughout the years that followed. On October 1, 1953, the United States and South Korea concluded a mutual defense treaty, formally signifying America's commitment to the preservation of South Korea's independence.

Getting Out

A quarter of a century later, Jimmy Carter campaigned for the presidency advocating, among other things, withdrawal of some of the 41,000 American troops that remained in Korea in 1976. As Carter moved to execute this withdrawal in 1977, however, he ran into unexpected congressional opposition, opposition not unlike that encountered by President Truman in the MacArthur affair.

First, the same differences over global strategy that were so noticeable in 1951 still existed largely beneath the surface in 1977, but with a significant change. In 1951, it was the doves who wanted to maintain the status quo; in 1977, it was the hawks.

Second, on May 19, 1977, the *Washington Post* published an interview with Maj. Gen. John K. Singlaub, chief of staff of the American military command in Korea, in which the general was quoted as saying, "if we withdraw our ground forces on the schedule suggested, it will lead to war." Singlaub was recalled and reassigned by the White House. He was given a hearing by a congressional committee, this time the Investigations Subcommittee of the House Armed Services Committee. These hearings, like the MacArthur hearings, were marked by controversy and ended inconclusively.

Also in May, the Senate Foreign Relations Committee, at the instigation of Senator George McGovern, D-S.D., added a policy statement about Korea to the bill authorizing appropriations for the State Department. The principal provision of this amendment was that "the United States should seek to accomplish, in accord with the President's announced intention, a complete withdrawal of United States ground forces from the Korean peninsula within four or five years."[9]

When the bill came before the Senate in June, this provision ran into a buzz saw of opposition. The debate was directed primarily to the merits of the issue — that is, whether withdrawing some or all of the troops from Korea was a sensible thing to do — but it also marked a new assertiveness by Congress with respect to the congressional role in deciding the issue. In order to avoid congressional repudiation of the president's policy — and more particularly to blunt an effort to enact some kind of prohibition on troop withdrawal — Majority Leader Robert C. Byrd offered a substitute amendment that watered down McGovern's support of the president. As it finally passed the Senate, the Byrd amendment had Congress declaring "that U.S. policy toward Korea should continue to be arrived at by joint decision of the President and the Congress" and that "any implementation of the foregoing policy should be done in regular consultation with the Congress."[10]

In 1973, Congress had passed over President Nixon's veto the War Powers Resolution — discussed on p. 126 — sharply circumscribing presidential authority to send troops abroad. Nixon based his veto on grounds of unconstitutional interference with the president's powers as commander in chief. Now Congress was going further and asserting its prerogative to circumscribe presidential authority to bring troops home. It argued in part from the precedent of the War Powers Resolution.

"I do not think this is strictly an executive branch decision," said Senator Sam Nunn, Georgia Democrat and prominent member of the Armed Services Committee. "Under the War Powers Act [sic], we talked a long time about the commitment of troops abroad. I should think that, by implication, we would have some control over the withdrawal of forces that are in a dangerous spot in the world." And, "If it works one way, it works the other."[11]

Some senators who had opposed the War Powers Resolution now also opposed the president's authority unilaterally to withdraw troops from Korea. During the hearings on war powers in 1972, the following exchange occurred:

> Senator Javits. So really you are opposed to my bill because you have less faith in the Congress than you have in the President; isn't that true?
> Senator Goldwater. To be perfectly honest with you, you are right.[12]

Now, in 1977, Goldwater argued that the president should send his requests about Korea "to the proper committees of Congress, and then we can hold hearings."[13]

And Senator James Allen of Alabama, arguing against the Carter policy, stated:

> We are turning our backs completely, as I see it, on the principle that was established in the Vietnam war debates, namely, that Con-

gress have a right to participate in decisions regarding the waging of war or foreign policy in general.

But here, we are abdicating our role. A role that was fought for here in the Congress.

I did not always support that. . . . I thought the President as Commander-in-Chief of our Armed Forces should have a right to dictate the other policy, but the wisdom of the Congress, in which I now concur, prevailed and Congress did assert unto itself the right to participate in foreign policy decisions.[14]

Congress returned to the subject in 1978. Various proposals to put firm limits on the withdrawal were rejected, but the military assistance bill expressed the view that "further withdrawal of ground forces of the United States from the Republic of Korea may seriously risk upsetting the military balance in that region and requires full advance consultation with Congress." The act also says that the president "should" transmit to Congress, 120 days before each phase of troop withdrawal, "a report on the viability of the withdrawal."[15] The use of the word "should" is curious; most reporting requirements use the stronger "shall."

In January 1979, new intelligence estimates showed greater North Korean military strength than had previously been thought. This finding increased doubts both in Congress and in the Pentagon about the wisdom of withdrawal. Finally, in July, the White House announced that further implementation of Carter's plan was being postponed until 1981. The total troop reduction from 1977 to 1979 was from 41,000 to 38,000.

EUROPE

Getting In

As part of its containment strategy against communism, the United States joined 11 other Western nations in establishing the North Atlantic Treaty Organization (NATO) early in 1949. Then, on September 9, 1950 (less than three months after American troops were committed to the defense of South Korea with little objection from Congress), President Truman announced approval of a "substantial increase" in American forces in Europe over the two American divisions already in Germany. On December 19, Truman said that this increase would be carried out as soon as possible.

This provoked a great debate in the Senate, which began on January 5, 1951, with a major foreign policy speech by Senator Robert Taft:

As I see it, members of Congress, and particularly members of the Senate, have a constitutional obligation to reexamine constantly and discuss the foreign policy of the United States. If we permit appeals to unity to bring an end to that criticism, we endanger not only the constitutional liberties of the country, but even its future existence [an argument that would be heard 15 years later with respect to Vietnam].[16]

The president, Taft asserted:

> . . .has no power to agree to send American troops to fight in Europe between members of the Atlantic Pact and Soviet Russia. Without authority, he involved us in the Korean war. Without authority, he apparently is now attempting to adopt a similar policy in Europe.[17]

Three days later, Senate Republican leader Kenneth Wherry of Nebraska introduced a sense of the Senate resolution (a resolution voted on by the Senate but without the president's signature and not having the force of law) that no American ground forces "should be assigned to duty in the European area for the purposes of the North Atlantic Treaty pending the formulation of a policy with respect thereto by the Congress."[18] This led to prolonged hearings by the Foreign Relations and Armed Services committees in the course of which the administration put a figure of four divisions on its planned increase.

As happened in the MacArthur controversy, the hearings and the Senate debate that followed were confused by two issues — the issue of substantive policy and the issue of the proper congressional role. Those who favored Truman's policy in Europe tended to take a broad view of the president's powers to act on his own. Those who opposed the policy tended to take a narrow view. The matter was complicated by the desire of the president's supporters to avoid any congressional action which, even though it approved the policy, might be taken as an assertion of the congressional right to do so, something which would establish — in their view — an unfortunate constitutional precedent. The end result was ambiguous and not wholly satisfactory to either side, though less so to those who supported a broad concept of presidential authority.

In March, following the hearings, the Foreign Relations and Armed Services committees reported two resolutions that were identical in language but different in form. One was a simple Senate resolution; the other was a concurrent resolution, that is, one requiring passage by both houses. The operative provisions of the resolutions approved the appointment of General Eisenhower as NATO commander and a "fair share" contribution of U.S. forces in NATO; asked the president to consult with the Senate Foreign Relations, House Foreign Affairs, and Armed Services committees in both houses before sending the troops abroad; and asked that the Joint Chiefs of Staff certify that other NATO countries were doing their share before U.S. troops were sent.[19]

The reasons for reporting two resolutions were complicated in a technical parliamentary sense, but they reflected the underlying substantive issues. A Senate resolution requires action only by the Senate; a concurrent resolution requires action by the House as well. Neither is submitted to the president for his signature and neither has the force of law. They are only formal expressions of the sense of the Senate or the Congress, as the case may be. If the Senate passes both a Senate and a concurrent resolution in the same terms, the Senate resolution can stand alone if the House fails to act. A concurrent resolution, being an expression of both houses of Congress, carries somewhat more weight; but the Senate often prefers not to share with the House its prerogatives in foreign affairs.

A third group in the Senate insisted that the action be taken in the form of a joint resolution. A joint resolution goes to the president for his signature and has the force of law. Thus, in the hierarchy of these things, a joint resolution is the most binding action; a simple Senate (or House) resolution, the least binding. Those who took the broadest view of the president's powers favored a Senate resolution; those who took the narrowest view favored a joint resolution.

These crosscurrents of opinion were reflected in the Senate votes. The simple Senate resolution passed by a vote of 69-21. The concurrent resolution passed by only 45-41 in the Senate, but languished to its death in the House. The Senate rejected the idea of a joint resolution, 31-56.

The Senate also adopted an amendment offered by Democrat John McClellan of Arkansas that no more than four divisions should be sent without the Senate's approval. The McClellan amendment was first rejected, 44-46. It was then reconsidered and agreed to, 49-43. The McClellan amendment had no force of law, but it was an assertion of Senate prerogatives that distressed the Truman administration.

Getting Out

Nevertheless, approximately 300,000 American troops, accompanied by 225,000 dependents, were stationed in Europe, most of them in Germany. Beginning in 1966, growing but unsuccessful agitation developed to bring some of them home. In a sense, it was a spillover of the then nascent Senate disillusionment with Vietnam. More directly, it was a consequence of the French withdrawal from the military side of NATO and a generalized feeling that the United States contribution to NATO was more than its "fair share" (the words of the 1951 resolution). Congressional sentiment for cutting American forces in Europe increased later as the dollar declined relative to the German mark, and it became more expensive to maintain the troops in the NATO area.

The most articulate spokesman for reducing American troops in Europe was Senate Majority Leader Mike Mansfield of Montana. In 1966, Mansfield, joined by 12 other members of the Senate Democratic Policy Committee, introduced a resolution expressing the sense of the Senate that American forces in Europe should be reduced. Despite the prominence of its sponsors, no action was taken on the resolution, and the issue of troop reduction, although raised annually, did not come to a head until 1971.

In that year, Mansfield shifted his strategy from Senate resolutions — in effect, recommendations to the president — to the power of the purse. In the amendment to a bill extending the draft, he proposed to limit funds to the amount necessary to support 150,000 troops. This would have meant a reduction of 50 percent, and it provoked a major debate in the Senate during which five alternative troop cut proposals were offered. All of them were less drastic than the Mansfield amendment, and all were defeated by a coalition of those who thought they did too little and those who thought they did too much. In the end, the Mansfield amendment itself was rejected by a vote of 36-61, but 60 senators voted for at least one of the proposals. The Nixon administration's all-out effort against troop reduction in Europe received a major assist from the Soviet Union in the form of the overture that led to Mutual Balanced Force Reduction (MBFR) talks in Vienna. This provided opponents of the reduction with the argument that the troops ought to be left in Europe as bargaining chips.

The Senate voted on the subject again in November 1971 when the Appropriations Committee added an amendment to the defense appropriation bill limiting funds to the level required for 250,000 troops. This was rejected, 39-54.

The effort to reduce troops in Europe in the 1960s and early 1970s moved from recommendations to limitations on money. It thereby avoided the constitutional argument that was raised by the McClellan amendment to the original troops to Europe resolution in 1951 and repeated in the debate on the War Powers Resolution in 1973. This was whether Congress has a power, other than the power of the purse, to control troop deployments.

Eleven of the senators who voted on the McClellan amendment, including McClellan himself, were still in the Senate for the vote on Nixon's veto of the War Powers Resolution. A consistent view of the relative powers of the president and Congress over the armed forces would have required the same vote — yea on the part of those favoring a restriction of the president's powers and nay on the part of those opposing a restriction. Only two senators, McClellan and Republican Milton Young of North Dakota, voted the same way both times, yea in each case.

The Senate in 1951 also included two future presidents and one future vice president — Lyndon Johnson, Richard Nixon, and Hubert Humphrey. Although Humphrey voted against the limitation on the president's powers implied in the McClellan amendment, 22 years later he voted for the tighter limitation contained in the War Powers Resolution. Johnson and Nixon, each of whom as president was to assert sweeping executive powers, split on the McClellan amendment. Johnson — consistent with his later actions — voted against it. Nixon voted for it, and then vetoed the War Powers Resolution.

Other senators who voted on the McClellan amendment and the War Powers Resolution were John Sparkman, J. William Fulbright, Russell Long, James Eastland, John Stennis, John Pastore, George Aiken, and Warren Magnuson. (Technically, Magnuson did not vote on the McClellan amendment, but he was paired against it.[20]) All of them changed from a less to a more restrictive view of presidential power.

VIETNAM

What brought about this change was the war in Vietnam, which in the late 1960s and early 1970s became the most divisive issue in the United States since the Civil War. The period was marked by a growing split between Congress and two presidents, a schism that culminated in the enactment of the War Powers Resolution over Nixon's veto in November 1973 and finally in use of the ultimate congressional power — the power to withhold appropriations.

The differences between Congress and the president originated in the substantive policy of American involvement in Vietnam. The argument over relative constitutional powers came later. Congress itself, like the country at large, was divided over Vietnam. The curve of opinion in Congress, like that of public opinion, progressed from acceptance of presidential policies, to opposition by a minority, to opposition by an overwhelming majority. A farsighted member of the House saw this development coming at a time when the American buildup was just beginning. "We can take one casualty per congressional district," he said privately. "We can maybe even take 10. But if it gets to be 100, Congress will stop it." That is precisely what happened. By the time Congress stopped it, American deaths totaled about 50,000, or a little more than 100 per congressional district.

Getting In

Congress paid strikingly little attention to the steps taken by the Johnson administration in 1965 to convert the American role in Vietnam from support and advice to active participation. The first of these steps came in February, when Johnson ordered the bombing of North Vietnam in retaliation for a Viet Cong attack on an American barracks (occupied by what technically were then still advisers). The second came in July when Johnson, after publicly agonizing over the decision, ordered an additional 50,000 American troops to Vietnam.

One reason for the almost silent congressional acquiescence was relief that those measures were not more far-reaching. Before the July decision, officials of the Johnson administration had talked about the possibility of calling up the reserves, raising taxes, and imposing controls on the economy. Compared to these proposals, sending an additional 50,000 regular army troops did not seem so drastic.

The same psychology had been at work to some extent the year before when Congress, to its later regret, provided a statutory basis for the war through the Gulf of Tonkin Resolution. This resolution was occasioned by a reported attack August 2, 1964, on the U.S. Navy destroyer *Maddox* while it was on what was described as a routine patrol in the Gulf of Tonkin off the North Vietnamese coast. On August 4, further attacks were reported on the *Maddox* and on the *C. Turner Joy*, which had joined it. There was no damage to the destroyers, but President Johnson ordered air strikes against North Vietnamese torpedo boat bases. The next day Johnson asked Congress for a joint resolution. In pertinent part, it read as follows:

> That the Congress approves and supports the determination of the President, as Commander in Chief, to take all necessary measures to repel any armed attack against the forces of the United States and to prevent further aggression.
> Sec. 2. The United States regards as vital to its national interest and to world peace the maintenance of international peace and security in southeast Asia. Consonant with the Constitution of the United States and the Charter of the United Nations and in accordance with its obligations under the Southeast Asia Collective Defense Treaty, the United States is, therefore, prepared, as the President determines, to take all necessary steps including the use of armed force, to assist any member or protocol state of the Southeast Asia Collective Defense Treaty requesting assistance in defense of its freedom.[21]

This resolution passed Congress August 7 — two days after Johnson requested it — by votes of 416-0 in the House and 88-2 in the Senate. Johnson was fond of carrying a tattered copy of it in his pocket and of showing it to anyone who questioned his authority, especially to members of Congress who had voted for it. He and other executive officials considered the resolution the "functional equivalent" of a declaration of war.

The immediate military response to the incidents of August 2-4 had been limited. This made Johnson look moderate, especially when compared to Senator Barry Goldwater, his Republican opponent in the 1964 presidential election.

Later on, however, a serious question developed of whether or not the resolution had passed Congress under false pretenses. A review of navy documents by the Senate Foreign Relations Committee revealed that the *Maddox* had not been on a routine patrol at all, but rather on a sensitive and provocative intelligence mission. There was even some doubt as to whether one of the reported attacks even occurred.

Congress repealed the Gulf of Tonkin Resolution in 1971. It may also be noted that this resolution was only one of five which Congress passed between 1955 and 1964 approving in advance the use of force in various parts of the world to achieve specified American objectives. The other resolutions concerned Formosa (passed 1955, repealed 1974), the Middle East (1957), Cuba (1962), and Berlin (1962).

Getting Out

For a number of years, Congress did no more than argue, albeit with increasing stridency, the merits of presidential policies in Vietnam. In other words, it hoped to effect change through persuasion, rather than through legislation. In major part, this was because, until the 1970s, the opposition was still not strong enough to muster a majority in Congress

for legislation significantly restricting the scope of American involvement. Many members of Congress who had doubts about the wisdom of
the involvement still felt compelled to support it because American
troops had already been committed.

As opposition to the war increased, so did congressional frustration
in trying to end it, and Congress turned to the power of the purse. A
significant step in that direction was taken in 1970, when in the Cooper-
Church amendment to the foreign military sales bill, Congress prohibited the expenditure of funds to support military operations in Cambodia after July 1, 1970. In a sense, this was symbolic inasmuch as by
that cutoff date the Nixon administration had already withdrawn
American ground forces from the country. It did, however, have the
practical effect of preventing the reintroduction of American air and
ground forces as the situation in Cambodia later deteriorated.

Throughout the months that followed, Congress utilized this same
approach toward American involvement in Indochina. In 1973 and 1974,
for example, no less than seven restrictions were placed on the use of
funds appropriated by Congress for American military activities in the
area. Typical of these restrictions was the language of the State Department Authorization Act of 1973:·

> Notwithstanding any other provision of law, on or after August 15,
> 1973, no funds heretofore or hereafter appropriated may be obligated or
> expended to finance the involvement of United States military forces in
> hostilities in or over or from off the shores of North Vietnam, South
> Vietnam, Laos, or Cambodia, unless specifically authorized hereafter
> by the Congress.[22]

Again, as with the Cooper-Church amendment, the immediate
practical effect of such measures in a sense was symbolic: the American
involvement was winding down. The question was whether it would have
done so anyway, or whether this disengagement was a response to growing congressional insistence. The congressional grip on the purse strings
may also have prevented a reinvolvement in the hectic days of the final
withdrawal in 1975.

THE WAR POWERS RESOLUTION

During this same period, Congress was nearing the end of more than
three years of consideration of the War Powers Resolution. The immediate inspiration for the early drafts of this measure was the American
incursion into Cambodia ordered by President Nixon in May 1970.

As it finally emerged from the legislative process in November 1973,
the War Powers Resolution was a complicated law in which a number of
disparate strands of congressional thought were woven together. There
was a general desire to restrain the president by ensuring a larger
congressional role in war-making, but the fulfillment of this desire was
sought by various routes.

Some saw the resolution as a restatement of what the Founding Fathers had intended, an intent which in this view had been distorted through congressional abdication. It was a way of forcing Congress to share the responsibility for sending Americans into combat. Others viewed the resolution as a way to delineate the powers of the president as commander in chief. (And some, such as Senator Thomas Eagleton, ended by opposing it because in their view it expanded those powers.) Still others, such as Senator Jacob Javits, viewed it as providing the basis for a compact between the president and Congress on how the totality of their combined powers would be exercised. (This concept was shattered when Nixon vetoed the resolution.)

The constitutional powers of the president as commander in chief to introduce the armed forces into hostilities "or into situations where imminent involvement in hostilities is clearly indicated by the circumstances" are defined by the War Powers Resolution, which finally became law over Nixon's veto. The powers "are exercised *only* pursuant to (1) a declaration of war, (2) specific statutory authorization, or (3) a national emergency created by attack upon the United States, its territories or possessions, or its armed forces." [Sec. 2(c). Emphasis supplied.] Note that this excludes a national emergency created some other way — for example, an attack on American civilians abroad, or an attack on merchant shipping (as happened in the *Mayaguez* case), or the perceived threat of an attack (as happened in the Cuban missile crisis).

In any event, the president "shall" consult with Congress "in every possible instance" beforehand. [Sec. 3.]

In the absence of a declaration of war, the president is to report to Congress within 48 hours of deploying the armed forces in three kinds of situations: when the forces are sent into hostilities or into situations where hostilities are imminent; when forces equipped for combat are sent to any foreign country (except for supply, replacement, repair, or training); and when they are sent in numbers which "substantially enlarge" combat equipped forces already abroad. [Sec. 4(a).]

With respect to the last two of these three situations, the president's report is the end of the matter. With respect to the first, Congress can order the forces withdrawn at any time by a concurrent resolution, which does not require the president's signature and is therefore not subject to his veto. Even without a concurrent resolution, the forces are to be withdrawn at the end of 60 days — in special cases, 90 days — unless Congress in the meantime has declared war, enacted some other specific authorization, extended the 60-day period, or is physically unable to meet. [Sec. 5.][23]

In the form in which it became law, the War Powers Resolution passed Congress in October 1973. President Nixon vetoed it on October 24, calling it "unconstitutional and dangerous to the best interests of our Nation."[24] Both houses voted to override the veto on November 7, the House by 284-135, the Senate by 75-18.

Gerald Ford shared Nixon's view that the resolution was unconstitutional and as a member of the House voted against it. Nevertheless, as president, Ford sent Congress the reports required by the resolution on four occasions: the evacuation of Danang, Phnom Penh, and Saigon in April 1975 and the rescue of the ship *Mayaguez* from Cambodian captors the following month. These four incidents were of short duration, ranging from less than three hours to eight days.

No question was raised about the operations in Danang and Phnom Penh. The evacuation of Saigon was controversial mainly because many in Congress thought it should have been carried out sooner than it was. The rescue of the *Mayaguez* was very controversial. Critics charged that it represented an overreaction by the Ford administration and that Congress had not been consulted. But nobody complained about the end result.

The Carter administration has not contested the constitutionality of the War Powers Resolution. Neither have any incidents clearly bringing the resolution into play arisen during the Carter administration. In May 1978, United States Air Force planes were used to transport French and Belgian troops, as well as military cargo, to Zaire. The following month, the air force carried Moroccan troops to Zaire. In both cases, the purpose was to repel an invasion by tribesmen from neighboring Angola and to restore order.

No reports were made to Congress, though some members were told beforehand. Some members, notably Representative Paul Findley, argued that reports should have been made. The International Security Subcommittee of the House Foreign Affairs Committee decided otherwise after hearing arguments from the State Department that the USAF crews were armed only with revolvers (and therefore not equipped for combat within the meaning of the resolution) and that they never got closer than 130 miles to the fighting. In August 1979, the Defense Department announced plans to airlift the foreign troops out of Zaire.

As we noted in Chapter 2, the War Powers Resolution has defects, and it has yet to be tested. Neither those who think it is unconstitutional nor those who think it is an appropriate exercise of congressional powers expect the Supreme Court to rule on it. And in truth, the resolution deals more with a political question than a legal one. The test, when and if it comes, will have as much to do with the nature of the crisis America faces abroad and with how seriously Congress takes its responsibilities as with presidential compliance.

BASE RIGHTS

Decisions to deploy troops abroad, and the corollary — the acquisition and protection of foreign base rights — have been a continuing preoccupation of American foreign policy since World War II. Deployment decisions are usually made on the basis of military strategy, but they have broader political effects as well, many involving Congress.

In the first place, the mere fact of the presence of large numbers of Americans in a foreign setting introduces an additional factor in the relations between the United States and the country in question. In many parts of the world, the Americans have more money and a higher standard of living than the local population. Some of them will inevitably run afoul of local laws or flout local customs. Their presence may become an issue in local politics and inevitably identifies the United States closely with the regime in power.

A decision to withdraw American troops and their dependents may have as many political ramifications as the decision to send them abroad initially. As in Korea and Germany, a proposed withdrawal may give the appearance of a lessening of United States interest in the country concerned and in its defense. Or, as in some other countries, it may signal the end of American aid programs to the governments. It will certainly signal the end of economic benefits to those who work for, or sell goods to, the Americans.

Quite apart from the issue of deployment, however, Congress has inextricably been involved in the question of base rights if in no other way than through appropriating the money to build the bases. In addition, most base rights agreements involve some kind of quid pro quo that requires appropriations, either directly or indirectly. The question also arises of whether these agreements should have the dignity of treaties or whether they can properly be consummated by executive action.

By the mid-1960s, the United States had 375 major foreign military bases and 3,000 minor facilities scattered around the world. In 1969-70, a special subcommittee of the Senate Foreign Relations Committee made a major study of these bases and their political implications. In its report, the subcommittee pointed out:

> It is the day-to-day implementation of policy which frequently and sometimes almost imperceptibly provides the building blocks for future commitments. . . . Once an American overseas base is established, it takes on a life of its own. Original missions may become outdated, but new missions are developed, not only with the intent of keeping the facility going, but often actually to enlarge it.[25]

The record of congressional participation in decisionmaking about foreign bases has been mixed. Since the Foreign Relations Committee study — an outgrowth of concerns aroused by the Vietnam War — Congress has been somewhat more alert to the implications of its actions. But generally speaking, Congress has not been as inquisitive as it should have been, and the executive branch has not been as candid as it should have been. Consequently, neither has adequately thought through the implications of foreign military bases and attendant cooperation by the United States with foreign military forces and governments. Most of the time, Congress has simply acquiesced in executive actions and not always on the basis of adequate information provided by the White House. A few examples will suffice to indicate the complexity of the problem.

When the Philippines became independent in 1946, the United States retained the rights to Clark Air Force Base and to a naval base at Subic Bay, both very large installations undergirding American power in the Western Pacific and East Asia. By the 1970s, following the reduction of American forces elsewhere in the area, they were the only major American bases south of Korea and Japan. When the American leases expired, the Philippine government was able to extract, as the quid pro quo for renewal, a five-year aid package worth $500 million, as well as concessions concerning the administration of the bases. This was done through an executive agreement, which was submitted to Congress for its information but not approval. Congress will have to face annually the question of appropriations.

The arrangement unavoidably tended to identify the United States with the Philippine government of President Ferdinand E. Marcos, who was ruling under martial law with scant regard for human rights (as explained in Chapter 7) and who was fighting two insurrections.

In Spain, the United States first obtained base rights in 1953 from the government of General Francisco Franco, who ruled the country from 1939 until his death in 1975. Supported by Germany and Italy, Franco had emerged victorious from the bloody Spanish civil war. Thereafter, he imposed on Spanish society a right-wing authoritarian regime that lasted more than a generation. The original purpose of American air bases in Spain was to provide bases for the B-47 bombers, then the largest strategic bomber in the air force inventory; but the B-47 had a relatively short range. The United States also acquired a submarine base and navy communications facility at Rota. The base agreement was regularly renewed as it expired, despite the fact that the B-47 was replaced by the longer range B-52, which in turn was replaced by U.S.-based intercontinental ballistic missiles.

The United States not only provided military and economic assistance to Spain (some $3.3 billion), but it also engaged in joint planning and joint military exercises with the Spanish government. In part, this was to meet the Spanish argument that the presence of American bases and U.S. forces made Spain a potential target for attack. But, as the Senate Subcommittee on Security Agreements and Commitments Abroad pointed out:

> Overseas bases, the presence of elements of United States armed forces, joint planning, joint exercises, or extensive military assistance programs represent to host governments more valid assurances of United States commitment than any treaty or agreement. Furthermore, any or all of the above instances of United States military presence all but guarantee some involvement by the United States in the internal affairs of the host government.

In November 1968, the then chairman of the Joint Chiefs of Staff, General Earle Wheeler, in a statement delivered in Madrid to representatives of the Spanish General Staff, formulated better than any statement by the subcommittee the concept being discussed here. At that time General Wheeler said, in a statement previously cleared by both the State and Defense departments, that the presence of United States troops on Spanish soil represented a stronger security guarantee than anything written on paper.[26]

The renewal of the Spanish base rights in 1970 through an executive agreement rather than a treaty encountered such opposition in the Senate that the next extension in 1976 was submitted as a treaty. Although not embodying a formal security commitment, it went far beyond the previous executive agreements in terms of U.S.-Spanish cooperation. It provided military assistance, sales, and other benefits to Spain amounting to $1.2 billion over a five-year period — more than one-third as much as had been provided over the preceding 23 years. In addition, the treaty expanded, formalized, and provided an institutional framework for activities that had been carried on in the past with respect to defense, economic questions, education and cultural affairs, and science and technology.

Now the Senate critics of the nation's involvement in Spain found that they had painted themselves into a corner. They had loudly insisted that the new Spanish arrangements be submitted to the Senate as a treaty. When this was done by the White House, many senators felt inhibited from voting against the treaty, despite doubts about some of its provisions.

Complicating the issue was the fact that Franco had died in November 1975. Among executive and legislative officials there was a general uneasiness about rocking the boat during the delicate and unpredictable transition period in Spanish politics.

In Ethiopia, the United States' desire for a communications facility at Asmara led to a commitment in 1960 to support a 40,000-man army and a statement "reaffirming" the United States' "continuing interest in the security of Ethiopia and its opposition to any activities threatening the territorial integrity of Ethiopia."[27] This was perhaps innocuous enough if read literally, but it resulted in America's choosing sides in a territorial dispute between Ethiopia and Somalia. It also allied the United States with Emperor Haile Selassie against an insurgency movement in the province of Eritrea, the province where Asmara was located. As part of the quid pro quo, the United States furnished Ethiopia with more than half a billion dollars in economic and military assistance (including jet fighter planes which the Ethiopians could scarcely keep airborne). Suggestions in the Senate that the United States cut out the aid program and give Haile Selassie cash instead — that is, pay rent for Asmara — were met by the response by the White House that the emperor insisted on the planes.

Mounting opposition to the Ethiopian dynasty finally led to its overthrow in September 1974. There followed a prolonged period of political upheaval and civil strife in the country. Fortunately, by the time the United States was forced out of Asmara by the new government, technological developments had made the Ethiopian base less important, and alternative base facilities were available.

PROBLEMS OF THE CONGRESSIONAL ROLE

Consultation

Quite apart from statutory requirements such as that contained in the War Powers Resolution, presidents are sensitive to congressional opinion for political reasons. Support in Congress for the president's moves can broaden the base of public support for American policy in the United States as well as abroad. Conversely, congressional opposition can complicate and frustrate a president's policies.

Although presidents are jealous of their prerogatives as commander in chief, they almost always go through the motions of consulting with Congress about major decisions on the use of troops abroad. (A notable exception was the Nixon incursion into Cambodia, and that was one of the reasons it provoked such an outcry on Capitol Hill.) Chief executives usually do this after the decision has been made so that it amounts to a policy *fait accompli*. They generally limit themselves to giving selected members information in advance of its public release.

This procedure is not at all what Congress has in mind when it demands to be consulted. The House International Relations Committee in its report on the War Powers Resolution reflected a widely held congressional view when it rejected "the notion that consultation should be synonymous with merely being informed." According to the committee:

> . . .consultation in this provision means that a decision is pending on a problem and that Members of Congress are being asked by the President for their advice and opinions and, in appropriate circumstances, their approval of action contemplated. Furthermore, for consultation to be meaningful, the President himself must participate and all information relevant to the situation must be made available.[28]

Even without these conceptual differences, the process of executive-legislative consultation itself involves difficult problems. The initiative almost always rests with the president, and the question immediately arises of which legislators should be consulted. Especially during crises or other occasions when time is a factor, and when considerations of national security information may be involved, it is obviously not practical to consult with Congress as a whole — through the device of a presidential message to a joint session, for example. There must be some selectivity in choosing legislators to be included — an exceedingly delicate issue among members of Congress. Most problems cut across rival committee jurisdictions (possibly involving personality conflicts on Capitol Hill), and the party leaders in the House and Senate must be included in such consultations as well.

Thus the executive branch faces a dilemma. The fewer the members of Congress involved in consultations, the less likely it is that there will be leaks of sensitive information, and the more likely a consensus will emerge from the discussions. But when consultations are limited to a small group, the decisions made are less likely to be representative of opinion in Congress as a whole — particularly in this era of growing dispersion of power on Capitol Hill. Furthermore, the smaller the group consulted, the more likely there are to be hurt feelings on the part of those left out. Finally, if Congress is not in session, some or all of the members to be consulted may not be in Washington or even in the country.

If there is to be meaningful consultation, there has to be, as the House International Relations Committee pointed out, a sharing with Congress of all relevant information. Not infrequently, the executive branch is reluctant to do this, in part because of a fear of leaks and in part because of a fear that *all* the relevant information might throw a different light on the matter than that in which the executive branch wants it to appear. The problem of leaks may be more an excuse than a reason for not engaging in consultations. Over any given time period, Congress certainly leaks no more, and quite possibly less, than the executive branch. Most of the time, Congress has shown no disposition to insist on access to all relevant information, although its record in this respect has improved somewhat in recent years.

It is equally true that many members of Congress are unwilling to devote the time not only to absorb all the relevant information but to consider seriously all the policy options available to the United States. It took the Kennedy administration a week to decide on its policy in the Cuban missile crisis. The members of Congress who were then "consulted" had less than an hour; yet one can scarcely imagine any of them being willing, even if given the opportunity, to devote a week to the problem in the midst of a political campaign.

This raises a question, despite congressional fulminations on the subject, of how much some members of Congress really want to be consulted. Particularly in crisis situations, there is a tendency in Congress to give the president the benefit of the doubt. There is also a reluctance to take the political responsibility for potentially disastrous decisions. Better, in this view, that the president should get the credit for something that turns out well than that an individual member of Congress should share the blame for something that turns out poorly. It was not for nothing that Truman had a sign on his desk reading, "The buck stops here."

Policy vs. Management

The increasing assertiveness of Congress about troop deployment raises the question of where to draw the line between broad policy on the one hand and day-to-day management or administrative decisions on the other. This not only involves constitutional problems that can be argued at length; it also involves the practical, more immediate problem of the allocation of time — a scarce commodity in Congress. The more Congress devotes itself to the minutiae of which troops are deployed where, the less it can address the larger policy questions with which it is better equipped to deal. The distinctions between these categories, however, is not always clear.

A fundamental question also arises about how Congress can enforce the decisions it makes. It is one thing for Congress to say that American troops cannot be sent abroad; in the long run at least, Congress can always enforce this decision, as it eventually did by withholding appropriations in the case of the Vietnam War. It is something else for Congress to say that, once troops are already abroad, they have to stay there — particularly in the face of opposition by a strong president who insists upon his prerogatives as commander in chief to bring them home. Theoretically, it might be possible for Congress to get its way by using the appropriations power, but the task of drafting such legislation would present formidable technical difficulties.

If Congress is to say, as the House Armed Services Committee did in 1978, that x thousand troops of the 2d Division are to be kept in Korea, then there is no reason it cannot say that y thousand troops of the 82d Airborne Divison are to be kept at Fort Bragg, North Carolina, or transferred to Fort Knox, Kentucky, or that z ships of the Atlantic Fleet are to be based at Guantanamo, Cuba. No one has seriously suggested this level of congressional involvement in military decisionmaking, although Congress has come close to it in ordering certain domestic bases kept open against the wishes of the White House and Defense Department.

Declarations of War

Increasing legislative assertiveness over troop deployments overseas in part represents an attempt to compensate for the erosion of the power of Congress to declare war, as explained in Chapter 2. This erosion occurred primarily because of changes in international relationships, in military technology, and in the nature of modern warfare.

At various times during the Vietnam War, for example, several senators considered introducing a declaration of war to focus the issue of America's involvement in the conflict more sharply. The idea did not, however, gain support on Capitol Hill. Legislators who opposed it believed that a declaration of war would have given American involvement in the conflict a legitimacy it otherwise lacked; and the declaration might have escalated the war to an even higher level of intensity, possibly involving a direct Soviet-American or Sino-American confrontation. There was also the practical and perplexing question of whom to declare war against — North Vietnam or the rather shadowy Viet Cong, or both?[29]

The United States fought the Korean War under the aegis of the United Nations. A declaration of war by Congress in that conflict would have presented the risk of grave consequences by triggering North Korean-Chinese-Soviet defense alliances. In both the Korean and Vietnam experiences, the absence of a declaration of war was one important way to *keep* a limited war limited. And in an age of megaton nuclear missiles, that is the only kind of war that can be tolerated.

Hawks vs. Doves

"Where you stand," Senator Hubert Humphrey once remarked, "depends on where you sit." Congress reasserts its powers over the armed forces, or acquiesces in the erosion of its powers, depending on its prevailing view of a particular presidential policy. Even those senators, such as Taft, who thought Truman exceeded his authority in Korea, muted their criticism because they approved of the substance of the policy if not of the procedure by which it was decided. A year later, during the MacArthur hearings, many of the same senators complained that Truman's conduct of the war was too restrained.

Most of the impetus behind the War Powers Resolution came from members of Congress who disapproved of the Nixon administration's policies in Indochina. And the members of Congress who are most vocal in asserting the power of Congress to keep troops in Korea are those who most strongly oppose the Carter policy of withdrawal.

Arguments over the proper role of Congress in connection with the armed forces usually center on the propriety of restraints on the president. As a legacy of Vietnam, and in the terminology of that era, the arguments tend to assume a division between doves in Congress and hawks in the White House and Pentagon. This does not necessarily accord with reality. There are numerous historical examples, going back to the War of 1812, when Congress has been more militant in dealing with other countries than the president.

History also provides abundant evidence that there is no monopoly on wisdom — or for that matter on bad judgment — at either end of Pennsylvania Avenue. Nor is there any guarantee that the president and Congress will not both be mistaken at the same time. It is the modest theory of the Constitution only that they are less likely to be.

NOTES

1. Dean Acheson, *Present at the Creation: My Years in the State Department* (New York: W. W. Norton & Co., 1969), p. 407.
2. Tom Connally as told to Alfred Steinberg, *My Name is Tom Connally* (New York: Thomas Y. Crowell Co., 1954), p. 346.
3. Harry S. Truman, *Memoirs*, vol. 2, *Years of Trial and Hope* (Garden City: Doubleday & Co., 1956), p. 338.
4. Acheson, *Present at the Creation*, p. 409.

5. Connally, *My Name Is*, pp. 347-348.
6. U.S., Congress, Senate, *Congressional Record*, 81st Cong., 2d sess., June 28, 1950, 96:9319-9323.
7. Acheson, *Present at the Creation*, p. 413.
8. Ibid., p. 414.
9. U.S., Congress, House, H. R. 6689, 95th Cong., 1st sess., as reported in the Senate; see also S. Rept. 95-194, pp. 26-27.
10. U.S., Congress, Senate, *Congressional Record* (daily edition), 95th Cong., 1st sess., June 16, 1977, pp. S9960, S9962, and S9963; the final version of the amendment is found in P.L. 95-105, Sec. 512.
11. Ibid., pp. S9946, S9948.
12. U.S., Congress, Senate, Committee on Foreign Relations, *Hearings on War Powers Legislation*, 92d Cong., 1st sess., 1972, p. 393.
13. U.S., Congress, Senate, *Congressional Record* (daily edition), 95th Cong., 1st sess., June 16, 1977, p. S9950.
14. Ibid.
15. P.L. 95-384, Sec. 23(d).
16. U.S., Congress, Senate, *Congressional Record*, 82d Cong., 1st sess., January 5, 1951, p. 55.
17. Ibid., p. 59.
18. U.S., Congress, Senate, S. Res. 8, 82d Cong., 1st sess.
19. U.S., Congress, Senate, S. Res. 99 and S. Con. Res. 18, 82d Cong., 1st sess.
20. A "pair" is a gentlemen's agreement between two lawmakers on opposite sides to withhold their votes on roll calls so their absence from Congress will not affect the outcome of record voting. If passage of the measure requires a two-thirds majority, a pair would require two members favoring the action to one opposed to it.
21. P.L. 88-408, August 10, 1964.
22. P.L. 93-126, Sec. 13, October 18, 1973.
23. P.L. 93-148, November 7, 1973.
24. U.S., Congress, House, H. Doc. 93-171, 93d Cong., 1st sess.
25. U.S., Congress, Senate, Committee on Foreign Relations, Subcommittee on Security Agreements and Commitments Abroad, *Security Agreements and Commitments Abroad*, 91st Cong., 2d sess., December 21, 1970, pp. 1, 19.
26. *Security Agreements and Commitments Abroad*, pp. 20-21.
27. Ibid., p. 9.
28. U.S., Congress, House, H. Rept. 93-287, 93d Cong., 1st sess.
29. The question of whether Congress should have declared war in the Vietnam conflict is discussed more fully in Senator Jacob K. Javits, "The Congressional Presence in Foreign Relations," *Foreign Affairs*, 48 (January 1970): 221-235.

6

The Intelligence Community

In its fundamentals, the relationship of Congress to the intelligence community is, or should be, no different from its relationship to other parts of the executive branch. The role of Congress is to provide basic legislative authority and then to oversee how that authority is used. Legislative oversight is a duty that Congress has imposed on itself. The law (2 U.S.C. 190d(a)) requires each standing committee of the House and Senate to "review and study, on a continuing basis, the application, administration, and execution of those laws, or parts of laws, the subject matter of which is within the jurisdiction of that committee."

But several factors make Congress' relationship to the intelligence community unique. One is the necessity for secrecy in an otherwise open government. Another is the failure of Congress to provide basic comprehensive legislation on intelligence activities. A third is the failure of Congress, until 1976 in the Senate and 1977 in the House, to exercise any true oversight. All of these factors combined to create in both the intelligence community and in Congress mental attitudes which made it a traumatic experience for both parties when Congress finally began to assert itself. The intelligence community had been conditioned by more than a quarter century of experience not to tell Congress what it was doing. And Congress had been conditioned not to ask.

For more than 25 years following passage of the National Security Act, which created the Central Intelligence Agency in 1947, Congress largely ignored the intelligence community. It allowed the National Security Agency and the Defense Intelligence Agency to be created by executive order. It voted for untold billions of dollars in hidden appropriations for intelligence activities with very few, if any, of its members knowledgeable as to either the amounts or the purposes of the funds. Those members actively concerned about the activities of the intelligence community were rebuffed by large majorities on the few occasions they tried to ask questions or to establish procedures for doing so.

During this period, Congress interested itself in the intelligence community only when something went so horribly wrong that it came to public view, as when the U-2 was shot down over the Soviet Union in 1960 and when the Bay of Pigs invasion of Cuba failed in 1961. These crises contributed to what was then still a minority view that Congress ought to do something to keep such things from happening. The emphasis was on preventing mistakes.

Further momentum developed in Congress in the early and mid-1970s with the revelations of CIA activities in Chile and of abuses by the CIA and the FBI of constitutional rights of American citizens. The first serious, broad-scale congressional investigation of the intelligence community (the Church committee in 1975-76) was directed almost wholly to the question of "illegal, improper or unethical activities."[1]

Senator Frank Church's investigation and a more raucous investigation of the intelligence community in the House laid the groundwork for the creation (in 1976 in the Senate and in 1977 in the House) of the permanent Intelligence committees. These committees were given legislative jurisdiction as well as broad powers of oversight. As it turned out, the exercise of these powers was a good deal more complicated than simply preventing mistakes and abuses.

DEFINITIONS

The intelligence community is knee-deep in glossaries, technical definitions, and acronyms. The House Intelligence Committee noted in 1978 that it had been "waging a steady campaign against the unnecessary use of acronyms," but added that "victories tend to be few and short-lived."[2]

Because the technical definition of "intelligence" is much more complicated, it is clearer for our purposes to think of "intelligence" as meaning simply "information" — the definition, by the way, that the army used to give it. Intelligence can be acquired in such mundane ways as reading a newspaper or in such exotic ways as taking a picture from space or planting a listening device in an official's office or by bribery or blackmail.

The American intelligence community consists of the governmental agencies engaged in collecting intelligence, either overtly or covertly; in analyzing it; and in countering the activities of foreign intelligence agents (such as the Soviet secret police) who might jeopardize American security. (The names and responsibilities of the specific agencies in the intelligence community were identified in Chapter 1.)

"Intelligence" is quite separate from "covert action" — except that the United States government is so organized that the same agency, the CIA, engages in both. Whereas intelligence is simply the collection of information — overtly or covertly, by fair means or foul, covert action has to do with sub rosa and theoretically nontraceable efforts to influence (sometimes to overthrow or subvert) foreign governments, groups, or economies. Covert action may involve the surreptitious dissemination of information, either true or false, but any collection of information is coincidental.

Whatever technique is used, covert action is done secretly because public identification of the United States government with the particular activity would be either counterproductive or embarrassing or both. Some examples of covert action that have become public are the secret subsidies of anti-Communist labor unions in Western Europe in the late 1940s and early 1950s, the overthrow of the Mossadegh regime and the restoration to power of the Shah in Iran in 1953, the overthrow of the Arbenz government in Guatemala in 1954, the abortive Bay of Pigs invasion of Cuba in 1961, and the attempts to destabilize the Allende government in Chile in 1970-73.

We are mainly concerned here with Congress' relationship to the CIA and the National Security Agency (NSA), the two most important members of the intelligence community from the point of view of foreign policy. These agencies not only provide most of the intelligence to the community and to policymakers; they also take most of the risks in collecting it. In addition, of course, the CIA is the covert action agency.

THE ERA OF NEGLECT

Of the agencies whose sole concern is intelligence and covert action, only the CIA was created by Congress. (The principal purpose of the National Security Act of 1947 that created the CIA was to provide for the Department of Defense.) The act made the CIA responsible to the president and put the agency under the general supervision of the National Security Council. The act also made the director of the CIA the director of Central Intelligence, thus giving him the responsibility for coordinating the activities of the intelligence community as a whole, as well as managing the CIA.

National Security Act Provisions

Four other provisions on the CIA in the National Security Act should be noted.[3] First, the CIA "shall have no police, subpena, law-enforcement powers, or internal-security functions." This restriction has generally been interpreted (perhaps too broadly) as meaning that the CIA is to have no domestic operations other than the administrative and analytical work that goes on in its headquarters. One of the factors which finally prompted Congress to begin investigating the activities of intelligence agencies was the revelation that the CIA had collaborated with local police departments in the United States and had investigated dissenters to America's involvement in the Vietnam War.

The second relevant provision of the National Security Act provides that the director of Central Intelligence "shall be responsible for protecting intelligence sources and methods from unauthorized disclosure."

Successive directors fell back on this authority for refusing to respond to questions from Congress. It has also been used as the excuse for some of the CIA's domestic activities.

Third, the CIA is "to perform, for the benefit of the existing intelligence agencies, such additional services of common concern as the National Security Council determines can be more efficiently accomplished centrally." The National Security Council is the highest-level executive agency for advising the president on national security problems.

Fourth, the CIA is to "perform such other functions and duties related to intelligence affecting the national security as the National Security Council may from time to time direct."

Since 1947, these catch-all provisions have been invoked as authority for numerous intelligence operations, some of which have subsequently aroused public and legislative opposition. They form the totality of the legislative authority for the CIA's intelligence gathering and covert action.

Because the act establishing the Department of Defense was also used as the legislative vehicle for creating the CIA an anomaly was created. This meant that jurisdiction over the CIA in Congress, both as to legislation and oversight, was lodged in the Armed Services committees, many of whose members were sympathetic with CIA activities. Yet the way the CIA does its job has at least as many political ramifications in the field of foreign policy as military ramifications in the field of defense. And the foreign policy committees in Congress for many years were effectively excluded from contact with the CIA.

The same situation prevailed with respect to the National Security Agency, which was established in the Defense Department by President Truman in 1952 and whose existence was scarcely acknowledged for years. NSA deals with signals intelligence — that is, intelligence derived from monitoring communications or electronic activities by foreign countries. It affects foreign policy not only through the intelligence it collects, but also through its methods of collection. For example, NSA needs listening posts in foreign countries, and these usually involve a quid pro quo. The American ship *Pueblo* was on an intelligence-gathering mission for NSA when it was seized by the North Koreans in 1968.

Following the passage of the National Security Act of 1947, subcommittees on the CIA, or on Intelligence (they were variously named), were created in the Armed Services committees of each house. Meetings were not announced, and they were infrequent. A subcommittee sometimes went a whole year without meeting. Similar subcommittees were created in the two Appropriations committees to provide funds for the CIA and, later, the NSA. These funds were concealed in appropriations for other agencies, mainly the Defense Department.

During a number of years in the 1960s, when Senator Richard Russell of Georgia was chairman of both the Armed Services Committee and of the Defense Appropriations Subcommittee, membership on the two Intelligence subcommittees overlapped so much that the two were, for practical purposes, merged. Only one staff member — the much over-worked staff director of the Senate Armed Services Committee — was permitted to attend the meetings, and he was forbidden to brief any other senators on what transpired.

CIA officials have maintained that all of the agency's significant actions were reported to these oversight committees. The members of the committees, however, were clearly not prepared to ask questions and usually accepted whatever they were told about intelligence operations. Massachusetts Republican Leverett Saltonstall, a member of an oversight committee for many years, once said flatly that there were some things about these activities that he did not want to know. Most legislators agreed with Saltonstall or, at the very least, were content to accept existing arrangements. So was the CIA which operated only under the restraints imposed by the National Security Council, and in the 1950s even the nature of these restraints was a tightly held secret.

Early Efforts by Mansfield

Some members of Congress, however, were uncomfortable about existing procedures for monitoring intelligence operations. The unease stemmed from a feeling that the CIA was inadequately supervised, that Congress was shirking its responsibilities, and that sooner or later this state of affairs would cause trouble for the United States abroad.

One of the most deeply concerned about this possibility was Senator Mike Mansfield, the Montana Democrat who later became majority leader. For a number of years after he came to the Senate in 1953, Mansfield introduced resolutions to create a CIA oversight committee modeled after the Joint Committee on Atomic Energy.

The joint committee was created by the Atomic Energy Act of 1946, a landmark piece of legislation that not only established the principle of civilian control of the atom, but also provided for congressional oversight. The act required the Atomic Energy Commission to keep the joint committee "fully and currently informed" of its activities. A similar provision with respect to the CIA would have overridden, so far as Congress was concerned, the director's statutory duty to protect intelligence sources and methods. For 30 years, until it was abolished in a congressional reorganization in 1977, the joint committee was widely regarded as a model of how Congress could responsibly and securely handle highly classified information.

The only time Mansfield was ever able to get a Senate vote on his resolution was in 1956 when it was rejected, 27-59. Ten years later, the Senate effectively killed a somewhat different resolution with the same purpose by voting 61-28 to refer it to the Armed Services Committee. On the face of it, things had not changed very much in a decade.

Although the two votes were almost identical, the underlying concerns in the Senate had changed. By 1966, evidence had accumulated that intelligence operations or covert actions could have adverse foreign policy repercussions. Two particularly sensitive situations deserve special mention.

The U-2 Incident

The program of U-2 flights over the Soviet Union was developed in the 1950s to give the United States an aerial reconnaissance capability by flying above the range of Soviet antiaircraft weapons and using what were then sophisticated cameras. The intelligence it produced was remarkable and valuable. In May 1960, on the eve of a scheduled summit conference, it turned out that the U-2 was no longer beyond the Soviet reach: The plane was shot down inside the Soviet Union, and its pilot was captured. After an initial period of confusion and contradiction, President Eisenhower admitted that the plane's real purpose was espionage, and Soviet Premier Nikita Khrushchev angrily canceled the summit.

The Senate Foreign Relations Committee held extensive hearings in closed session and published a censored version. Administration witnesses refused to answer the key question: What was the plane looking for the day it was shot down? The answer was crucial to a determination of whether the intelligence that it hoped to acquire was sufficiently important to justify the political risk of failure on the eve of a summit. It was also crucial to a determination of what would have been lost if the flight had been postponed until after the summit.

Nevertheless, the administration was more forthcoming in responding to the committee's interest than it had previously been. Throughout most of the 1950s, CIA directors had even resisted requests to brief the Senate Foreign Relations Committee on intelligence analysis, let alone on intelligence itself. This reluctance was somewhat diminished after Secretary of State John Foster Dulles reminded his brother, CIA Director Allen Dulles, that he, Allen, could not give public speeches around the country and then refuse to appear before the Foreign Relations Committee. But the CIA, supported by the White House, generally took the position that it would deal only with the Armed Services and Appropriations committees. The U-2 incident made the first notable breach in this position.

It was the political consequences of the U-2 affair that first aroused the interest of the Foreign Relations Committee. The committee's review raised disturbing questions about the extent to which foreign policy consequences were taken — or not taken — into account in the process of approving intelligence operations. A program consisting of several U-2 flights over a period of months had been personally approved by the president, but he had not concerned himself with individual flights within the overall program. The flight that was shot down was scheduled on technical considerations of the weather without regard to the political considerations of the approaching summit conference. The success of previous flights had bred complacency about the success of this one.

The Bay of Pigs

By 1960, the Eisenhower administration became convinced that if the Castro regime survived much longer in Cuba, it would so consolidate its power that it could never be dislodged and that Soviet power would be established in the Caribbean. At that time, this seemed totally unacceptable. Accordingly, plans were made for a covert action in which the CIA would secretly train and support a group of Cuban exiles to overthrow Castro.

The plans and training were well advanced when the Kennedy administration took office in January 1961. After some hesitation, Kennedy gave the go-ahead. The invasion was launched in April 1961 and promptly ended in disaster with the American involvement clearly revealed.

Again the consequences were primarily political — acute embarrassment for the United States — and again it was the Foreign Relations Committee, not Armed Services, which investigated. The closed hearings, in which the executive branch cooperated, went on for weeks. They did not prove very much beyond the fact that President Kennedy had received and acted on the basis of some very bad advice. The hearings did serve, however, to increase senatorial skepticism of the intelligence community and of the methods by which it was supervised. (The Bay of Pigs also increased Kennedy's skepticism about the same problem; he shortly moved to improve White House control over intelligence activities.)

It also developed that the only good advice Kennedy received about the Bay of Pigs undertaking had come from Congress, but not through any established channel for congressional-executive communication. Because of a combination of circumstances — the most important being the personal relationship between Kennedy and Senator J. William Fulbright — the president invited Fulbright to join him in a meeting with his advisers to discuss the projected invasion of Cuba before the decision was made to proceed. Fulbright was the only person present to speak out against the plan.

A further incident is also worth reporting here as an indication of congressional inconsistency in approaching oversight. The Foreign Relations Committee, as noted, spent weeks rehashing the failure of the Bay of Pigs mission. After the success of American policy in the Cuban missile crisis the following year, Secretary of State Dean Rusk all but begged the committee to investigate the performance of the intelligence community and of the administration in crisis management. The committee was not interested. The point is that Congress as a general rule tends to be more interested in investigating failures than successes.

The McCarthy Resolution

In 1966, Senator Eugene J. McCarthy of Minnesota picked up the campaign for more effective oversight of the intelligence community that Mansfield had carried on almost single-handedly for so long. In January, McCarthy introduced a resolution authorizing the Senate Foreign Relations Committee to make a "full and complete study" of the influence of the CIA on American foreign relations. This came in the aftermath of the U.S. intervention in the Dominican Republic the preceding year and at a time of growing doubts about American involvement in Indochina and about what the role of the CIA was there.

During consideration of the McCarthy resolution by the Foreign Relations Committee, the resolution was changed to provide for a new committee — to be called the Committee on Intelligence Operations, and to consist of three members each from the Senate Appropriations, Armed Services, and Foreign Relations committees. In effect, the new resolution would have expanded the existing oversight subcommittees of Appropriations and Armed Services (which for practical purposes operated as a single subcommittee) by adding three members from Foreign Relations.

The Foreign Relations Committee tried to bring this about informally, and Fulbright privately asked Russell if he would not agree to adding members from Foreign Relations. Russell consulted with the Appropriations-Armed Services group and reported the general feeling that it would be unwise to increase the size of the committee. Later Russell said that if the size were increased, seniority would have to govern the selection of the members added from Foreign Relations. This was unsatisfactory to Fulbright because it would have excluded Senator McCarthy, the sponsor of the idea.

So the matter went to the Senate for a vote in July and was referred to the Armed Services Committee where, as expected, it languished. Then the following January, as the 90th Congress was being organized, Senator Russell invited three members of the Foreign Relations Committee to attend meetings of the CIA oversight committees. Ironically, the three he invited — Fulbright, Bourke Hickenlooper of Iowa (the ranking Republican member), and Mansfield (the majority leader) — were not chosen according to seniority. Mansfield was junior to John Sparkman of Alabama. Members of the Foreign Relations Committee did not find the new arrangement satisfactory. The Intelligence subcommittees, as noted, met infrequently and were inadequately staffed.

An important factor at work throughout this period was trenchantly described in 1971 by Francis Wilcox, former chief of staff of the Senate Foreign Relations Committee and a former assistant secretary of state:

What is basically involved is something it pains the Senate to talk about — personality differences and bureaucratic jealousies. To be blunt about it, and perhaps to overstate it, neither the CIA nor the people who now watch over it fully trust the people who want to watch over it; and the people who want to watch over it do not fully trust either the agency or its present watchers.[4]

THE BEGINNING OF REAL OVERSIGHT

After these false starts, what prodded Congress out of its lethargy about overseeing the intelligence community was a series of events in the early and mid-1970s. One impetus was provided by revelations stemming from the Watergate affair. Other reasons were more directly related to developments in foreign policy.

Chile

In 1972, columnist Jack Anderson published internal documents of the International Telephone and Telegraph Company indicating that ITT had tried to persuade the CIA to intervene in Chilean politics in 1970 to prevent Socialist Salvador Allende from becoming president. The Senate Foreign Relations Committee responded by creating the Subcommittee on Multinational Corporations to investigate this report and also to conduct an in-depth study of multinational corporations in general.

A year later, in March 1973, the subcommittee held lengthy hearings which revealed that ITT had indeed sounded the alarm all over Washington at the time of Allende's election in September 1970. The company had even offered to furnish as much as $1 million for the expenses of clandestine American intervention, but had found no takers. Past and present CIA officials testified that the agency had a policy of not accepting contributions from private businesses. John McCone, a director of ITT and a former director of the CIA, was one of the officials who testified to this effect.

Notwithstanding ITT's efforts, Allende had taken office in 1970. He soon encountered a sea of troubles — most of them of his own making — but some of them complicated by a cutoff of American credits, both private and public. The Nixon administration never made any secret of its dislike of Allende, but maintained that the policies it was following to impede his regime were all open and aboveboard.

In September 1973, six months after the ITT hearings, Allende was overthrown in a bloody coup d'état. The unseen hand of the CIA was again suspected and again denied. The Subcommittee on Western Hemisphere Affairs of the Senate Foreign Relations Committee held closed hearings. At the hearings, CIA Director William Colby reported in greater detail than had ever been done before (but still incompletely) about CIA activities in Chile. In this version, the agency's principal activity was the covert funneling of subsidies to certain political parties, newspapers, and groups opposing Allende. The objective was to enable the opposition to survive until the next regularly scheduled Chilean presidential election in 1976, at which time it was hoped that a non-Socialist candidate could be elected (since Allende was constitutionally unable to succeed himself). This satisfied the subcommittee, or at least its chairman, Senator McGee of Wyoming, that the anti-Allende coup had been the work of local Chilean forces.

The following spring — 1974 — Colby testified again, in somewhat greater detail, before the CIA subcommittee of the House Armed Services Committee. The transcript of that testimony was read in June by Representative Michael Harrington, a Boston Democrat and outspoken liberal. Harrington was not a member of the Armed Services Committee, but he was taking advantage of a law that gives any member of the House or Senate access to any records of a committee of the house in which he serves.

Harrington was outraged by the Colby testimony. In July, he sent letters demanding investigations of CIA activities in Chile to Representative Thomas Morgan, chairman of the House Foreign Affairs Committee, and to Senator Fulbright, chairman of the Senate Foreign Relations Committee. Neither took any action. Fulbright replied that CIA activities in Chile were not so different from CIA activities in other countries and that the remedy lay in an effective joint committee of Congress "with full authority to examine the CIA and control it." Fulbright conceded that he could not get the votes to establish such a committee.

In September, Harrington's letter, containing the substance of Colby's hitherto secret testimony, leaked to the press, and an uproar ensued. Senator Frank Church, who had presided over the ITT hearings but who had not been present for the later Colby testimony, felt that he had been deceived and that information had been withheld from him.

The Hughes-Ryan Amendment

Partly inspired by the Chile affair, Congress used the 1974 foreign aid bill as the vehicle to require that covert actions (as distinguished from purely intelligence operations) conducted "by or on behalf of" the CIA be reported to "the appropriate committees of the Congress." The amendment by which this was accomplished was the handiwork of Democratic Senator Harold E. Hughes of Iowa (a member of the Armed Services Committee) and Democratic Representative Leo J. Ryan of California.

The Hughes-Ryan amendment named the Senate Foreign Relations and the House Foreign Affairs committees as two of the committees to receive the reports; the other "appropriate committees" were not specified in the amendment. By general agreement, they have been defined to be the Appropriations and Armed Services committees in each house and later — after they were established in 1976 and 1977 — the two permanent Intelligence committees as well.

The amendment also tightened administrative control of covert action by requiring, as a precondition, that the president find "that each such operation is important to the national security of the United States." The report to the committees is to be made "in a timely fashion" and is to include "a description and scope" of the activity.[5]

The CIA had long maintained that it already reported covert actions to its oversight subcommittees in Appropriations and Armed Services, although given the infrequency of the meetings of those subcommittees the timeliness of the CIA reports could be seriously questioned.

The foreign policy committees in the House and Senate then had to figure out the mechanics of how they would receive the information required from the executive branch. They also had to decide what, if anything, they would do with the information after they received it.

The House Foreign Affairs Committee (or International Relations Committee, as it was known from 1975 through 1978) has not revealed its procedures. In the Senate Foreign Relations Committee, it was agreed that the reports would be received orally from the director of the CIA by the chairman and ranking minority member, with the committee's chief of staff present and authorized to brief any other committee member who asked. Not many did.

The calendars of the Foreign Relations Committee reflect five meetings of the chairman and ranking minority member with the director of the CIA in 1975, six in 1976, three in 1977, and one in 1978. The number of meetings and the number of covert actions undertaken by the CIA are not necessarily related, however. Some meetings were simply to review all covert actions then being carried out. And some covert actions required more than one meeting.

In practice, the question of what to do about the reports came up only if a member disagreed with a particular covert action. The member's recourse, in this case, was to present any objections, not to the CIA, but to higher political authority — namely, the State Department or the president. The few members who were really interested in CIA activities found this procedure frustrating.

Covert action (technically called "special activities" since President Carter's 1978 Executive Order) is a means to achieving a policy objective. In 1975 and 1976, three covert actions aroused the apprehensions of one or more members of the Senate Foreign Relations Committee. In two of these, the concerned senators had no particular quarrel with the policy objective, but they believed that over the long term the United States and the two foreign countries involved would be better off if the situations were allowed to work themselves out without intervention by American intelligence agencies. The senators also felt that the risks of possible disclosure were too great to justify the activity in question. In one of these cases, a senator felt so strongly the action in question was mistaken that he wrote a letter about it to President Ford — and never got an answer. As it turned out, one of the actions was successful, the other partially so.

Angola

The third case involved the African country of Angola which, at the end of 1974, found itself on the verge of achieving independence from Portugal after 14 years of guerrilla warfare. Differing tribal loyalties and ideological disputes sharply divided the political factions in Angola. Agreements among them concerning the government that was to replace Portuguese authority proved to be short-lived.

United States covert involvement in Angola began in a very small way, mainly through the payment of a cash subsidy to one of the non-Marxist leaders and his group. By July 1975, this initially limited involvement was rapidly escalating, as was the fighting in Angola where one faction was receiving support from the Soviet Union (later from Cuba as well) and another from South Africa. Ultimately, America's intervention entailed a budget of millions of dollars and consisted of supplies as well as money. As involvement grew, the African Affairs Subcommittee of Foreign Relations, headed by Senator Dick Clark of Iowa, expressed its concern directly to Deputy Secretary of State Robert Ingersoll in an inconclusive meeting.

By November, congressional concern had reached the point that the full Foreign Relations Committee summoned CIA Director Colby and Under Secretary of State Joseph Sisco for a session on Angola; in December, the Subcommittee on Foreign Assistance received more detailed briefings from executive officials on the American role in Angola. To the embarrassment of the committee and the irritation of the CIA, substantial portions of both meetings were leaked to the press. As a result, Colby fired off a letter to the committee implicitly threatening to stop cooperating with it. As Colby's letter put it, "publicity of this sort obviously casts serious doubts on my ability to provide sensitive information to the Foreign Relations Committee, its subcommittees, and its staff."

As all of this was happening, the Defense Department appropriations bill, with its hidden funds for the CIA, was making its way through Congress. Senator John Tunney, who had not been privy to any of the secret briefings on the CIA, but who read the newspapers, offered an amendment in the Senate prohibiting use of any funds in the bill "for any activities involving Angola directly or indirectly." It was agreed to, 54-22, on December 19, and the House concurred, 323-99, on January 27, over the strenuous objections of the Ford administration. This is the only time that Congress has acted formally and publicly to end a covert action.

CONGRESSIONAL INVESTIGATIONS

Meanwhile, both the House and Senate proceeded with separate investigations of the intelligence community. In each instance, the focus was on past misdeeds, but ultimately the inquiries led to the establishment of permanent committees in each house charged with oversight of the community as a whole.

The Church Committee in the Senate

Early in 1975, by a vote of 82-4, the Senate established the Select Committee to Study Governmental Operations with Respect to Intelligence Activities — a name that the resolution creating it said was given "for convenience of expression"![6] It was headed by Senator Church, who had presided over the original investigation of CIA-ITT activities in Chile. In 16 months, between January 1975 and April 1976, the Church committee published 17 volumes of reports and hearings dealing with everything from domestic intelligence activities of questionable legality to assassination plots targeted against foreign leaders.

The Church committee soon discovered how extraordinarily difficult it is, even with full access to files and records, to learn the full truth about covert actions in the past. This applies to both executive management and legislative oversight of the intelligence community. Intelligence is a highly compartmentalized business. In order to enhance security and to preserve plausible deniability, intelligence officials are often given to speaking, and especially to writing, in ambiguous circumlocutions.

It was not until after the Church committee had completed its work that all the facts about CIA involvement in Chile came out — and even then no one could be sure it was the full story. The State Department, the American embassy in Santiago, and eventually the Congress knew about CIA subsidies for Allende's opponents; they did not know that President Nixon had directly instructed CIA Director Richard Helms to "destabilize," as it was put, the situation in Chile so much that Allende could not continue in office.

Knowledge of this plan of action was to be tightly restricted to the CIA and specifically was not to be revealed to the State Department and to the embassy, despite the fact that they were charged with conducting American policy in Chile. It was for denying the existence of these activities before the Foreign Relations Committee that Helms was subsequently fined $2,000 when he pleaded nolo contendere to Justice Department charges of failing to testify "fully . . . and accurately." What emerged from the Church investigation was that although in a technical sense the CIA might not have been involved in the coup which overthrew Allende, its whole course of action in Chile for three years had been designed to create a situation in which such a coup would occur.

The principal result of the Church committee was twofold: the creation of a standing committee on intelligence, oriented more to continuing oversight than to investigations of past misdeeds; and a recommendation for legislative charters for all intelligence agencies, spelling out permissible and impermissible behavior. Drafting these charters has proven to be more difficult than it once appeared.

The Pike Committee in the House

In contrast to the quiet, but ultimately sensational, work of the Church committee, the House was kept in turmoil for a year and a half over how to go about substantially the same job.

On February 19, 1975, the House voted 286-120 to create a Select Committee on Intelligence. Lucien Nedzi of Michigan, the chairman of the Armed Services Committee's Special Subcommittee on Intelligence, was named chairman of the new committee. Its members included Harrington, who had earlier made such a fuss about Chile, and Ronald Dellums of California, another acerbic critic of the CIA. The members fell to quarrelling among themselves almost at once. It took three months to hire a staff director. In June, Nedzi resigned as chairman and the House rejected his resignation by a vote of 64-290.

Then, in July, the House took the extraordinary action of abolishing the committee and creating another one with the same name and terms of reference but without Nedzi and Harrington. This committee was headed by Otis Pike of New York. The Pike committee spent the fall of 1975 brawling with the administration over access to classified documents. Ostensibly, the issue was the committee's insistence on its right to declassify them, but, in fact, personalities were at the bottom of the dispute.

In the first place, the administration suspected the committee of leaking confidential information. In the second place, it was edgy over the law giving any member of the House access to any records of a House committee. Harrington had already acknowledged leaking some of the information in press reports about the CIA's activities in Chile and had been reprimanded by the Armed Services Committee, but he was unrepentant.

The matter was brought to the House Committee on Standards of Official Conduct, known as the ethics committee. The Armed Services Committee voted 16-13 to deny Harrington access to confidential information, notwithstanding the law, pending a ruling by the ethics committee. That committee voted 7-3 to do nothing, on the grounds that the Armed Services transcript that Harrington leaked had not been taken at a legal meeting. (There had been no notice, no vote to go into executive session, and no quorum.)

The difficult issue of declassification has troubled successive Congresses and administrations since the 1950s. Government procedures for classifying and declassifying information are controlled, not by law, but by executive orders. The Freedom of Information Act provides for ultimate judicial determination of whether a document is properly classified; but the procedure is a cumbersome one, not readily applicable to Congress, and usually the courts have been reluctant to overrule the intelligence community.

Congress, with reason, thinks the executive branch overclassifies information. The executive branch, also with reason, thinks that Congress is careless in handling classified information. Although members of Congress have frequently felt frustrated by executive insistence on maintaining classifications on information, most of the time they have been willing to accept, however reluctantly, the executive point of view, or at least to negotiate about it. Not so the Pike committee which, in September 1975, released some documents pertaining to the Yom Kippur War with phrases that the administration wanted deleted.

President Ford then angrily demanded that the committee return all the classified documents that it had been furnished and vowed that no more would be produced "until the committee satisfactorily alters its position." The committee refused to return the documents it had and requested new documents on the Tet offensive. Even before the release of the Yom Kippur material, the committee had directed a subpoena to CIA Director Colby for the Tet documents. The administration offered to supply some of them, but only on the condition that their confidentiality would be respected. Pike initially refused to accept them on this basis, but he eventually backed down.

In October and November 1975, the Select Committee on Intelligence fired off four subpoenas to Secretary of State Henry Kissinger — one for a 1974 memo by the State Department's Cyprus desk officer, one for State Department documents relating to covert action from 1962 to 1972, one for National Security Council records on covert actions approved since 1965, and one for NSC documents pertaining to Soviet compliance with SALT I arms control agreements.

The committee during this period was quarrelling internally as well as with the Ford administration. It divided 8-5 on accepting a compromise about the Cyprus memorandum, and it voted 10-3 to cite Kissinger for contempt of Congress for refusing to supply the covert action documents requested. President Ford then invoked the doctrine of executive privilege. The matter was resolved when a small delegation from the committee received an oral briefing in the White House about covert CIA activities.

(According to the doctrine of executive privilege, the president has the right to maintain the confidentiality of documents relating to the internal functions of the administration. The doctrine has never been precisely defined, although it has generally been respected by both Congress and the courts, which themselves assert analogous legislative and judicial privilege. A famous exception is the 1974 Supreme Court decision that President Nixon must comply with a subpoena for tapes of White House conversations sought for as evidence in the Watergate investigation.[7])

There were more and wilder antics to come. On January 23, 1976, the Pike committee voted 9-4 to release its final report despite administration objections that it contained material that should remain classified. Three days later, before it was released, a summary of the report appeared in the *New York Times*. On January 29, the House took the extraordinary action of voting 246-124 to prohibit the committee from releasing a report containing classified material until it had been "certified by the President as not containing information which would adversely affect the intelligence activities of the Central Intelligence Agency" or other agencies.[8] Then, on February 11, the *Village Voice* in New York published a 24-page supplement containing lengthy excerpts from the report. Two days later CBS correspondent Daniel Schorr confirmed that it was he who gave a copy of the report to the *Voice*.

Schorr's refusal to say where he got the copy set off yet another acrimonious investigation. The House Committee on Standards of Official Conduct tried, and predictably failed, to determine Schorr's source. It also delayed, for more than a year, House action to create a permanent intelligence committee. In the meantime, the Pike committee published its recommendations:

- That the House create a permanent intelligence committee;
- That the president put an overall figure for the intelligence community in his budget;
- That transfers and reprogramming of intelligence funds be subject to the approval of the Intelligence and other committees;
- That the General Accounting Office be empowered to investigate and audit intelligence agencies on the same basis as other agencies;
- That a Foreign Operations Subcommittee be created by statute in the National Security Council to deal with covert action and hazardous collection of intelligence;
- That the intelligence community be reorganized to separate the director of central intelligence from the CIA, and the National Security Agency from the Defense Department; to abolish the Defense Intelligence Agency; and to prohibit the recruitment by the intelligence community of American citizens associated with religious, educational, or communications organizations.

THE PERMANENT OVERSIGHT COMMITTEES

The Church committee issued its final recommendations April 26, 1976. On May 19, by a vote of 72-22, the Senate created the successor Select Committee on Intelligence.

Further action in the House was delayed for more than a year by the turmoil over the Pike committee's activities and by the futile search for Daniel Schorr's source for the committee report that he gave to the *Village Voice*. Finally, in July 1977, by a vote of 247-171, the Permanent Select Committee on Intelligence was established.

Although the resolutions creating these two committees (S. Res. 400 and H. Res. 658) are basically similar, there are a few important differences. One of these concerns the partisan political makeup of the committees. The Senate resolution assures the minority party of seven of the 15 seats on the committee, regardless of its strength in the Senate. The House resolution is silent on the subject of minority representation, a fact which largely accounts for the number of votes against it. As a consequence, the 13-member House committee in the 96th Congress had nine Democrats and four Republicans, a ratio roughly reflecting party strength in the full House.

Both resolutions provide for overlapping memberships with the Appropriations, Armed Services, Foreign Relations (Foreign Affairs in the House), and Judiciary committees, the last being included because of its jurisdiction over the FBI. In the Senate, two members from each of these committees (one Democrat and one Republican) are to be assigned to Intelligence; in the House, only one. In the Senate, the vice chairman is elected by the minority members of the committee; no provision is made for a vice chairman in the House. In both the House and Senate, the majority and minority leaders are ex officio members without votes.

Another difference is in the jurisdiction of the two committees. The resolution creating the Senate committee specifically excludes from its definition of intelligence activities "tactical foreign military intelligence serving no national policymaking function." The resolution creating the House committee, on the other hand, specifically includes "intelligence-related activities." This is a technical term which in general means tactical military intelligence.

One final difference should be noted. While the Senate resolution goes as far as it can, short of a law, to make sure the committee is kept "fully and currently informed," the House resolution is silent on this point. This omission has not been of any practical consequence so far, and given the firm hold of the House committee on the intelligence community budget, it is not likely to be.

Continuous service of a member is limited on both committees — to eight years in the Senate, to six years in the House. This limitation is designed as a safeguard against co-option, the subtle process by which the overseen persuade their overseers to become their handmaidens. This problem is particularly noticeable among the regulatory agencies of the government, and it has existed, at one time or another and to one degree or another, in the relations between most other congressional committees and the executive agencies for whose legislation they are responsible. Prior to 1975, it certainly existed with respect to the Appropriations and Armed Services committees, on the one hand, and the CIA on the other.

Senator Daniel Inouye of Hawaii, the first chairman of the Senate Select Committee on Intelligence, resigned as chairman (while continuing on the committee) at the end of 1977. In a report to the Senate he stated:

> I believe rotation of Chairmanship is the best way to assure that the combination of close detailed work with the agencies and a vigilant attitude toward their activities can be maintained. I am resigning because I believe it is important for the Senate and for the intelligence agencies who are under the charge of the Select Committee to have overseers who come to the issues as I have come to them — with an open, fresh and relatively objective point of view, so necessary for the important task of oversight.[9]

In addition, although no rule requires it, there is a policy in the Senate committee of rotating staff members and staff assignments, though not on a fixed timetable. These safeguards against co-option carry a price in the loss of continuity and expertise gained through long experience. It is as important to know what questions to ask as it is to be "open, fresh and relatively objective."

Only time will tell whether the Intelligence Committee has struck the right balance, but it is interesting to note that in 1977 consideration was given to establishing the principle of rotating members and chairmen in all Senate committees. In this respect, the practice of the Intelligence Committee may be a harbinger of broader changes in congressional organization.

Declassification Procedures

In establishing the Intelligence committees, both the House and Senate for the first time tried to provide a means for resolving disputes with the executive branch over declassification of documents. The procedures in the two houses differ only in minor details and are as follows:

First, the committee must vote to publish the information in question and notify the president it has done so. Second, the president, within five days, must personally notify the committee in writing of his objections to publication and his reasons. He must also certify that the threat to the national interest of publication outweighs the public interest in disclosure. Third, the committee must either accept the president's objections or vote to refer the question of disclosure to the Senate or the House, as the case may be. In the House, this is accompanied by a recommendation of the committee; in the Senate, it is not. Fourth, under the somewhat different timetables specified in the resolutions, the matter is considered in closed session.

In the Senate, a vote is then taken in public session to approve publication in whole or in part, to disapprove publication in whole or in part, or to refer the matter back to the committee. In this last case, the committee makes the final determination. In the House, the vote is taken on whether to approve the recommendations of the committee. If the recommendations are disapproved, the matter is referred back to the committee for further consideration.

The only important difference in these procedures is that in the House, the ultimate decision on the committee's recommendations is reserved for the House as a whole. The Senate as a whole can make the decision if it wants to, but it also has the option of passing the buck back to the committee.

These declassification procedures have never been tested, but as designed, they have several advantages. They ensure that the objections of the executive branch will be those of the president himself rather than those of a lower ranking official. The procedures also ensure that the House and Senate as a whole will have an opportunity to give the president's objections thoughtful consideration. In the end, the decision rests with Congress — not with the president or the executive branch.

Intelligence Appropriations

Both the House and the Senate Intelligence committees get their real power from their legislative jurisdiction over authorizations for appropriations for the intelligence agencies and from provisions in the resolutions specifically prohibiting appropriations that have not been authorized. This means that the committees not only have access to information about the secret intelligence budget, but they also can approve or disapprove it, in whole or in part.

Subcommittees of the Appropriations committees have always been in this position, of course, but the Intelligence committees are taking the job more seriously. They consider the budget on a line item basis, which means that they vote separately on each major category of expenditure including, importantly, each covert action project.

The authorization bill resulting from this process is unique in that it says "funds are hereby authorized to be appropriated," but does not contain any figures. These are included in classified reports of the two committees, reports that are made available to the Appropriations and Armed Services committees and to the executive branch.

The published portions of the bill contain only the authorizations for the intelligence community staff and the CIA Retirement and Disability System. For fiscal year 1980, these amount to approximately $12 million and $52 million, respectively. (The House committee bill for fiscal 1980 also publicly specified $13.4 million for the FBI to counter terrorism in the United States.)

The appropriations subsequently made pursuant to the authorizing legislation are still concealed in the Defense Department appropriation bill. There has been much discussion of whether at least an overall figure for the intelligence budget should be published, and both the House and the Senate have specifically directed their Intelligence committees to study the question.

One of the recommendations of the Pike committee in the House was that the president include an overall intelligence figure in his budget. The Church committee in the Senate voted 6-5 to let the Senate decide if the figure should be public, a decision that the Senate has shown no inclination to make. The House committee in 1979 voted specifically not to reveal the overall figure. This congressional reluctance is curious in light of the fact that CIA Director Stansfield Turner has repeatedly said that he has no objection to releasing a single, inclusive figure.[10] (It is even more curious why, then, Turner does not release it himself.)

There is clearly an anomaly in the existence of a secret law in a country governed on the basis of public laws. On the other hand, even an aggregate total would give other countries an indication of the level of the American intelligence effort. Variations in the total from year to year have sometimes been substantial as large new projects are undertaken or old ones are phased out (e.g., the war in Laos) or as expensive new technology is developed. Such information would at least provide a basis for guessing what American intelligence is up to and would give foreign intelligence services an indication of where to look. A further, less persuasive, objection to publishing an overall figure is that pressures would then mount for publication of a more detailed breakdown.

It may fairly be said that since the establishment of the two Intelligence committees, the intelligence budget has been subject to a more searching congressional review than ever before. The committees' ultimate power, of course, lies in withholding money or in prescribing the purposes for which it is to be spent. But the committees — like those operating in public — have gone further and have used their classified reports on the authorizing legislation to give policy guidance to the intelligence community. In its report on the 1980 bill, for example, the Senate committee stated:

> The committee expects that the classified report, although not available to the public, will have the full force of any Senate report, and that the intelligence community will comply with the guidelines and directions contained therein.[11]

Congressional committees generally think of their reports as having more force than is actually the case. They certainly do not have the force of law. The influence of the reports varies from time to time and from agency to agency, an important factor being whether the agency wishes to comply and whether it thinks it can get away with noncompliance. Secrecy makes it impossible to measure this influence in the intelligence community.

On the face of it, Congress has delegated extraordinary powers to its Intelligence committees. Yet it is no more power than the Appropriations and Armed Services committees once had and failed to exercise.

(The Appropriations committees still have it; they actually provide the money which the Intelligence committees authorize.)

Furthermore, any member can read the Intelligence committees' classified reports, although few legislators actually do. If the member does not like them, he or she can precipitate a debate in closed session; if enough legislators are persuaded to agree, the committees can be over-ridden. This has never happened. Except for the fact that the debate would take place in closed session, the procedure is not significantly different from that which is followed with respect to any other issues considered by a House or Senate committee.

CONCLUSION

No more dramatic example of the new congressional assertiveness with respect to foreign policy is to be found than in the changed relationship between Congress and the intelligence community. The change was slow in coming and was more the result of an evolutionary process than a single event, although the Watergate crisis accelerated the trend.

Congress investigated, but did nothing about, such earlier mis-adventures as the U-2 flight and the Bay of Pigs invasion. Then, in the immediate aftermath of Vietnam, the atmosphere changed. Controversial policies in Chile and Angola and abuses of constitutional rights in the United States combined to effect this change. Underlying the congressional concern was the implicit notion that if Congress had known about these and other questionable activities, it would have prevented them. This belief was re-enforced by the example of Senator Fulbright's advice to the Kennedy administration not to undertake the ill-fated Bay of Pigs venture. In some of these cases, there was also congressional resentment over having been hoodwinked by executive officials.

One of the weaknesses of the old system of intelligence oversight lay within Congress itself. In most instances, some legislators were knowledgeable of misdeeds or questionable behavior by intelligence agencies, but they did nothing about it — nothing, at any rate, that appears on the public record. There is, of course, no guarantee that these lapses will not happen again. Members of Congress are no more infallible than officials in the executive branch. But the more formalized structure of the legislative oversight mechanism, and the fact that more people are now involved in it, make that prospect less likely than in the past.

The basis of congressional concern about the intelligence community has nearly always been political — that is, concern on Capitol Hill about the consequences of failures. This concern has been mainly directed to covert action, less so to intelligence collection and analysis. With the two Intelligence committees now voting on line item authorizations for covert actions, Congress, or at least the members of the committees, will share the burden of future intelligence failures. In the past, Congress has generally been reluctant to assume this kind of responsibility, and it may be questioned whether legislative attitudes have changed fundamentally.

Effective legislative oversight, however, involves a great deal more than simply keeping intelligence operations and related policy decisions from going awry. Legislative oversight is also concerned with making things go right, or making them go better. In the attention the Intelligence committees have given to the quality of the intelligence product and analysis in recent years, they have demonstrated their awareness of broader concerns.

Late in the summer of 1979, the House and Senate Intelligence committees were confronted with the question of how the presence of a brigade of Soviet troops in Cuba could have gone undetected for a period of several years by the intelligence community, and whether restrictions imposed by the White House on U-2 overflights had contributed to that failure.

At the end of 1979, one of the most urgent tasks of the House and Senate Intelligence committees remained the long-awaited statutory charters and guidelines for intelligence operations. (In 1978, Congress did pass the Foreign Intelligence Surveillance Act, but this had more to do with constitutional process in the United States than with foreign policy.) The committees face a difficult problem: How detailed should the law governing intelligence activities be? The more detailed the law is, the less operational flexibility is left for the intelligence community. Yet the more flexibility left to its members, the greater the possibility for abuse or bad judgment in intelligence activities.

The Intelligence committees of Congress thus have a long agenda. A checklist would include such difficult and complex questions as:

• What kinds of intelligence ought to be collected? What are the political risks involved in collecting it? What information is vital to maintaining national security and to assessing long-range trends in the international system? And what information is of marginal interest, focusing too much on current (and perhaps relatively unimportant) events?

• What can be done, or needs to be done, to insulate agencies belonging to the intelligence community from executive pressures to shape their activities and reports according to what the president and his principal subordinates want to hear? (For many years, critics charged, intelligence reports on developments in Iran merely reinforced the existing policies of the administration.) The best safeguard perhaps was the establishment of the two Intelligence committees in Congress, with memberships broadly spanning the political spectrum. Yet even this change is likely to provide only minimum protection against biased intelligence activities if Congress fails to use the committees effectively.

• Are there feasible alternatives to covert action, particularly on a scale so large that it is impossible to keep it secret? If the United States drastically reduces the number of covert actions (as it has) but does not dismantle its capability for undertaking them, how does the national government keep its covert action operatives occupied, trained, and ready when they are needed?

• Should certain intelligence activities be excluded regardless of circumstances because they offend American ideological values and ethical concepts? It is generally agreed that peacetime assassination attempts should be ruled out, but other activities raise more difficult questions. Is it acceptable for the CIA to use scholars, clergymen, or media correspondents to achieve its objectives? If it does so, and this fact becomes known (as has occurred in the past), then legitimate scholars, clergymen, and correspondents fall under suspicion that they are really CIA agents — a suspicion they encounter routinely in many foreign countries today. But if the CIA does not do so, then the forms of cover available to intelligence agents are significantly reduced.

• What should be the relationship of the CIA to American business firms and activities abroad? Many Americans with experience overseas can provide important information to the intelligence community. Yet, again, for intelligence agencies to utilize this resource places all American business activities abroad under suspicion.

• What sorts of trade-offs can reasonably be made for allowing American intelligence agencies (such as the National Security Agency) to collect information in foreign countries? To gain this concession, should the United States routinely exchange intelligence data and reports with foreign intelligence agencies? Should America allow foreign governments cooperating with it to carry on intelligence operations within the United States?

Today, the Intelligence committees of Congress are well staffed, and thus far there has been no serious leak of classified information. Members of the committees take their jobs seriously. The House committee, under Chairman Edward P. Boland of Massachusetts, has proceeded soberly and responsibly. The Senate Intelligence Committee, under Chairman Birch Bayh of Indiana, has played a useful role in the treaty-making process. Its thorough investigation squelched charges that the Panama Canal treaties had been tainted by the compromise of intelligence operations, and it helped clarify the issue of verification in connection with the SALT II arms control agreements. Some proposed intelligence activities have been abandoned because of questions raised by the committees.

For several years, there have been no major debates of intelligence issues, no front-page stories of scandals such as shook the nation (and the intelligence community) in the early 1970s. With the intelligence process necessarily shrouded in secrecy, an outside observer cannot be wholly confident of judgments based on evidence from the public record. But at least Congress now has an institutional structure and an adequate staff to meet the challenge of supervising American intelligence operations. All the returns are not yet in, but a hopeful and helpful start has been made in solving an extremely difficult problem for the American democracy.

NOTES

1. U.S., Congress, Senate, S. Res. 21, 94th Cong., 1st sess., agreed to January 27, 1975, establishing the Select Committee to Study Governmental Operations with Respect to Intelligence Activities.
2. U.S., Congress, House, Permanent Select Committee on Intelligence, H. Rept. 1795, 95th Cong., 1st sess., October 14, 1978, p. 16.
3. The National Security Act of 1947, 50 U.S.C. 403(d).
4. Francis O. Wilcox, *Congress, the Executive, and Foreign Policy* (New York: Harper & Row, 1971), p. 86.
5. Sec. 662 of the Foreign Assistance Act of 1961 as amended, 22 U.S.C. 2422.
6. U.S., Congress, Senate, S. Res. 21, 94th Cong., 1st sess., agreed to January 27, 1975.
7. *United States v. Nixon* 418 U.S. 683 (1974).
8. U.S., Congress, House, H. Res. 982, 94th Cong., 2d sess., agreed to January 29, 1976.
9. U.S., Congress, Senate, Select Committee on Intelligence, *Report to the Senate on the Work of the Senate Select Committee on Intelligence,* n.d., p. 15.
10. U.S., Congress, House, Permanent Select Committee on Intelligence, *Intelligence and Intelligence-Related Activities Act, Fiscal Year 1980.* For the additional views of Congressman Romano L. Mazzoli, see Part I of H. Rept. 96-127, p. 10.
11. U.S., Congress, Senate, S. Rept. 71, 96th Cong., 1st sess., April 18, 1979, p. 2.

7

The Human Rights Issue

The issue of how much weight should be given to human rights in American foreign policy originated in Congress and has been pressed on a succession of presidents including Jimmy Carter who himself emphasized the issue in his 1976 campaign. The issue first arose as a simple argument over American support of dictators. It became possibly the most tangled web of American foreign policy, full of confusion, contradiction, and inconsistency — and not without a measure of moral posturing, bordering at times on hypocrisy. Nevertheless, it is a peculiarly American issue, and it has brought to a focal point many of the dilemmas of post World War II foreign policy.

Congressional interest in the human rights issue has been notable, among other things, for the attention given to bilateral relations with other countries and the neglect shown for multilateral agreements to promote human rights. Initially, congressional efforts to influence human rights policy were fundamentally directed to putting a certain distance between the United States and oppressive regimes. This is different from actively promoting, as the multilateral agreements seek to do, the improvement and extension of human rights. As the issue developed, this distinction became blurred, and Congress eventually adopted the broader and more positive goal for bilateral policies. But Congress did not become any more supportive of multilateral agreements.

In many respects, human rights has become more an argument over unrelated questions than a substantive issue. Members of Congress opposed to a policy of détente with the Soviet Union cite the Soviet record on human rights. (Yet the same members often tend to overlook the equally abysmal human rights record of the Chinese.) Similarly, members of Congress who disliked the Somoza regime in Nicaragua emphasized its flouting of human rights. But those who feared Cuban involvement in Nicaragua talked instead about Castro's human rights violations.

Despite the complexities and subtleties of the human rights question, the trend in Congress in the 1970s was to give greater weight to human rights issues in formulating and administering American foreign policy. Congress was well ahead of the Nixon and Ford administrations in this respect, and at times it even outran Jimmy Carter, who proclaimed in his January 20, 1977, inaugural address, ". . .[O]ur commitment to human rights must be absolute. . . . The powerful must not persecute the weak, and human dignity must be enhanced."

THE ORIGINS OF CONGRESSIONAL CONCERN

Concern over the kinds of governments the United States became closely identified with overseas began to manifest itself in Congress during the late 1950s, particularly with respect to Latin America where dictatorships were being ousted by democratic governments. The United States had long been criticized by liberals, both at home and throughout Latin America, for having supported the dictators. (The degree and nature of support varied; what some of the critics meant was that Washington had not actively aided those groups seeking a dictator's overthrow — quite a different matter.)

The criticism reached its most dramatic point in May 1958, when Vice President Richard Nixon, on a tour of South America, was set upon by mobs in Caracas, Venezuela. On his return, it was Nixon who set forth what remains the most sensible diplomatic formula for the United States: "A handshake for dictators; an abrazo [embrace] for democrats."

Congressional involvement in human rights questions, however, was largely rhetorical until the late 1960s. By that time, the wheel of Latin American political history had taken another turn, moving away from democratic governments and back toward the old pattern of dictatorships.

The human rights issue was first posed with painful clarity in Brazil in the aftermath of a military takeover of the government in April 1964. The previous government had led Brazil into a chaotic situation with inflation running 100 percent a year or more. The new government adopted economic policies that started Brazil on the road to what was widely described as a miracle of economic development. Using draconian measures of repression, it also energetically set about a transformation of Brazilian political institutions.

Predictably, these two policies led to opposite reactions in the United States. The business community and the Johnson administration hailed the sound economic policies and the favorable treatment of foreign investment evident in Brazil under the new regime. Others deplored the disregard for civil liberties and the growing reports of torture by Brazilián authorities. The reaction of the State Department was to down-play the reports of human rights violations and to continue its warm embrace of the new government.

The situation in Brazil focused attention on one of the minor activities of the Agency for International Development — its public safety program. This program had been started a few years before to help selected developing countries deal with growing problems of public order, ranging all the way from street demonstrations to terrorist activities. The purpose of AID's public safety program was to provide equipment (tear gas and radios were two of the most popular items) and training for foreign police and paramilitary forces in techniques of crowd control and investigative work. One of the countries receiving this kind of foreign aid was Brazil.

As reports of police torture in Brazil increased, charges were made that the AID public safety team was somehow involved in these abuses. Given the difficulty during this period of distinguishing between the Brazilian police and military, the American military mission in the country was also implicated in these charges. Some of the accusations were quite specific — that torture techniques were part of AID's program of instruction and that torture devices were among the equipment supplied Brazil by the United States.

No reliable evidence was ever found to substantiate these charges. Indeed, the object of AID's public safety program was precisely the opposite — to teach the techniques and to supply the equipment needed for effective law enforcement *without* the use of torture. But the accusations of American complicity in Brazilian violations of human rights persisted. They were made in connection with other countries as well. In Uruguay, for example, an American public safety adviser was kidnapped and murdered by terrorists who accused him of complicity in police brutality.

By 1971, Senator Frank Church, then chairman of the Latin American Subcommittee of the Foreign Relations Committee, was sufficiently exercised about such complaints to hold comprehensive hearings on United States policy toward Brazil. These hearings, augmented by subsequent staff reports on Guatemala and the Dominican Republic, demonstrated, at least to the satisfaction of Church and some of his colleagues, that the basic problem of the American public safety program was one of public relations. Police forces in Brazil, Guatemala, and the Dominican Republic were undoubtedly guilty of using excessive force against citizens — to put the most charitable interpretation on the evidence. Through its public safety program, the United States was identified with these excesses. The program had been designed to transfer American techniques of law enforcement, but sufficient account had not been taken of the fact that the transfers were made to countries where the police operated without the political and judicial restraints to which they are subject in the United States.

A movement thus began in the Senate to abolish the public safety program. It eventually succeeded in 1974 after overcoming stiff bureaucratic opposition and some resistance in the House.

CONGRESS ACTS ON HUMAN RIGHTS

Chile

Just as events in Chile brought a turning point in congressional relations with the intelligence community, so they altered Congress' response to the problem of international human rights.

The overthrow of President Salvador Allende's regime in September 1973 ushered in a period of mass arrests and imprisonment incommunicado without charges for long periods. This was accompanied by the inevitable allegations of mistreatment and torture of prisoners. Some of these allegations were impressively documented.

The Nixon administration reacted to the overthrow of Allende and the emergence of the new military government in Chile much the same way the Johnson administration had reacted to the new government in Brazil in 1964. Although the Nixon embrace was perhaps a trifle less fervent, the administration made no secret of its approval of the downfall of the Allende government (while deploring the fact that the president had been killed in the process), and it loosened the strings on American loans and grants to Chile.

The initial congressional action (as distinguished from oratory) toward those developments was quite mild. The Foreign Assistance Act of 1973, approved December 17, contained two provisions that did no more than express the sense of Congress. Expressions of the sense of Congress are intended as guidance to the executive branch and do not have the force of law. They are frequently the result of legislative compromise over stronger proposals which, if cast in mandatory language, would provoke debate and opposition. They are, in short, a means of avoiding a test of strength in Congress while at the same time getting some kind of a policy on record. They often also indicate that majority support does not exist in Congress for stronger measures, and the administration can usually expect not to be called to account if it does not take the sense of Congress seriously. That was not, however, the case in this instance.

The two human rights provisions in the Foreign Assistance Act of 1973 dealt with the question of political prisoners in general and with the problem of human rights in Chile in particular. With respect to political prisoners in all countries, it was the sense of Congress that the president should deny foreign aid to any government "which practices the internment or imprisonment of that country's citizens for political purposes."[1]

With respect to Chile, Congress had more to say. It was the sense of Congress that the president should:

● "Request the Government of Chile to protect the human rights of all individuals, Chilean and foreign," with respect to "the granting of asylum, safe conduct, and the humane treatment or release of prisoners";

• "Support international humanitarian initiatives by the United Nations High Commissioner of Refugees and the International Committee of the Red Cross to insure the protection and safe conduct and resettlement of political refugees, the humane treatment of political prisoners, and the full inspection of detention facilities under international auspices"; and

• "Request the Inter-American Commission on Human Rights to undertake an immediate inquiry into recent events occurring in Chile."[2]

After the passage of the Foreign Assistance Act of 1973, Congress became steadily more assertive about Chile and enacted a series of specific limits on aid that could be given that country. In 1974, it placed a limitation of $25 million on military assistance. In 1975, it put a ceiling of $90 million on economic assistance including housing guarantees and sales of surplus agricultural commodities. (During the 1960s, American assistance to Chile had sometimes been twice that amount.)

In 1976, Congress prohibited any kind of military assistance, sales, exports, or training, and economic assistance was limited to $27.5 million (not including grants of surplus agricultural commodities distributed by charitable organizations). American aid could be doubled if the president made certain certifications to Congress in writing, certifications Congress did not expect the president to be able to make. They were that the Government of Chile:

• "Does not engage in a consistent pattern of gross violations of internationally recognized human rights, including torture or cruel, inhuman, or degrading treatment or punishment, prolonged detention without charges or trial, or other flagrant denials of the right to life, liberty, or the security of person";

• "Has permitted the unimpeded investigation, by internationally recognized commissions on human rights (including the United Nations Commission on Human Rights and the Inter-American Commission on Human Rights of the Organization of American States) of alleged violations of internationally recognized human rights. . ."; and

• "Has taken steps to inform the families of prisoners of the condition of and charges against such prisoners."[3]

The Ford administration's foreign policy throughout this period was dominated by Secretary of State Henry Kissinger, who greeted each new congressional initiative on human rights with resistance which varied proportionately to the specificity and stringency of the initiative. In this, Kissinger was reacting in a typically bureaucratic fashion. Regardless of who has been secretary, the State Department has never liked binding policy directives or limitations from Congress. (There are rare exceptions to this in cases when the department is seeking to bolster its negotiating position with a foreign country and wants to be able to say, in effect, "Look, we understand your position, but Congress has tied our hands." Even in these cases, the department does not like to have its hands tied too tightly.)

In the case of human rights, Kissinger made the usual bureaucratic plea for diplomatic flexibility. He argued that public protests of human rights violations were likely to be counterproductive and that more could be achieved through quiet diplomacy. In the abstract, there is much to be said for this argument. Sovereign governments ordinarily do not respond well to public criticism, let alone preaching from other governments, particularly when it is directed at something they regard as a domestic matter.

The trouble with the argument in this case was that nobody in Congress believed Kissinger was really conducting any quiet diplomacy aimed at improving the human rights of Chileans or anybody else. When Senator Claiborne Pell, who had been particularly outraged by the Johnson and Nixon administrations' embrace of a repressive government in Greece, asked Kissinger to cite some examples of quiet diplomacy, the secretary demurred that it would be inappropriate to do so in public. Pell accepted that objection and invited the secretary to submit a classified memorandum. It took the State Department eight months to find a handful of examples.

It must also be remembered that these exchanges took place as the full story of the CIA's maneuvers in Chile was beginning to unfold. If Kissinger had had any shred of credibility left in the human rights area, Congress (or at least the Senate) might well have accepted his argument for quiet diplomacy. But he did not, and Congress took the bit in its teeth on the human rights question. In doing so, it subsequently complicated life for the Carter administration, which ironically had promised to put more emphasis on human rights in American foreign policy.

A General Human Rights Policy

The enactment of limitations on aid to Chile (and also to Korea and Uruguay) for human rights reasons paralleled a congressional attempt to formulate a general policy relating foreign aid to a recipient government's human rights practices. This attempt was complicated by the variety of kinds and purposes of foreign aid.

It is one thing to cut off military assistance, sales, and training for Uruguay (as Congress did in 1976), a small, remote country of little, if any, geopolitical importance. It is another thing entirely to cut off a much larger aid program for the Philippines (which Congress has never done), where the observance of human rights is scarcely better than in Uruguay, but where the United States is beholden to the government for large American air and naval bases.

It is one thing to cut off aid to a repressive government for economic infrastructure projects (such as road building or harbor construction) or for balance of payments support; it is the government that is hurt first and most. It is something else to cut off shipments of food; then it is the people the government is oppressing who suffer most.

Congress attempted to deal with this problem by distinguishing between security assistance, on the one hand, and food and development assistance on the other. (In the jargon of foreign aid, security assistance is military aid, including military credit sales and training, and economic assistance directly related to military or political purposes. Development assistance is aid directly related to economic development.)

Security Assistance. The Foreign Assistance Act of 1974 expressed the sense of Congress that:

> . . .except in extraordinary circumstances, the President shall substantially reduce or terminate security assistance to any government which engages in a consistent pattern of gross violations of internationally recognized human rights, including torture or cruel, inhuman or degrading treatment or punishment; prolonged detention without charges; or other flagrant denials of the right to life, liberty, and the security of the person.[4]

In cases in which assistance was proposed or furnished to such governments, the president was to inform Congress of the extraordinary circumstances necessitating the assistance. In determining whether a government consistently violated human rights, consideration was to be given to the extent of its cooperation in permitting unimpeded investigations "by appropriate international organizations."

This left the president considerable leeway in determining what circumstances were "extraordinary." The requirement for these to be reported to Congress gave Congress the chance to second guess him and tended to ensure that presidential definitions of "extraordinary" would not be whimsical.

Congress rewrote this section of the Foreign Assistance Act of 1974 in 1976, tightening the standards and procedures. Now, for the first time, Congress did more than withhold aid from human rights violators. It declared that "a principal goal of the foreign policy of the United States shall be to promote the increased observance of internationally recognized human rights by all countries." Previously, security assistance to human rights violators was prohibited except in "extraordinary circumstances," as determined by the president; now it was prohibited except in specified circumstances. This change ensured a larger foreign policy role for Congress.

In the first place, security assistance programs generally were to be formulated and conducted "in a manner which will promote and advance human rights and avoid identification of the United States, through such programs, with governments which deny to their people internationally recognized human rights and fundamental freedoms. . . ."

In the second place, the materials presented to Congress by the executive branch justifying the request for security assistance programs were to include "a full and complete report" on the human rights practices of each country for which such assistance was proposed. In preparing the report, consideration was to be given to "the relevant findings of appropriate international organizations" and the extent to which proposed recipient governments cooperated in permitting unimpeded investigations by such organizations.

In the third place, on request from Congress with respect to any country, the secretary of state was to submit an additional, more detailed statement responding to seven specific areas of concern set forth in the law. If the statement from the secretary was not forthcoming in 30 days, all security assistance to the country was to be cut off until the statement was transmitted or Congress specifically authorized assistance to be resumed.[5]

Congress tinkered with the law again in the International Security Assistance Act of 1978. For governments consistently and grossly violating human rights, security assistance could not be provided to the police, domestic intelligence agencies, or similar law enforcement agencies, nor could licenses be issued for the export of crime control and detection equipment. Neither could members of the armed forces of such a country receive American military education or training. In each case, exceptions were made if the president certified to Congress that extraordinary circumstances existed. Although Congress had ordered the demise of the AID public safety program in 1974, the 1978 revisions went one step further in preventing the export of crime control and detection equipment (even through commercial channels) to governments with bad human rights records.

Finally, in 1979 Congress added the carrot to the stick in its approach to human rights. It directed that in allocating security assistance funds "the President shall take into account significant improvements in the human rights records of recipient countries, except that such allocations may not contravene any other provision of law."[6]

This made explicit what had long been implicit in the legislative requirements for withholding aid from governments that violate human rights. The withholding implied that if human rights performance improved, the aid would be restored. Now Congress as much as said that explicitly. But it left unanswered the weight that should be given to this consideration in the totality of American interests presumably served by security assistance programs.

Development Assistance. In 1974, Congress had attempted to shift the thrust of foreign aid programs from large infrastructure projects (e.g., hydroelectric dams) to activities that more directly and immediately affected the lives of the poor (e.g., food production, health, education). The following year, when Congress considered the matter of development assistance to governments violating human rights, it faced the problem of how to punish those governments without at the same time punishing the people they were mistreating, among whom needy people were presumably suffering the most. The answer it came up with was to cut off aid to the governments unless the aid was directly benefiting the needy.

This answer at best proved only partially satisfactory. To the degree that the United States helps the needy in a country, it relieves the government of that country of its own obligations to do so. More to the point, it relieves the government of having to face the consequences of not doing so — consequences that are likely to take the form of internal political pressures, social unrest, and possible economic collapse. All of these would be likely to hasten the replacement of the offending government, perhaps by one less oppressive.

Furthermore, it is next to impossible to operate an aid program, even one limited to helping the needy, without dealing with the country's government. The worse a government's record is with respect to human rights (especially in the Third World), the worse it is also likely to be with respect to honesty and efficiency in public administration.

A case in point is Haiti, which has been chronically misgoverned, especially during the oppressive regime (1957-71) of President François Duvalier. Under the dictatorship of "Papa Doc," as he was called, it was impossible for the United States even to carry out free food distribution programs without becoming entangled in red tape and demands for payoffs by government officials. This is why the Kennedy administration stopped trying to operate an aid program in Haiti.

In the International Development and Food Assistance Act of 1975, Congress stated that no development assistance could be provided to any government consistently engaging in gross human rights violations "unless such assistance will directly benefit the needy people in such country."[7] Congress had just said the year before that development assistance was supposed to be aimed at helping the needy in any event. But the new provision did serve to give a new dimension to human rights legislation, and it required the president to report annually on what he had done about it.

In 1977, Congress broadened the scope of the report required and made the secretary of state, rather than the president, responsible for submitting it. The annual report must deal with the status of human rights in each country receiving development assistance, and it is to include steps that have been taken "to alter United States programs . . . in any country because of human rights considerations."

The report for 1978, submitted to Congress in 1979, covers 115 countries. No individual steps are mentioned, although the report makes the general statement that assistance levels have been adjusted "to recognize good human rights performance and to manifest our concern over human rights violations."[8] (In 1979, Congress further broadened the reporting requirement and made it applicable to all countries that are members of the United Nations, regardless of whether they were receiving foreign aid.)[9]

The 1977 legislation also earmarked $750,000 of development assistance funds "for studies to identify, and for openly carrying out, programs and activities which will encourage or promote increased adherence to civil and political rights . . . in countries eligible" for economic development assistance. For fiscal year 1979, this development assistance was increased to $1.5 million, but the earmarking was dropped; the president was only "encouraged to use not less than" this total.

Food. In 1977, through amendments to the Agricultural Trade Development and Assistance Act (popularly known as P.L. 480), Congress linked human rights and the sale of surplus agricultural commodities:

> No agreement may be entered into to finance the sale of agricultural commodities to the government of any country which engages in a consistent pattern of gross violations of internationally recognized human rights . . . unless such agreement will directly benefit the needy people in such country.

Congress also produced guidelines as to what would, or would not, benefit the needy:

> An agreement will not directly benefit the needy people unless either the commodities themselves or the proceeds from their sale will be used for specific projects or programs which the President determines would directly benefit the needy people of that country. The agreement shall specify how the projects or programs will be used to benefit the needy people and shall require a report to the President on such use within six months after the commodities are delivered.[10]

These guidelines are lacking in specificity, but they serve to underline the point that regardless of the indirect benefits to governments and others from P.L. 480 sales, the direct benefits must go to the needy. This is perhaps easier to require in legislation than it is to carry out in administrative practice.

The balance of the 1977 provision contained by now familiar points: the Senate Agriculture and the House Foreign Affairs committees could require the president to "submit in writing information demonstrating that an agreement will directly benefit the needy people in a country"; a government's willingness to cooperate in international investigations was to be considered in assessing its human rights record; and the president was to report annually on the steps taken to implement the provision.

Multilateral Aid Programs. It was in connection with multilateral aid programs that the chickens hatched by congressional distrust of the Nixon-Kissinger policy in Chile came home to roost in the Carter administration.

In 1976, Kissinger's last year as secretary of state, the United States executive directors of the Inter-American Development Bank and the African Development Fund were directed, by law, "to vote against any loan, any extension of financial assistance, or any technical assistance to any country which engages in a consistent pattern of gross violations of internationally recognized human rights . . . unless such assistance will directly benefit the needy people in such country." The United States Governor of the Bank (i.e., the secretary of the treasury) could be required to explain how proposed assistance would benefit the needy. In the case of the African Development Fund, the ban applied also to countries "providing refuge to individuals committing acts of international terrorism such as the hijacking of an aircraft."[11]

Limiting aid to that which directly benefits the needy is a tougher standard for multilateral lending agencies than for the bilateral aid program. The multilaterals are more likely to finance large capital projects such as port improvements or industrial development programs, in which it is more difficult to show direct benefits to the needy.

In 1977, in one of its first major battles with Congress, the Carter administration tried unsuccessfully to get these provisions out of the law and to keep them from being applied to other multilateral agencies — the International Bank for Reconstruction and Development (World Bank), the International Development Association, the International Finance Corporation, and the Asian Development Bank. The administration had come to power in 1977 with a program of its own to emphasize human rights, not only in connection with aid but throughout the whole broad sweep of foreign policy. Faced with making day-to-day operating decisions, it now adopted the traditional executive branch posture of seeking as much diplomatic flexibility as possible, relying on its oft-repeated commitment to human rights as evidence of its good faith.

The Carter administration argued that such flexibility would strengthen its negotiating position and would result in more, rather than less, global progress toward respect for human rights. In effect, this was the same argument that Kissinger had made for quiet diplomacy. The Senate, which had always been more sympathetic to this argument than the House, was now willing to accept it; so was the House Committee on Banking, Finance and Urban Affairs. But the House as a whole would have none of it.

In the end, the House prevailed. As enacted, the law required the United States to oppose any assistance to countries consistently engaging in gross violations of human rights or providing refuge to aircraft hijackers, unless the assistance was "directed specifically to programs which serve the basic human needs of the citizens of such country."

The 1977 law also introduced a positive emphasis on human rights, as distinguished from the approach of denying benefits to countries violating rights. The United States was called upon to use "its voice and vote" in the international financial institutions to advance the cause of human rights, and it was encouraged to channel assistance toward countries other than those with bad human rights records. In addition, the secretary of state and the secretary of the treasury were directed "to initiate a wide consultation designed to develop a viable standard for the meeting of basic human needs and the protection of human rights and a mechanism for acting together to insure that the rewards of international economic cooperation are especially available to those who subscribe to such standards and are seen to be moving toward making them effective in their own systems of governance."[12]

This law covered all international financial institutions in which the United States participates except the International Monetary Fund. With respect to that institution, a 1978 law simply directs the secretary of the treasury to report annually to Congress on the status of human rights in each country which draws on funds made available under the IMF's Supplementary Financing Facility.

Summary. In trying to fine tune aid programs to fit human rights policies, Congress has applied the tightest standards to security assistance and multilateral programs, the loosest to development assistance and food aid.

A valid distinction can be made in the case of security assistance, because it is directly related to military or political objectives and therefore more closely identifies the United States with the recipient government. But Congress has also directed that security assistance programs be formulated and conducted to promote human rights. It has not done this with respect to development assistance and food aid, although it has with respect to multilateral programs.

Development assistance programs can be more easily designed to promote human rights than security assistance programs. Development assistance programs could, for example, provide help through judicial reform or legal education — although this assistance would scarcely qualify as directly benefiting the needy. Congress has, in fact, authorized development assistance money to develop programs to promote human rights, but without saying how.

ORGANIZATION OF THE STATE DEPARTMENT

In 1975, the State Department established by administrative action the position of coordinator for humanitarian affairs (with a total staff of two) in the office of the deputy secretary of state. As one result of the congressional suspicion that Henry Kissinger's quiet diplomacy on human rights was really no diplomacy at all, the new position was provided for by law in 1976 and was made a presidential appointment subject to confirmation by the Senate. The coordinator was to be responsible to the secretary of state for matters pertaining to human rights and humanitarian affairs in the conduct of foreign policy, including those relating to refugees, prisoners of war, and members of the armed services missing in action. Finally, the human rights reports to Congress with respect to security assistance were to be the responsibility of the coordinator.[13]

In 1977, Congress upgraded the position of coordinator to the status of assistant secretary. The expanded duties of the assistant secretary for human rights and humanitarian affairs included:

• Gathering "detailed information regarding humanitarian affairs and the observance of and respect for internationally recognized human rights" in countries affected by foreign assistance requirements;
• Preparing the statements and reports to Congress required in connection with security assistance;
• Making recommendations to the secretary and to the administrator of AID regarding compliance with human rights requirements of the foreign aid legislation; and
• Performing "other responsibilities which serve to promote increased observance of internationally recognized human rights by all countries."[14]

The secretary of state was also directed to send Congress, by January 31, 1978, "a comprehensive report on the Office of the Assistant Secretary for Human Rights and Humanitarian Affairs, including its current mandate and operations, the mandate and operations of its predecessor offices, and proposals for the reorganization of the Department of State that would strengthen human rights and humanitarian considerations in the conduct of United States foreign policy and promote the ability of the United States to participate effectively in international humanitarian efforts."[15] That report concluded, not surprisingly, that "the present structure provides an effective way to assure consideration of human rights and humanitarian considerations in the conduct of United States foreign policy."[16]

The statutory creation of this office and its subsequent upgrading to the level of assistant secretary were acts of more than ordinary bureaucratic significance. Congress spelled out the duties and responsibilities of the office to a greater extent than is normal with respect to assistant secretaries of state. This provided a focal point for human rights concerns in the executive branch. It gave the new assistant secretary a legislative mandate. More particularly, it created a vested bureaucratic interest in human rights. The assistant secretary for human rights and humanitarian affairs has a constituency in Congress, and members of Congress interested in human rights have a constituency in the assistant secretary's office.

The arrangement not only centralizes, in terms of organization, concern for human rights in the State Department. It not only gives the assistant secretary a measure of bureaucratic independence. It also ensures that a voice advocating consideration of human rights is going to be heard in the department's policymaking process. As this has worked in practice, the role of the assistant secretary for human rights and humanitarian affairs in policy decisions has been the source of irritation to the State Department's geographic bureaus.

COMMUNIST COUNTRIES

The Trade Act of 1974

The main purpose of the Trade Act of 1974 was to provide the president with authority to engage in a new round of international trade negotiations aimed at stimulating world commerce through mutual reductions in both tariffs and nontariff barriers to trade. One of the additional purposes was to authorize the extension of most-favored-nation treatment to Communist countries, most of which had been excluded from it by earlier legislation.

Under most-favored-nation treatment, a country is guaranteed that, with respect to tariffs on any particular item, it will be treated the same as the nation which receives the best treatment. Inasmuch as the United States extends most-favored-nation treatment to most countries, the term is a misnomer. It suggests special treatment which does not exist. It is the absence of most-favored-nation treatment which is discriminatory.

Implementation of the trade agreement negotiated in October 1972 between the United States and the Soviet Union was dependent on the extension to the Soviet Union of most-favored-nation status. An earlier U.S.-Soviet agreement settling the Soviet's lend-lease debt from World War II was also dependent on the trade agreement.

The trade bill was designed, among other things, to make possible the implementation of these agreements. It was considered in 1973 and 1974 in the larger context of debate over the Kissinger policy of détente with the Soviet Union. The issue of human rights was injected into this debate by an argument over linking most-favored-nation treatment with Soviet emigration practices. At issue was the desire of many Soviet Jews to resettle in Israel.

In 1972, the Soviets began levying steep exit taxes on emigrants holding advanced academic degrees, a group which included many Jews. The Soviet rationale was that the taxes would repay the cost of the free education which such persons had received and from which Soviet society would no longer benefit if the persons emigrated. The Soviets also denied exit visas on national security grounds to persons who had had access to classified information. Other restrictions were also applied, the most common one being simple inaction on applications for emigrant visas.

The issues of détente and emigration came together in a confusing way. Americans opposed to détente were also generally opposed to closer trade relations with the Soviet Union and were skeptical that such relations would result in net economic or political benefits to the United States. On the contrary, it was felt that the trade bill, on balance, would benefit the Soviet Union and that this provided leverage to the United States in forcing Soviet concessions on emigration.

The Jackson-Vanik Amendment

"To assure the continued dedication of the United States to fundamental human rights," Senator Henry M. Jackson of Washington and Representative Charles A. Vanik of Ohio, both Democrats, offered an amendment to the Trade Act of 1974.[17] After this rhetorical beginning, the Jackson-Vanik amendment proceeds to outline specific provisions. Products from "any nonmarket country" shall not be eligible for most-favored-nation treatment. Nor shall any such country participate in any United States government program "which extends credits or credit guarantees or investment guarantees directly or indirectly."

The amendment also states that the president shall not conclude "any commercial agreement" with any such nonmarket economy country if the president determines that the country: (1) "denies its citizens the right or opportunity to emigrate"; (2) "imposes more than a nominal tax on emigration or on visas or other documents required for emigration, for any purpose or cause whatsoever"; or (3) "imposes more than a nominal tax, levy, fine, fee, or other charge on any citizen as a consequence of the desire of such citizen to emigrate to the country of his choice."

Once the president makes the determination that a country engages in the emigration restrictions cited, there are two ways it can be removed from the ban on credits and most-favored-nation treatment. One is a presidential finding and report to Congress that the country is no longer restricting emigration. The report has to include "information as to the nature and implementation of emigration laws and policies and restrictions or discrimination applied to or against persons wishing to emigrate," and it has to be updated semiannually.

The other way is through a presidential waiver of the ban with respect to a particular country. The waiver authority is severely circumscribed. In the first place, the president has to convince Congress that the waiver will substantially promote the objectives of free emigration, but also and more importantly, that he "has received assurances that the emigration practices of that country will henceforth lead substantially to the achievement" of such objectives. In the second place, tight provisions exist for congressional review of the waiver, which has to be approved by both houses. The waiver procedure also has to be repeated annually.

A separate provision of the Trade Act deals in a similar way with any Communist country which "denies its citizens the right or opportunity to join permanently through emigration, a very close relative in the United States, such as a spouse, parent, child, brother, or sister."[18]

The Jackson-Vanik amendment posed a complex set of issues. There was general sympathy for the plight of Soviet Jews and members of Congress were reluctant to oppose anything that looked like it would ease that plight. Yet real doubts existed that the amendment, in fact, would do so. As Secretary of State William P. Rogers put it to the Ways and Means Committee in May 1973, the best hope for a satisfactory resolution of Soviet emigration practices "will come not from the confrontation formal legislation would bring about, but from a steady improvement in our over-all relations.[19] This was essentially the same quiet diplomacy argument that Kissinger was to make later with respect to human rights legislation in connection with foreign aid.

Throughout the debate, the Soviet Union repeatedly made it clear that it regarded its emigration practices as an internal matter and not an appropriate subject for international negotiation. Yet once the issue had been raised in Congress, it was taken as a political imperative that some provision on the subject go in the trade bill. The problem for the administration and its supporters thus became one of finding language that would satisfy a majority in Congress without driving the Soviets to scuttle the trade agreement and perhaps to clamp down on emigration even more. The task was complicated by the fact that some members of Congress no doubt wanted to use an emigration amendment as a device to kill most-favored-nation treatment for the Soviets, or at least would not care if that proved to be the result.

During most of 1973 and 1974, two sets of negotiations were in progress: negotiations between Kissinger and the Soviet Union and negotiations between Kissinger and the Jackson-Vanik forces on Capitol Hill. By October 1974, it appeared that an agreement had been reached. It was formalized in an exchange of letters between Secretary Kissinger and Senator Jackson.

"[O]n the basis of discussions that have been conducted with Soviet representatives," Kissinger wrote to Jackson, "I should like on behalf of the Administration to inform you that we have been assured that the following criteria and practices will henceforth govern emigration from the USSR." There then followed six understandings, the most important of which were that there would be no discrimination in issuing exit visas, that no punitive measures would be taken against applicants for emigration, and that the tax on exit visas which had been suspended would remain suspended.[20]

Jackson went further. He said the agreement assumed that the annual rate of Soviet emigration would rise from the 1973 level of about 35,000 and in the future would correspond to the number of applicants. (The rate in 1974 was about two-thirds that of 1973.) He also said that 60,000 emigrants a year would be the "minimum standard" of compliance in order for the president to certify to Congress that Soviet practices were leading to substantially free emigration. He added that this was based on assurances from Soviet leaders.

In testimony before the Senate Finance Committee on December 3, Kissinger said, in effect, that Jackson was overstating the matter. According to Kissinger, his own letter to Jackson had been based on "clarifications" given to him and President Ford by Soviet officials. No commitments "either in form or substance" had been made by the Soviet Union. Jackson's letter, Kissinger said, contained interpretations and elaborations "which were never stated to us by Soviet officials," and there was no Soviet "commitment as to numbers."[21]

The Senate passed the Jackson amendment by a vote of 88-0 on December 13. Five days later, the Soviet Union denied it had given any specific assurance, as Senator Jackson had indicated. To the contrary, Moscow asserted that the number of emigrants was declining. It released the text of an October 26 letter to Kissinger from Foreign Minister Andrei A. Gromyko, calling the Jackson-Kissinger exchange a "distorted picture of our position as well as what we told the American side on that matter." Gromyko restated the longstanding Soviet position that the emigration issue was a wholly domestic one.[22]

Both houses agreed to the conference report on the trade bill December 20, and Ford signed it January 3, 1975. On January 14, Kissinger announced that the Soviets had rejected the conditions of the Jackson-Vanik amendment and consequently would not implement the 1972 trade agreement.

There the matter stood. Jewish emigration from the Soviet Union decreased in 1975 and in ensuing years, but it increased markedly in 1979 to a level of 4,000 a month, possibly because the Kremlin wanted to improve the climate for Senate consideration of SALT II and also possibly because it wanted to be sure that the Soviet Union received most-favored-nation treatment if China did.

This latter possibility arose as a consequence of the normalization of U.S. diplomatic relations with the People's Republic of China at the beginning of 1979. Those who are opposed to détente with the Soviet Union tend to favor it with China, but the emigration practices of the Peking government were even more restrictive than those of the Soviet Union. Now, however, Peking loosened those restrictions, and unmanageable hordes of Chinese flooded into Hong Kong. Their emigration from China was legal, but their immigration into Hong Kong was not. In response to a request from the British government, Peking tightened its emigration controls somewhat.

Arriving in Peking for a visit to China, Jackson said China should be accorded most-favored-nation treatment and called for congressional approval of the Sino-American trade agreement signed in Peking July 7, 1979.[23] Carter submitted the agreement to Congress October 23. It was approved by Congress January 24 and most-favored-nation status for China became effective February 1, 1980.

The Commission on Security and Cooperation in Europe

On August 1, 1975, following two years of negotiations, the leaders of 34 countries plus the Vatican signed in Helsinki the Final Act of the Conference on Security and Cooperation in Europe. The occasion was deemed of sufficient importance for President Ford to go to Helsinki himself to sign it on behalf of the United States.

The Helsinki Agreement concerns a broad range of issues — military security, economics, science and technology, the environment, and human rights, to name a few. Not legally binding, it is more than anything else a statement of good intentions by the signatories.

The human rights provisions aim to facilitate "freer movement and contacts," the reunification of families, marriage between citizens of different states, travel for personal or professional reasons, improvement in the circulation of information and in working conditions for journalists, and cooperation and exchange in the fields of culture and education.[24]

During the long negotiations, the United States put particular emphasis on the human rights provisions as a means of getting the Soviet Union and the other Communist countries of Eastern Europe on record, even though they were not legally committed to that protection.

Not being a treaty, the Helsinki Agreement did not require the consent of the Senate, but in order to give itself a role in overseeing implementation of the agreement, Congress in 1976 established the Commission on Security and Cooperation in Europe. The commission consists of 15 members — six from the House, six from the Senate, and one each from the departments of state, defense, and commerce.

This congressional initiative was not welcomed by the Ford administration, which delayed appointing the executive branch members on the grounds that such a mixed executive-legislative commission possibly violated the separation of powers. A more important factor, both in the congressional action to create the commission and in the Ford administration's reaction to it, was the atmosphere prevailing in the wake of the Jackson-Vanik amendment. A substantial group in Congress did not trust the administration to hold the Soviets' feet to the fire on human rights. And the administration feared that Congress would use the commission to interfere further, as the administration saw it, in U.S.-Soviet relations. As it has turned out, this has not happened.

The purpose of the commission is "to monitor the acts of the signatories which reflect compliance with or violation of the articles" of the agreement. Another function is "to monitor and encourage the development of programs and activities of the United States Government and private organizations with a view toward taking advantage of the provisions ... to expand East-West economic cooperation and a greater interchange of people and ideas between East and West."[25]

A principal reason for creating the commission was to give Congress a mechanism and a forum for watching and calling attention to Soviet treatment of Jews and dissidents. This has indeed been the main focus of the commission's activity, but by no means the only one. The commission has also concerned itself with the desire of 10,000 Soviet evangelical Christians to emigrate and with the situation in Eastern Europe generally. In 1979 it was at work on a major report, following hearings, on American compliance with the Helsinki agreement, particularly in the area of human rights.

INTERNATIONAL HUMAN RIGHTS AGREEMENTS

Although Congress set up a commission to monitor Soviet compliance with the nonbinding Helsinki Agreement, the Senate has consistently refused to approve multilateral human rights treaties. June 1979 marked the thirtieth anniversary of the Genocide Convention on the Senate Foreign Relations Committee calendar. No other treaty has been pending for so long. (Pending bills and resolutions die at the end of a Congress every two years; treaties stay before the Senate until they are either acted on or returned to the president.)

Genocide emerged as one of the crimes against humanity for which leaders of the Axis Powers were tried during and after World War II.[26] The Convention on the Prevention and Punishment of the Crime of Genocide was adopted unanimously by the United Nations General Assembly on December 9, 1948, and formally signed by the United States. President Harry S. Truman sent it to the Senate with a request for advice and consent to ratification on June 16, 1949. A subcommittee of the Foreign Relations Committee held hearings in 1950 and recommended that the convention be approved, but no action was taken by the full committee.

There the matter stood for 20 years. Then, in response to a renewed push by the Nixon administration, further hearings were held. This time the Foreign Relations Committee reported the convention favorably to the Senate with the recommendation that it be approved with understandings and a declaration, but the Senate did not consider it. The convention was reported again in 1971. The Senate actually debated it in 1972, but did not vote.

The major effort to secure Senate action on the convention came in 1973-74 and succumbed to a filibuster. Two motions to end the debate failed by almost identical votes of 55-36 and 55-38. (It takes 60 votes to invoke cloture against a filibuster.) The votes indicated that, even without a filibuster, the convention was well short of the two-thirds majority needed for approval. The Foreign Relations Committee again reported the convention favorably in 1976 and held further hearings on it in 1977. There the matter rests.

Seldom has there been such a large tempest in such a small teapot. The Genocide Convention seems innocuous enough. All it does is outlaw the crime of "genocide," a word which was coined in the aftermath of the Nazi campaign against the Jews to mean murder of a whole race. Yet there is intense opposition to this simple proposal to outlaw a crime that nobody defends. Certainly there is no more basic human right than the right not to be killed because of one's race.

Senatorial opposition to the Genocide Convention has many sources, most of them stemming from apprehension that it would injure the federal system in the United States. Genocide, this argument runs, is mass murder. Murder is already a crime in every state in the union. Further action on the subject is not part of the federal government's business. In addition, opponents of the convention have never been at a loss to find technical provisions in it which form the basis for legalistic quibbles.

Yet none of these considerations seems sufficient to explain the public's emotional response to the genocide debate. The reaction has very little to do with the language of the convention itself. On one side, there is the deep feeling that the United States ought to join most of the rest of the world in a solemn statement of international law repudiating Hitler's holocaust. On the other side, there is the fear that the convention is somehow part of a plot to bring about world government, and that it could be used to pillory the United States for its treatment of Indians, blacks, or other minorities.

Another consideration has been important in the reluctance of the Senate to advise and consent to human rights treaties generally. This is that most of the rights which are dealt with by these treaties are already protected in the United States either by the Constitution or by federal statute. Certain other rights specified in the treaties are viewed by senators more as economic or social goals — for example, the right to health and education.

Out of approximately 40 international treaties in force with respect to human rights, the United States is a party to only ten. Most of the others have not even been submitted to the Senate, and some have not been signed by the United States.

In keeping with his inaugural promises, President Carter submitted four international human rights treaties to the Senate in 1978 — the International Convention on the Elimination of All Forms of Racial Discrimination, the International Covenant on Economic, Social and Cultural Rights, the International Covenant on Civil and Political Rights, and the American Convention on Human Rights. No action had been taken by 1979.

CONCLUSION

The multifaceted practice of diplomacy involves balancing frequently contradictory national interests, such as military security, access to essential raw materials, the protection of American business abroad, the growth of foreign trade — and the protection and promotion of human rights. The line between standing up for human decency and meddling in another country's internal affairs is exceedingly fine. Violations of human rights can range from occasional roughing up of a prisoner by police to systematic torture and mass murder. At what point in this spectrum does international concern become appropriate?

And what is a human right anyway? Congressional attention has focused on the right not to be physically abused; but the Jackson-Vanik amendment involves the right to emigrate, and the American government through both the president and the Congress has spoken out on the treatment of Soviet dissidents — an issue essentially involving free speech.

To much of the Third World, however, human rights encompass what many Americans regard not as rights so much as desirable social or economic goals — education, housing, and medical care. The inclusion of these subjects in international agreements is one reason for the Senate's reluctance to approve them. In its human rights reports to Congress, the Carter administration has adopted the broader definition — one respect in which the executive branch has gone further than Congress.[27]

A further difficulty is avoiding the appearance of self-righteousness or hypocrisy. The United States' own record with respect to human rights, particularly with respect to racial discrimination, is far from flawless. The history of Soviet Jewry is scarcely sadder than the history of American Indians.

Nevertheless, the record is clear that the United States generally enjoys better relations with countries where there is a decent respect for the individual than with those where there is not. The most prominent example, of course, is America's relations with its European allies and with countries like Canada and Australia, but the point applies to other countries as well.

The emphasis on human rights issues in the 1970s was in part a reaction to the neglect these issues suffered during the Cold War period when considerations of national security were paramount. But it was more than that. It followed the flowering of the civil rights movement in the 1960s and the national disillusionment over Vietnam.

Exactly how to implement a human rights policy in the 1980s remains a question. Short of military intervention, the options available to the United States (from the less to the more drastic) include:

- Private diplomatic representations;
- Public criticism;
- Reduction or termination of foreign aid or credits;
- Call for action by an international organization (actions ranging from a condemnatory resolution to international sanctions);
- Recall of the American ambassador;
- Severance of diplomatic relations;
- An embargo of trade.

All of these options are available to the executive branch, but only some of them (public criticism, reduction of aid, trade restrictions) are available to Congress. Taking any of these actions on behalf of human rights may mean a sacrifice of some other foreign policy objective. Nor is there any guarantee that human rights observance by other countries actually will be improved. But these actions do make it clear that the United States considers human rights practices a significant factor in its foreign relations — and it is Congress that has taken the initiative in shaping U.S. foreign policy with human rights issues in view.

NOTES

1. The Foreign Assistance Act of 1973, Sec. 32, P.L. 93-189, approved December 17, 1973.
2. Ibid., Sec. 35.
3. The International Security Assistance and Arms Export Control Act of 1976, Sec. 406, P.L. 94-329, approved June 30, 1976.
4. The Foreign Assistance Act of 1974, Sec. 46, P.L. 93-559, approved December 30, 1974.
5. The International Security Assistance and Arms Export Control Act of 1976, Sec. 301(a). This section in its present form is Sec. 502B of the Foreign Assistance Act of 1961, as amended.
6. The International Security Assistance Act of 1979, Sec. 4, P.L. 96-92, approved October 29, 1979.
7. The International Development and Food Assistance Act of 1975, Sec. 116, P.L. 94-161, approved December 20, 1975.
8. U.S., State Department, *Report on Human Rights Practices in Countries Receiving U.S. Aid,* submitted to the Senate Foreign Relations and House Foreign Affairs committees, February 8, 1979, p. 6.
9. The International Development Cooperation Act of 1979, P.L. 96-53, approved August 14, 1979.
10. The Agricultural Trade Development and Assistance Act of 1954, as amended, Sec. 112, added by the International Development and Food Assistance Act of 1977.
11. P.L. 94-302, approved May 31, 1976, Secs. 103 (a) and 211.
12. P.L. 95-118, approved October 3, 1977, Sec. 701.
13. The International Security Assistance and Arms Export Control Act of 1976, Sec. 301(b), P.L. 94-329, approved June 30, 1976.
14. The Foreign Assistance Act of 1961, as amended, Sec. 624(f)(1), added by the Foreign Relations Authorization Act, Fiscal Year 1978, 91 Stat. 846.
15. The Foreign Relations Authorization Act, Fiscal Year 1978, Sec. 109(a)(7), P.L. 95-105, approved August 17, 1977.
16. U.S., State Department, *Report of the Secretary of State to the Congress of the United States Regarding the Operations and Mandate of the Bureau of Human Rights and Humanitarian Affairs,* submitted to the House Foreign Affairs Committee, January 31, 1978, p. 21.
17. The Trade Act of 1974, Sec. 402, P.L. 93-618, approved January 3, 1975.
18. Ibid., Sec. 409.
19. U.S., Congress, House, Ways and Means Committee, "Trade Reform" Hearings on H.R. 6767, The Trade Reform Act of 1973, 93d Cong., 1st. sess., May 9, 1973, p. 165.
20. *The New York Times,* October 19, 1974, p. 10.
21. U.S., Congress, Senate, Finance Committee, *Hearing on Emigration Amendment to the Trade Reform Act of 1974,* 93d Cong., 2d sess., December 3, 1974, pp. 53-54.

22. *The New York Times,* December 19, 1974, pp. 1, 18.
23. *The New York Times,* August 8, 1979.
24. U.S., State Department, *Conference on Security and Cooperation in Europe: Final Act,* Publication No. 8826, August 1975.
25. P.L. 94-304, approved June 3, 1976.
26. See Gerhard von Glahn, *Law Among Nations: An Introduction to Public International Law,* 3d ed., (New York: Macmillan Publishing Co., 1976), pp. 713-715.
27. *Report on Human Rights Practices in Countries Receiving U.S. Aid,* pp. 2-3.

PART III

Conclusion

P art I (Chapters 1 and 2) provided a general discussion of the respective roles of the executive branch — focusing upon the powers of the
president — and of Congress in the foreign policy process. In Part II
(Chapters 3 through 7), five specific issues from recent American diplomatic experience were selected to illustrate Congress' foreign policy role
since the Vietnam War. These case studies had two common elements:
they dealt with significant questions confronting the United States in
foreign relations, and they identified one or more important prerogatives
of Congress and the president in the foreign policy field.

In the final chapter of this study — Part III — our purpose is twofold. First, it is to identify congressional behavior patterns in the recent
era of legislative activism in foreign relations. What approaches has
Congress taken to a series of diverse external problems? In what respects
has Congress' approach in recent years marked a change from the long
preceding period of legislative acquiescence in presidential diplomatic
leadership?

Second, what are the more noteworthy long-term implications of an
active and independent role by Congress in foreign affairs? In order to
answer that question, we must consider the factors that have sustained
congressional assertiveness in confronting foreign policy questions. How
durable are these factors? Are they likely to provide momentum for
forceful legislative initiatives in foreign relations in the years ahead? Or
can they be expected to diminish, as memories of the Vietnam conflict
recede and as the United States confronts new and difficult problems in
the international system? On balance, what has been the impact of an
assertive Congress upon American diplomacy?

The era of congressional dynamism in foreign policy was to no in-
considerable degree an inevitable outgrowth of the Vietnam War. That
traumatic experience brought about a reappraisal of the whole process of
reaching foreign policy decisions. In Southeast Asia, the United States
found itself embroiled in a massive military conflict because of a series
of separate, unrelated, and often modest steps — an approach to foreign
policy sometimes called "incrementalism."

In effect, this was an outcome which "just happened" as the result
of no conscious or deliberate design by policymakers or American citi-

zens. (In fact, officials in Washington frequently denied their intention of expanding America's responsibility for the defense of South Vietnam, even while they were in the process of doing so!) In time, however, the United States found itself saddled with the dominant responsibility for the Vietnam War effort — primarily because officials in Washington and informed citizens failed at each stage to perceive the cumulative effect of a series of isolated steps which collectively produced America's involvement in that conflict.

Congressional critics of the American role in the Vietnam War have often led the legislative branch to exert its powers in the foreign policy field since the late 1960s. Yet, ironically, in time these members of Congress may confront the same pervasive criticism that they leveled against executive policymakers. The forceful exercise of legislative prerogatives has unquestionably — and in some respects, profoundly — affected the conduct of American diplomacy. But are the consequences of Congress' diplomatic activism those which officials in Washington (including some legislators) and the American people intend? Has the forceful intrusion of Congress into the foreign policy realm enhanced American diplomacy, or has it placed new obstacles in the path of diplomatic success?

Such questions are important for officials engaged in the foreign policy process, for authorities on the American governmental system, and for informed citizens alike. Our answers often must be tentative; they are perhaps inescapably conditioned by underlying value judgments; and they cannot anticipate the conditions that will confront the United States in its relations with some 150 independent nations. With due recognition of these uncertainties, Chapter 8 presents an assessment of Congress' overall impact upon the American foreign policy process.

8

Congressional Assertiveness and Foreign Affairs: A Balance Sheet

A recent British ambassador to the United States was asked what surprised him most about the conduct of American diplomacy. He replied, "The extraordinary power of your Congress over foreign policy. . . ."[1]

Executive policymakers have increasingly acknowledged the crucial role that Congress plays in the foreign relations of the United States. Although before entering government service Henry Kissinger was dubious about undue legislative influence in foreign affairs, as secretary of state he called for "a new national partnership" between the president and Congress in dealing with international issues.[2] President Richard M. Nixon, in a report to Congress on foreign policy in the 1970s, underlined the importance of executive-legislative cooperation:

> Charged with constitutional responsibilities in foreign policy, the Congress can give perspective to the national debate and serve as a bridge between the Executive and the people.[3]

Indicative of the executive desire for cooperation with Congress during the 1970s was the growth of the State Department's legislative liaison staff by some 50 percent.[4]

Although executive officials and informed students of American foreign policy are becoming increasingly aware of the expanding role of Congress in foreign policy, they are are often far from enthusiastic about the disturbing implications of congressional diplomatic assertiveness. Presidents Johnson, Nixon, Ford, and Carter vocally opposed legislative efforts to limit their powers abroad and to exercise constitutional and historical prerogatives they believed belonged to the executive branch. From the perspective of the White House, former Michigan Congressman Gerald R. Ford lamented that congressional activities not infrequently impeded America's ability to achieve its foreign policy objectives:

The pendulum has swung so far that you could almost say we have moved from an imperial Presidency to an imperiled Presidency. Now we have a Congress that is broadening its powers in foreign relations too greatly.[5]

According to other commentators, recent experience has demonstrated that when Congress becomes actively involved in foreign relations, it is "often determined to play havoc with foreign policy implementation."[6]

What have been the principal causes of recent congressional activism in the foreign policy field? What can be identified as the most significant consequences of a forceful legislative role in American foreign relations? And what will be the future balance between executive and legislative influence in the foreign policy process? These three important and interrelated questions provide the framework for discussion in the concluding chapter of our study.

CONGRESSIONAL ASSERTIVENESS: BACKGROUND AND CAUSES

According to the provisions of the Constitution, as we saw in Part I, Congress possesses a number of prerogatives allowing it to influence foreign relations. Congress must appropriate funds needed for innumerable programs in foreign affairs. It has the power to declare war; and it must raise and support the armed forces. The Senate has two unique functions not shared with the House of Representatives: the requirement that treaties receive the advice and consent of the Senate; and that the president's appointments be confirmed by the Senate. From the founding of the American republic, therefore, it was envisioned that Congress would be involved in the solution of diplomatic problems, although in many important respects the exact scope and nature of its involvement was left to be determined by experience.

The powers of the chief executive in foreign relations expanded significantly over the course of time — leading by the mid-1960s to a condition of virtually unchecked presidential authority diplomatically. The steady accretion in the president's diplomatic influence became particularly pronounced after the United States emerged as a superpower at the end of World War II. Perhaps the most remarkable fact about this growth in presidential authority in foreign relations was how seldom it was challenged by Congress. In fact, during several eras, the enhancement of presidential power could only have occurred with the explicit or tacit *concurrence* of Congress. The Roosevelt administration's conduct of World War II and the escalation of the Vietnam War under Presidents Kennedy and Johnson are two examples.

Today the era of congressional passivity or acquiescence in presidential decisions in the foreign policy field has ended. As a former official of the Johnson administration has expressed it:

In the present world situation, far greater congressional and public involvement in formulating our foreign policy seems to me not only right but nearly inevitable.[7]

One reason for greater congressional involvement in foreign policymaking is the interrelationship between foreign affairs and domestic issues. According to a former member of the House of Representatives, "foreign and domestic policy have merged into a seamless web of interlocking concerns."[8]

Since the New Deal program in the 1930s, the American society has also witnessed what might be called a "legislative explosion" of vast dimensions. Untold thousands of new laws have been enacted by Congress during the past half-century. An increasing proportion of Congress' time is devoted to adding to this list, to making needed changes in existing legislation, and to overseeing the administration of the laws already enacted. Much of this activity is based upon the premise that the solution to pressing national problems lies in the enactment of legislation.[9]

In America's approach to problems beyond its own borders since World War II, basically the same tendency can be discerned. The Truman administration's adoption of the "containment" strategy for resisting Communist expansionism in 1947 committed the United States to a new diplomatic role inescapably enhancing the powers of Congress in foreign affairs. For over a generation thereafter, the continuity of American foreign policy — from ongoing economic and military assistance programs, to the defense of NATO, to America's contribution to the United Nations and other international organizations — has depended upon favorable action by Congress. Moreover, congressional behavior in confronting closely related domestic issues, such as the level of taxation, overall government spending, and the development of natural resources, has directly affected America's relations with other countries.

Internal Changes in Congress

A number of identifiable changes have occurred within Congress in the past ten years that contributed to legislative activism in foreign affairs, and we will examine three of them.

Diffusion of Power on Capitol Hill. Partly as a result of efforts to reform congressional procedures, the problem of dispersed power within the House and Senate has become increasingly acute in recent years. As we noted in Chapter 2, most congressional committees are involved in some aspect of foreign affairs, and their jurisdictions over foreign policy issues frequently overlap. Congressional deliberations today seem more disunified than at any other stage in American history. According to an experienced observer of the Washington scene:

Never since the Senate defied Woodrow Wilson on the importance of creating a League of Nations . . . has the Congress . . . seemed as parochial, personal or divided as it does now.[10]

Individual legislative committees have been subjected to the same process of internal disunity and decentralized decisionmaking characteristic of Congress as a whole. A leading example has been the Senate Foreign Relations Committee. In 1979, the *New York Times* ran the headline "Strain and Rivalry Plague Senate Foreign Relations Panel." Two forces have impaired its unity and influence: successful challenges by other congressional committees to its once pre-eminent position and continuing disagreements within the committee concerning the authority of its chairman, the powers and responsibilities of its subcommittees, and the composition of its staff. By the late 1970s, efforts by Senator Frank Church to restore the once unrivaled position of the Senate Foreign Relations Committee in dealing with foreign policy questions had met with only limited success.[11]

Expansion of Staff. A second change affecting Congress' ability to play a more assertive role in foreign policymaking is the expansion of legislative staff. In mid-1979, Senator William Proxmire confounded his colleagues by conferring the "Golden Fleece Award" for questionable expenditures of taxpayers' money on none other than Congress itself. In Proxmire's view, Congress had earned this distinction; the House and Senate staff had grown during the past decade from 10,700 to 18,400 people, an increase of some 70 percent. The cost of maintaining this legislative bureaucracy had climbed from $150 million to $550 million annually. Ten years earlier, the average number of staff employees for each senator was 34. By 1979, 68 employees was the average.[12]

Today, members of the House and Senate can no longer legitimately complain about staff shortages on Capitol Hill. As one study of Congress has asserted:

> Congress, in the last five years, has developed a virtual counter-State Department composed of predominantly young, experienced and aggressive experts who are out to make their own marks on the foreign policy map.[13]

A greatly expanded staff has had a twofold impact upon Congress' role in foreign affairs. A larger staff provides Congress the *means* to assert its own independent position vis-à-vis the executive branch with regard to major international questions. It also supplies national legislators with a new *incentive* to become active in a field where, during an earlier period, they often had neither the interest nor the expertise to become deeply involved.

Staff expansion has also added momentum to centrifugal tendencies within Congress itself. Hardly a committee or individual member of Congress lacks (or is unable to acquire) adequate staff assistance in dealing with international issues. As one commentator has observed, now each member of the House and Senate is better equipped than ever "to go his separate way and establish his own domain of power and prestige."[14]

Increased Participation by the House. Until the period of the Vietnam War, the House of Representatives usually played a subordinate role in the foreign policy process. Although members of the House sometimes chafed at their inferior position vis-à-vis the Senate in external policymaking, they were normally content to accept understandings worked out between executive officials and influential senators and Senate committees with jurisdiction over foreign policy questions.[15] In recent years, however, the era of passivity by the House in foreign relations has ended. As we saw in the case study on the Panama Canal treaties in Chapter 3, the House strenuously objected to being excluded from the treaty-making process.

Increased participation by the House in foreign affairs can be explained on several grounds other than mere jealousy of the Senate's constitutional prerogatives. The growing interrelationship between domestic and external problems, for example, dictates a more dynamic role by the House in diplomatic decisionmaking. As never before, Congress is called upon to enact legislation and to appropriate funds for implementing foreign policy proposals and programs. Advocates of greater House influence are convinced that it can make a vital and distinctive contribution in Congress' deliberations on international questions. Since its members must stand for election every two years, the House provides the kind of "recurrent plebiscite on the foreign policy of the United States" that no other institution of the American government can contribute.[16]

External Influences on Congress

Legislative activism in foreign affairs has not only been influenced by changes within Congress. Several new forms of external pressure have also contributed significantly to this tendency. Congressional activism has been given considerable momentum by the nature and dynamics of American public opinion, by increased lobbying efforts by interest groups, and by lobbying on the part of executive agencies. Let us examine each of these external influences on Congress in turn.

Public Opinion. Since the Wilsonian era, public opinion has emerged as an influential force affecting the course of American diplomacy. Mounting public opposition to Russian expansionism, for example, was a potent factor inducing the Truman administration to adopt the policy of containment against the Soviet Union. Conversely, a generation later, growing public disenchantment with the nation's role in Southeast Asia was crucial in the Nixon administration's decision to terminate the war in Vietnam. In both instances, legislators were instrumental in communicating the nature and force of public sentiment to executive officials.

In keeping with the idea that Congress is the most representative branch of the American government, legislators believe that viewpoints expressed in the House and Senate provide the most authoritative expression of public thinking available to the president and his advisers. The House International Relations Committee emphasized this point in a 1977 report on Congress and foreign policy:

> Congressmen, by being in continuous contact with the people and representing their disparate interests and concerns, have served not only to insure democratic control over the foreign policymaking process, but have also been the conveyors of sometimes ambivalent and occasionally vociferous public opinion.
>
> Recent events have demonstrated that without a genuine public consensus of support, the executive branch cannot legitimately and effectively pursue any foreign policy.[17]

Congress' perception of its relationship to public opinion as it bears upon foreign relations has several specific implications. Many legislators believe it is uniquely incumbent upon Congress to foster public awareness and better understanding of foreign policy issues. As the chairman of the Senate Foreign Relations Committee defined its responsibilities in 1979, the committee had an obligation to "stimulate public debate"; it was the "main forum" for promoting public discussion of external policy questions.[18]

Alternatively, some legislators believe it is the responsibility of Congress to confront executive policymakers with public sentiment concerning a particular course of action in foreign affairs. For example, in 1978, Senate Majority Leader Robert C. Byrd joined other critics on Capitol Hill in opposing the Carter administration's policies towards Southern Rhodesia, now Zimbabwe-Rhodesia. Justifying his position, Senator Byrd said, "A lot of people just doubt that the Administration is right" on the Rhodesian question.[19]

The American people do not, however, speak with a unified voice. Popular attitudes towards foreign relations since the Vietnam War have been marked by confusion, bewilderment, and contradictions. The "anti-Communist consensus" — once the cornerstone of American postwar diplomacy — has been seriously eroded. Yet, as their opposition to Soviet expansionism in Afghanistan demonstrated, the American people after the war did not eschew all interventionist behavior abroad; they were not oblivious to the security of the nation's allies and friends; nor did they lack concern about America's overall leadership position in global affairs.[20]

In all segments of American society — not excluding the executive and legislative branches of government — calls for diplomatic caution and restraint often alternate with calls for decisive initiatives abroad to counterbalance, for example, growing Soviet influence in Africa or pervasive disregard for America's diplomatic interests in the Third World. Even toward a single important issue like détente with the Soviet Union, American attitudes oscillated between approbation and fear of many of its consequences.[21] As one commentator has pointed out:

We may simply have to learn to conduct foreign policy for a very long time without a single unifying theme on which to base a broad national consensus. Both the nature of the problems abroad and their diverse impact on American public opinion at home now point strongly to such a conclusion.[22]

A national consensus is also lacking on such issues as the operations of the intelligence community and human rights practices abroad. As we noted in Chapter 6, Congress responded to the American people's apprehensions about certain questionable activities of the CIA and other members of the intelligence community. Yet as demonstrated by developments like the Iranian revolution and the discovery of a large Soviet military presence in Cuba, many legislators questioned the adequacy of American intelligence operations and called for their improvement. Congress has been extremely active in promoting human rights abroad. Yet the legislative branch, reflecting American public opinion on the issue, has consistently refused to support economic and military sanctions against South Africa, and the sanctions once favored by the White House against Zimbabwe-Rhodesia were lifted.[23]

Towards these and other issues, the public has approached major international questions since Vietnam eclectically, pragmatically, and with a good measure of common sense. As one commentator explained:

Faced with some different ideas and a changing world, Americans chose eclectically what they thought made sense and rejected what they thought didn't.... Such, then, has been the pattern of accommodation, eclecticism and shameless synthesis that the American public has demonstrated in recent years.... Exposed to new doctrines [in foreign policy], the public made careful choices.... They put their choice to one essential test: *Did it make common sense?* If it did — fine. If not — back on the shelf.[24]

Inevitably, Congress' approach to foreign policy issues is heavily colored by these dominant characteristics of American public opinion.

Lobbying by Interest Groups and Foreign Governments. While lobbying is not a new phenomenon in the nation's history, some members and former members of Congress believe that legislators have become increasingly responsive to the campaigns of well-funded and highly organized pressure groups.[25]

A number of factors have produced a favorable environment for pressure group activity in recent years: the expanding role of government in all spheres of American life; the lack of a public consensus in the United States on foreign policy issues; the decline of party identification by citizens and the weakening of party discipline on Capitol Hill; the emergence of "single issue" politics (in which one issue, like gun control or abortion, can dominate a political campaign); and the growing diffusion of power within the House and Senate. One recent study called attention to the "385 standing committees and subcommittees [of Congress] being pursued by more than 1,300 registered lobby groups." Instead of America's traditional two-party system, there now appeared to exist on Capitol Hill "a 385-party system."[26]

Lobbying by foreign governments, whose efforts are frequently supported by internal pressure groups, has also had momentous consequences for recent American foreign policy. Foreign governments have learned to appeal White House decisions in foreign affairs to the often more sympathetic legislative branch. Governments abroad now routinely ignore the once firmly established principle that the president is "the sole organ" of the nation in its relations with other countries.[27]

Many foreign governments today have a direct stake in supporting a more active and independent foreign policy role by Congress.[28] As we saw in Chapter 4, the pro-Israeli lobby has repeatedly mounted intensive campaigns to have Congress block or reverse White House decisions thought inimical to Israel. Several years later, the white-ruled government of Southern Rhodesia undertook what was described as a "high-powered lobbying campaign on Capitol Hill" designed to lift economic sanctions against it imposed by the White House.[29] And pro-Libyan groups enlisted President Carter's brother Billy as their spokesman in their attempt to influence both executive and legislative officials.

Lobbying by the Executive Branch. Lobbying by executive agencies in behalf of the president's programs and policies can be another crucial factor in determining Congress' role in the foreign policy process. Most executive agencies have one office that is primarily responsible for communicating to Congress the views of the executive branch. For example, within the State Department the "legislative liaison" function is performed by the Office of Congressional Relations. And sometimes executive agencies also form alliances with private citizens' organizations to influence attitudes both within Congress and throughout American society.[30]

A correlation exists between effective lobbying activities by the executive branch and the level of congressional activism in foreign affairs, as illustrated by the record of the Carter administration. On numerous occasions, President Carter and his advisers complained about congressionally imposed restraints upon executive management of foreign affairs. Yet no administration in modern history appeared to be less interested in generating support for White House measures on Capitol Hill, and in promoting executive-legislative cooperation in external affairs, than President Carter's. Neither the president nor most of his aides had ever held national legislative office, and events revealed that legislative liaison enjoyed very low priority in the Carter White House.

President Carter's aides were not only inexperienced in legislative relations; in some instances, their tactics in dealing with legislators generated real resentment and irritation on Capitol Hill.[31] For example, early in 1979, Defense Department officials followed the president's orders and refused to lobby in the House and Senate for a moderate increase in military spending — despite requests from pro-Carter forces on Capitol Hill that this move was essential in gaining Senate support for the SALT II arms control agreement with the Soviet Union.[32] As a result of prodding by members of Congress — and developments in Iran and Afghanistan — the Carter administration eventually agreed to a considerable increase in American defense spending, and by 1980 relations with Congress had improved.

The failure of a president and his subordinates to engage in effective legislative liaison activities produces a condition tailor-made for legislative diplomatic activism. It assures not only that Congress will exert its viewpoints and prerogatives forcefully in the foreign policy process; it also virtually guarantees that congressional efforts will be episodic, uncoordinated, and inconsistent.

Leadership Failure in the White House

A deep-seated anxiety exists on Capitol Hill and among many segments of the American public that the influence of the United States abroad has declined in recent years.[33] This deterioration has been attributed by many critics to failure by the executive branch to provide wise and effective leadership in foreign relations.

Advocates of a more forceful congressional role in external affairs have brought two somewhat contradictory indictments against recent chief executives. Presidents Johnson and Nixon were denounced for *using* the vast powers of the presidency in behalf of ill-conceived foreign policy ventures, as in the Vietnam conflict. By contrast, Presidents Ford and Carter have been criticized widely for *failing to use* the powers at their command to respond forcefully and successfully to external challenges, such as the Soviet Union's troop buildup in Cuba and its invasion of Afghanistan. In both cases, critics believe that a precipitous decline in American power and influence abroad has resulted.

Who is to blame for the erosion of American power overseas? Since the period of the Vietnam War, few legislators have been in doubt about the answer: the president and his advisers in the executive branch. A succession of chief executives led the United States into the Vietnam morass — at a cost of some 360,000 American casualties and untold billions of dollars in direct and indirect expenditures. The Nixon administration prolonged the conflict long after the outcome of the war had been determined. The ensuing collapse of the government in South Vietnam, and North Vietnam's subsequent attempt to impose its hegemony throughout Southeast Asia, conveyed a regional and global impression of American weakness.

After the American ambassador to Afghanistan was killed early in 1979, one reporter found a pervasive belief on Capitol Hill that the White House had not been "firm enough in publicly defending American interests" overseas. The opinion of the Senate Minority Leader Howard

Baker of Tennessee was perhaps not untypical. Americans, Baker contended, were tired of being "pushed around" by other countries. They wanted the president "to be firmer, more consistent, a little less smiling, and Mr. Nice Guy." Baker and other Republicans accused the Carter administration of "presiding over the decay of American influence and the decline of American military power."[34]

With the 1980 national elections approaching, such reactions from members of the political opposition were perhaps predictable and tinged with self-interest. Yet basically the same sentiments were being expressed among members of the president's own party inside and outside Congress.

Late in 1979, the Senate Foreign Relations Committee, after prolonged investigations, approved the SALT II arms limitation treaty with the Soviet Union — but made its consent contingent upon a significant increase (as much as $40 billion in the next five years) in American defense spending.[35] Senator Frank Church, Chairman of the Senate Foreign Relations Committee, spearheaded a move to link ratification of SALT II with the removal of Soviet military forces from Cuba. At a minimum, Church demanded further assurances from the White House that Soviet forces were "not engaged in a combat role" and did not endanger hemispheric security. Senate Majority Leader Byrd insisted on providing the opportunity for a long list of other senators to serve as cosponsors of this popular measure.[36] As debate on SALT II and on the new Panama Canal treaties demonstrated, legislators want to be able to claim credit for protecting the security and diplomatic interests of the United States, particularly when they believe it is being neglected by the president.

Divisions within the executive branch have invited strong legislative initiatives in foreign affairs. As one American political commentator lamented:

> The misconduct of foreign affairs in the United States has lately become something of an international scandal. You can seldom pick up a newspaper these days without reading about some self-appointed Secretary of State who is embarrassing the country.[37]

President Carter's secretary of state, his chief national security adviser, and his special envoy to the Middle East all held different views on the appropriate steps to be taken in resolving the Arab-Israeli conflict. In other instances, members of the White House staff, the State Department, and the Defense Department have given conflicting assessments of the implications of détente for the United States. These and other examples of continuing, and often serious, intraexecutive conflicts must be included among the major causes of legislative activism in foreign relations.

Insofar as fundamental policy disagreements and bureaucratic infighting among executive officials weaken the president's leadership position, Congress is irresistibly tempted to fill the ensuing vacuum. Moreover, disunity within the executive branch is bound to exacerbate the problem of disunity within Congress itself in approaching diplomatic questions.

Late in 1979, one of President John F. Kennedy's former White House aides, Theodore C. Sorensen, made an earnest appeal to President Carter to "regain control" over the foreign policy machinery. In Sorensen's view:

> Effective control over the conduct of foreign affairs is slipping away from Jimmy Carter, and that is sad to see . . . because a coherent and effective American foreign policy requires Presidential leadership.[38]

Recent experience has shown that unless and until a unified foreign policy approach is supplied by the chief executive, the diplomacy of the United States will be marked by drift, ineffectualness, and the decline of national power abroad.

CONGRESSIONAL ASSERTIVENESS: CONSEQUENCES AND IMPLICATIONS

What impact has a more assertive and independent diplomatic role by Congress had upon American foreign policy? What have been its consequences — both positive and negative — upon the conduct of foreign relations by the United States? These questions will be examined in the light of our case studies and of other examples of Congress' recent dynamism in the foreign policy field.

Independent Legislative Initiatives

Until the period of the Vietnam War, it was a clearly established principle that negotiations with foreign governments were an executive prerogative. For example, longstanding precedent supports the view that the president or his designated agent "makes" or negotiates treaties with other governments. One of the earliest enactments of Congress was the Logan Act, which prohibits certain unauthorized negotiations between Americans and foreign officials. Although such contacts today have become frequent — and no citizen has ever been prosecuted for violating its terms — the Logan Act remains the law of the land.[39]

In practice, from the period of World War II until the 1970s, legislators were frequently involved in the conduct of diplomatic negotiations — but nearly always at the invitation of the president. Today, the appointment of legislators as members of American negotiating teams is an accepted technique for creating bipartisan support for the nation's foreign policy. In the spring of 1979, the Carter administration attempted to win widespread congressional support for the proposed SALT II agreements with the Soviet Union by allowing "26 Senators, 14 Republicans and 12 Democrats, including opponents and critics, and 46

members of the House of Representatives, to sit in on the arms negotiations in Geneva."[40]

The novel feature of Congress' involvement in diplomatic negotiations today is the tendency of legislators to engage in them *independently* — without White House approval, and sometimes in the face of
presidential opposition. In 1979, Senator Jesse Helms, a member of the
Senate Foreign Relations Committee, sent two staff members to London
to participate participate directly in diplomatic discussions designed to
end the longstanding civil conflict in Zimbabwe-Rhodesia. Senator
Helms' justification was candid: "I don't trust the State Department on
this issue."[41]

Another newsworthy example of Congress' direct intervention in
foreign relations occurred after Iranian students seized the American
embassy in Tehran on November 4, 1979, and held some 50 Americans
hostage. After early White House efforts to gain the release of the hostages failed, Representative George Hansen, R-Idaho, undertook his own
self-appointed peace mission to Iran, where he visited the hostages and
sought to obtain their release. Hansen's efforts also failed, and his unauthorized negotiations during the crisis were criticized by executive
and legislative officials alike, who feared his initiatives would under-
mine the president's authority and would provide evidence of disunity
within the American government during the crisis.[42]

Independent diplomatic efforts by Helms, Hansen, and other members of Congress appear to have established the precedent that legislators may now engage in the negotiating process freely. Perhaps legislators do so on the theory that — in the absence of overt White House
objection — they have the president's tacit approval. In any case, the
practice is bound to raise questions abroad about who is ultimately in
charge of American foreign policy and about how durable agreements
reached with a variety of American officials are likely to be.

The recognition of other governments is another area — long regarded as an executive province — into which Congress has intruded
during the past decade. Early in 1979, several senators attempted to
make President Carter's decision to recognize the People's Republic of
China (PRC) contingent upon Peking's pledge not to use force in exerting its longstanding claim to sovereignty over Taiwan. In effect, these
legislators wanted to threaten the PRC with withdrawal of American
recognition if it attempted to seize Taiwan by force.[43] While the president and his advisers were mindful of congressional concern about the
future of Taiwan, they were unwilling to condition American recognition
upon the PRC's behavior in the matter.

Another recent example of independent congressional initatives involves Zimbabwe-Rhodesia. Several members of the Senate Foreign
Relations Committee proposed sending a team of private citizens, chosen by the committee, to observe forthcoming elections in that country
— an unusual step designed to compel the White House to recognize a

new, politically moderate regime that might supersede the incumbent white-dominated government. Executive officials opposed this congressional initiative on the grounds that it encroached upon the president's traditional diplomatic prerogatives and because it was an evident attempt by some legislators to divert American foreign policy in Africa away from closer identification with revolutionary movements.[44]

Expansion of Treaty-making Role

As we noted in Chapter 2, the Senate has relied upon its constitutional prerogatives in the treaty-making process to assert its influence in the diplomatic field, and the House has sought to use other prerogatives (like its dominant role in the appropriations process) to compensate for the Senate's constitutionally unique position. Several significant aspects of congressional involvement in the negotiation and ratification of treaties have come to the fore in recent years. In contrast to the early postwar period, the Senate has shown that it is determined to construe its role in the treaty process actively.

Two examples during the 1970s — the new Panama Canal treaties and the SALT II arms limitation accords — are cases in point. In both instances, Senate deliberations on these agreements were prolonged, thorough, and in the end extremely influential. Insofar as these cases provide a reliable guide to Senate action in the future, foreign governments must now come to terms with the fact that the era of pro forma Senate participation in treaty-making has ended. International agreements reached with executive officials may be — and for important international accords, they likely will be — changed to reflect Senate viewpoints.

The normalization of relations between the United States and the People's Republic of China led to another novel interpretation of the Senate's prerogatives in treaty-making: senatorial insistence that the existing American defense treaty with Taiwan (the Republic of China) could only be terminated with congressional approval. In a case initiated by some 25 senators, a United States district court ruled late in 1979 that President Carter's scheduled termination of the Taiwan defense pact was unconstitutional, since no provision existed for legislative participation in the decision. A few weeks later, however, this decision was overruled by a United States court of appeals, whose finding was ultimately sustained by the Supreme Court. In keeping with judicial precedents on foreign policy questions, the Supreme Court again reaffirmed the president's pre-eminent position as the official spokesman for the United States in foreign affairs.[45]

The Pattern of Overseas Commitments

Since World War II, Congress has been determined to play a more influential role in the assumption and maintenance of America's overseas commitments. Has there been a consistent pattern of legislative activity concerning these overseas obligations? For the most part, the answer is no. Congress has curtailed some of them; it has expanded others; and it has maintained still other international commitments largely intact. Most importantly, Congress has insisted far more adamantly than ever before that the nation's international obligations be made a matter of public record.

First, let us examine overseas commitments that have been cut or curtailed by Congress since the late 1960s. The Vietnam War was terminated by act of Congress (although in the Nixon administration's view, that process had already begun before Congress directed it). In the ensuing years, adverse congressional sentiment blocked the White House from extending foreign aid to North Vietnam.

By enacting the War Powers Resolution in 1973, Congress imposed several new limitations upon the authority of the chief executive to use the armed forces; yet, as we saw in Chapter 5, congressional enforcement of the terms of the War Powers Resolution has been less than stringent. Towards Angola, Congress denied the White House authority to use military force and to carry on covert intelligence operations. And in several foreign countries with repressive governments that jeopardized the rights of their citizens, Congress has — or threatened to — cut off American aid and trade.

The limitations imposed by Congress upon the president's management of foreign affairs, however, are a two-way street. Beginning with the Johnson administration, every chief executive has complained about congressionally imposed restrictions upon presidential freedom of action in foreign relations. President Nixon and his national security adviser, Henry Kissinger, were persuaded that — except for congressional interference in the conduct of the Vietnam War — executive policymakers could have obtained a much more advantageous settlement of the conflict.[46]

On other occasions, however, executive policymakers have found actual or potential congressional restraints upon their freedom of action diplomatically useful. Former Secretary of State Kissinger has recounted several instances in which the president and his advisers used the threat of a severe congressional reduction in America's overseas commitments as a diplomatic gambit in negotiating with foreign governments. And the Nixon administration repeatedly informed the NATO allies that unless they increased their contribution to the defense of Western Europe, Congress would almost certainly reduce America's troop contribution to NATO.[47]

Since the Vietnam War, congressional activism in foreign affairs has not infrequently taken the opposite course: expansion of the nation's overseas obligations. Congress has accepted most military base agreements negotiated by executive officials with foreign countries. It did not block efforts by the White House to augment American military power in the Indian Ocean area. Nor were there significant congressional objections to American fleet movements off the Arabian peninsula, in an evident attempt by the White House to demonstrate Washington's support for friendly regimes in the Middle East. Similarly, Congress has made unequivocally clear its opposition to any reduction of American combat forces in South Korea.

By 1980 — after the seizure of the American embassy in Iran and the Soviet Union's massive military incursion into neighboring Afghanistan — support was evident on Capitol Hill for the acquisition of new naval bases in the Persian Gulf, along with the creation of a powerful military strike force capable of protecting American defense and security interests in foreign settings.

Congress has also maintained largely intact a number of long-standing American overseas commitments. While the funds provided for the purpose vary from year to year, Congress continues to appropriate funds for the foreign economic and military aid programs of the United States. Although the level of American economic assistance, as a percentage of the nation's gross national product, has declined in recent years, needy countries can continue to rely upon the United States to make a significant contribution in meeting their foreign assistance requirements. Similarly, America's allies abroad can usually depend upon the availability of arms aid and training programs to strengthen their security.

For several years, the House and Senate have resisted moves to reduce the number of troops America supplies to NATO. Moreover, despite sporadic criticisms of the United Nations in Congress, both chambers continue to support American membership in the U.N. and to provide a substantial portion of the funds required for the operations of U.N. agencies.

Congressional insistence that the formal and informal overseas obligations of the United States be reported to Congress and made a matter of public record must be reckoned among the more notable results of legislative activism in foreign affairs. Prolonged legislative deliberations on the new Panama Canal treaties, for example, raised public consciousness and helped produce favorable public sentiment in behalf of the agreements. On one of the most sensitive questions in executive-legislative relations — the president's use of the armed forces for diplomatic ends — Congress has demanded both that it be kept informed of White House actions and that it have an influential voice in the long-term disposition of troops abroad.

Both by law and by executive order, intelligence agencies must now report more fully than in the past to committees of Congress on their operations. Owing in no small measure to congressional initiatives, contemporary American foreign policy is governed now, more than in any previous era of history, by the Wilsonian principle of "open convenants, openly arrived at." Henry Kissinger's visit to the Chinese mainland in 1971 on behalf of the Nixon administration was remarkable, not only because it inaugurated the new era of rapprochement in Sino-American relations, but because it was a diplomatic initiative by the executive branch that was kept secret, for several months, from Congress.[48]

To the degree that a better informed Congress and citizenry provide a more secure foundation for effective diplomacy, legislative insistence upon maximum publicity for international commitments has clearly been a gain. The Vietnam War experience demonstrated convincingly that public support is indispensable for military and diplomatic success abroad.

Problems with Congressional Policymaking

Although Congress has adopted a more assertive role in foreign affairs, it may be doubted that the nature of congressional decisionmaking lends itself to effective foreign policy management. A former State Department official has called legislative power in foreign policy a "blunt instrument," which not infrequently has resulted in "a series of uncoordinated actions that annoyed the Secretary of State more than it advanced coherent policy." On some occasions, legislators have threatened to paralyze American foreign policy unless the White House abandoned or changed a proposed course of action.[49] According to some of President Carter's aides:

> Congress ties the President's hands on foreign policy, scrutinizing and criticizing every move he makes, sometimes jeopardizing relations with our allies and unpredictable foes.[50]

Even individuals with legislative experience have expressed concern about Congress' intrusion into the foreign policy field. "I confess to increasingly serious misgivings about the ability of the Congress to play a constructive role in our foreign relations," said former Senate Foreign Relations Committee Chairman J. William Fulbright. Fulbright added, ". . . those of us who prodded what seemed to be a hopelessly immobile herd of cattle [Congress] a decade ago, now stand back in awe in the face of a stampede."[51] Other legislators have expressed similar apprehensions. When a young, liberal senator was asked what he expected Congress to be accomplishing in foreign affairs, he replied, "We're going to find some way to foul up foreign policy."[52]

Unquestionably, Congress possesses the ability to "foul up foreign policy." The nation's recent diplomatic record provides several examples. Prolonged opposition to the new Panama Canal treaties in the House of Representatives raised questions at home and abroad about the constancy and unity of American foreign policy. The congressional response to the discovery in August 1979 of a large contingent of Soviet troops in Cuba was equally confusing and ambiguous.[53] One national news journal concluded that the Kremlin was "notoriously loath to let

U.S. Senators beat them with sticks" on the Cuban question. Mishandling of the whole affair in Washington, the article concluded:

> ... not only casts still more doubt on the leadership of the Carter administration but also raises a longer-term and more disturbing question about whether the Congress — recently so assertive about playing a bigger role in foreign policy — can help solve crises rather than manufacturing and aggravating them.[54]

Congress often approaches external policymaking as an exercise in lawmaking, and that may be one reason why its assertive role in foreign affairs has not always been productive. According to a former State Department official, by the end of the 1970s Congress had imposed "more than 150 statutory limitations on the United States' relations with foreign countries." Commenting on the congressional tendency to envision diplomatic questions in legal terms or as legal contests, he added:

> ... foreign policy has become almost synonymous with lawmaking. The result is to place a straitjacket of legislation around the manifold complexity of our relations with other nations.[55]

By contrast, success in diplomacy nearly always requires skills sometimes not found in lawmakers, such as understanding the point of view of other countries, flexibility in bargaining, secrecy, and ambiguity.

Although an advocate of bipartisan executive-legislative collaboration in foreign affairs, Senator Arthur Vandenberg was also concerned about some of the implications of Congress' forceful intrusion into the foreign policy field. On one occasion he warned:

> I think the Senate is entitled, at any time it pleases, to ... tell the Executive what it thinks concerning foreign affairs. But I think it would be a tragic and unfortunate thing if the habit ever became general or too contagious. ...[56]

Implicit in Vandenberg's admonition is a distinction, although somewhat ill-defined, between an expanded legislative voice in *policy formulation* and in the *conduct or execution* of foreign affairs. The former is a province in which Congress can and should participate. The day-to-day management of foreign relations, however, is another matter. This is not a realm into which the legislative branch should intrude regularly, nor is it really equipped to do so. Nevertheless, as one study pointed out, Congress has appeared "determined to play havoc with policy implementation."[57]

Foreigners have always found unique and bewildering the American system of separation of powers among three coordinate branches of government. But in no previous era has the foreign policy process in the United States perhaps proved so mystifying and frustrating for outsiders. Recent diplomatic experience has shown that agreement with the administration, even when the president's party controls Congress, often counts for little. After arriving at understandings with executive officials, foreign negotiators often have "to enter into separate external relations with the American Congress, and renegotiate . . . the agreement reached."[58]

Most governments endeavor to arrive at a unified foreign policy position *before* they enter into negotiations with other states. In the United States, however, a unified position among policymakers is often arrived at only *after* understandings have been reached with foreign governments. One Soviet spokesman recently asked: "With whom in America can we have dealings?" For foreign officials, it is "still not clear who exactly in the U.S. can speak in international relations on behalf of the United States."[59]

CONGRESSIONAL ASSERTIVENESS: PROBABILITIES AND PROSPECTS

What is the future of congressional assertiveness in American foreign relations? Has it become a permanent feature of the foreign policy process in the United States, or is it merely a phase that will be followed in time by a new era of executive dominance in external affairs? A number of diverse and contrary factors will determine the answers to these questions in the years ahead.

Factors Favoring Expanded Role

A persuasive case can be made for the contention that Congress will continue to exercise a powerful — and in some instances a decisive — voice in foreign affairs for the indefinite future. Executive officials, foreign governments, and the public must come to terms with this possibility.

Global and Domestic Setting. Among the forces engendering and sustaining an energetic role by Congress in foreign affairs, none is perhaps more important than the changing nature of the "global agenda." In the second half of the twentieth century, unique and often extremely difficult issues have come to the forefront of international concern — global economic stability, the pressing needs of the less developed societies, the increasingly acute world food shortage, runaway population growth throughout most of the Third World, and worldwide environmental problems. Today, the solution to these major international and regional problems requires active participation by Congress.

In the United States and in most other countries since World War II, the role of government has expanded to meet these challenges. This trend is both exemplified and sustained by the volume of legislation produced by Congress in the postwar era. One way of looking at Congress' diplomatic activism, therefore, is to say that the legislative branch is finally taking the same approach in dealing with external affairs that it has taken toward domestic issues since the New Deal; Congress is attempting to solve major public policy questions by enacting legislation and by relying upon other powers incident to lawmaking, such as its oversight function.

The assertiveness of the House and Senate in foreign relations can also be attributed to the American cultural milieu within which Congress operates. Since the early 1960s, sweeping changes have occurred in American life styles, in traditional modes of thought, and in behavior norms. On all fronts, customs and long-established practices have been challenged.[60] Perhaps more in the political realm than in other sectors of American life, established authority has come under attack. Demands are heard on all sides that political decisionmaking be made more democratic. And American voters today are more independent, often refusing to identify themselves with either major political party.

In the post-Vietnam War period, there is a deep-seated feeling of disillusionment and skepticism about the results achieved in domestic and foreign affairs by the nation's leaders. In this milieu, the possibility of a fundamentally different approach to foreign relations — with Congress playing a decisive role in the process — finds many advocates on Capitol Hill and throughout the nation as a whole.

Executive Encouragement. As much out of necessity as conviction perhaps, executive officials today frequently support a more dynamic and meaningful role by Congress in foreign relations. The president, the secretary of state, and other high-ranking executive officials at times have called upon legislative officials to join them in creating a unified approach to foreign policy issues.[61]

Moreover, the attitude of executive officials toward congressional activism in foreign affairs is often highly variable and eclectic. While executive officials routinely complain about congressional restrictions upon the president's authority, in particular instances they have favored forceful legislative intrusion in the diplomatic arena.

Early in 1979, Frank Church, the chairman of the Senate Foreign Relations Committee, bluntly notified officials of Saudi Arabia that the United States expected their diplomatic support in its efforts to resolve the Arab-Israeli conflict. Church informed the Saudi government — apparently with the full encouragement of executive officials — that unless the Saudis supported U.S. efforts, there would be a major congressional review of American foreign policy toward the Middle East. (For several months, State Department officials had been reluctant to convey such a warning directly to Saudi Arabia.)[62]

An even more dramatic example of executive encouragement of congressional activism was provided by former National Security Adviser and Secretary of State Henry Kissinger when he testified before the Senate Foreign Relations Committee in July 1979 on the SALT II strategic armaments agreements. Kissinger encouraged what one commentator called "congressional forays into the foreign-affairs power of the executive" by urging the Senate to make ratification of the accords contingent upon a significant increase in American defense spending — a move not favored by the White House at that time.[63]

Congress' Accomplishments. The positive results Congress has achieved in foreign policy are another factor that has sustained congressional activism in foreign affairs and may continue to do so in the years ahead. Advocates of a more forceful and independent legislative role in foreign affairs believe Congress' track record is good. They are convinced that Congress extricated the nation from the Vietnam War and, by enacting the War Powers Resolution in 1973, decreased the likelihood of future Vietnams to mar the nation's diplomatic record. Similarly, it was the Senate that protected American security interests by insisting upon changes in the Panama Canal treaties as negotiated by the executive branch. Owing in large part to Congress' efforts, the American intelligence community is now under tighter control, and respect for human rights by other governments has been promoted abroad.

Congress' accomplishments can also be viewed in more general terms. First, Congress has helped reverse the trend toward virtually unchecked executive authority in the field of foreign relations by insisting that major diplomatic undertakings since the Vietnam War be considered and supported by the executive and legislative branches of the government.

Second, congressional influence has been a potent force in changing the direction of American diplomacy. It has reversed America's tendency toward overcommitment abroad, and it has taken steps to prevent a recurrence of this pattern in the future. Through a variety of means, Congress has compelled the White House to become more discriminating and selective in the assumption of overseas responsibilities.

Third, Congress has broadened the base of foreign policymaking by demanding that legislative and public opinion be brought to bear early in the stage of policy formulation — not merely (as in the Vietnam War) after diplomatic defeats have been sustained. Moreover, as illustrated by continuing legislative oversight of intelligence activities and of executive efforts to promote human rights abroad, Congress has successfully demanded that public opinion play a continuing role in the evolution and periodic re-examination of the nation's diplomatic record. Such consultation is vital in assuring that American foreign policy possesses the kind of legitimacy required for its continued public support and its compatibility with underlying American values.

Factors Favoring Restraint

A number of short-run and long-term factors, however, point to restraint and possibly a reversal in the pattern of legislative activism witnessed since the Vietnam War. Initially, we need to be reminded that a forceful and independent role in foreign affairs by legislative bodies is a distinctive phenomenon among modern governments, confined almost entirely to the American system. In nearly all other countries, the tide has been running strongly in the contrary direction; other national legislatures have steadily lost the power to act independently, especially in the foreign policy field.

In Great Britain, France, West Germany, Japan, and other democracies today, the responsibility for managing foreign affairs is vested almost solely with executive officials. In the rare cases when the legislative body does successfully challenge the incumbent government's foreign policy, a political crisis (followed by new national elections) normally ensues. The experience of many countries suggests that the successful conduct of foreign relations inherently militates against a high degree of legislative activism and independence.

Cycles in Diplomatic History. Moreover, the forceful assertion of Congress' powers in foreign relations has been a cyclical occurrence in the nation's diplomatic experience. The "War Hawks of 1812" who demanded and got another war with Great Britain had many members on Capitol Hill. Following the end of the Mexican War in 1848, Congress once more asserted its influence dynamically in foreign affairs. And the period before and after World War I marked another era of congressional assertiveness.

The cyclical nature of Congress' diplomatic militancy — and of the ensuing struggle between executive and legislative officials for primacy in foreign affairs — may be explained in various ways. No single existing theory adequately accounts for it. To some extent, congressional assertiveness in foreign relations may be related to the oscillating isolationist and interventionist moods of the American people toward international affairs.[64]

Alternatively, it may be a function of the political balance between the executive and legislative branches and of the shifting political tides within the American society. For reasons that are even now difficult to explain satisfactorily, the zenith of bipartisan cooperation in foreign affairs in the postwar era was reached under the Truman and early Eisenhower administrations — when the presidency and Congress were controlled by different political parties. President Truman had much greater success in arriving at a constructive working relationship with a Republican-controlled Congress on foreign policy than President Carter experienced with a House and Senate controlled by his own political party![65]

Problems with Executive-Legislative Consultation. The nature of consultation between policymakers in the executive and legislative branches of government is a significant factor in determining the outcome of efforts to achieve constructive bipartisan collaboration on major foreign policy issues. Yet, as the discussion of consultation in Chapter 5 noted, there is the problem of when to consult — before or after the president has decided upon a particular diplomatic course of action. There is the additional question of which members of congress should be included in such discussion and of deciding who really represents Congress and can arrive at understandings in its name.

Even if the problems of when and whom to consult can be solved, a third serious inhibition upon successful executive-legislative consultation remains. What responsibility do members of Congress incur by participating in consultation on foreign policy issues? Does a policy decision resulting from such consultations become "their" decision, fully as much as the president's?

More specifically, does concurrence in a particular intelligence mission by selected members of the House and Senate make Congress as a whole responsible for its success or failure? Does a president's consultation with a selected group of legislators, in adherence to the terms of the War Powers Resolution, make Congress equally responsible with the executive branch when American military forces are used for diplomatic objectives?

If the answer to such questions is yes, how can this be reconciled with Congress' traditional role as a critic of executive policies, especially when they miscarry? Alternatively, if the answer is no, what inducement does an incumbent president have to consult legislators on particular diplomatic questions, when they refuse to share with executive officials responsibility for the outcome of a proposed policy?

The success or failure of executive-legislative consultation may also be determined by individual personalities. During the late 1940s, Secretary of State Dean Acheson and other executive officials worked harmoniously and effectively with influential legislators like Senator Arthur H. Vandenberg and Tom Connally to formulate diplomatic undertakings (such as the Marshall Plan) acceptable to the White House and Congress. Although these officials often belonged to different political parties, an atmosphere of mutual trust and respect governed their deliberations. Agreements reached between them nearly always were subsequently supported by majorities in the House and Senate.[66]

By contrast, during the Johnson administration, legislative and executive officials were often far from agreement on foreign policy issues. Senator J. William Fulbright outspokenly criticized White House policies toward Vietnam, the Dominican Republic, and other areas. The animosity and distrust that existed between Johnson and the Senate Foreign Relations Committee chairman served as a major deterrent to constructive executive-legislative relations in the foreign policy field.

Public Attitudes towards President and Congress. "Capacity in government," one informed student of the American system has said, "depends, in the United States as elsewhere, on leadership."[67] By the beginning of the 1980s, the American people's desire for clear and firm White House leadership in meeting the nation's internal and external problems was unmistakable. Surveys of public opinion also revealed genuine concern among citizens about the apparent deadlock between the president and Congress in dealing with urgent national issues.[68] In the public mind, the president was expected to exert leadership on Capitol Hill and to use the powers of his office to impose unity upon a divided government.[69]

Even congressional voices were heard in the chorus calling upon the chief executive to exhibit forceful and dynamic diplomatic leadership. Senator Adlai Stevenson, D-Ill., declared that in recent years, Congress had excelled at the game of "kick the President" — perhaps an understandable reaction on Capitol Hill to abuses of presidential power. Yet, Stevenson informed his colleagues, Congress' weaknesses "will come back to haunt us. I want a strong executive."[70]

A resurgence of executive authority rather than congressional militancy in foreign affairs may be the wave of the future. According to one interpretation, a factor likely to restrain Congress is that both the political "left and right want a strong Presidency, the left in domestic affairs, the right for foreign policy." This study of contemporary executive-legislative relations concluded:

> ... Americans not only prefer Presidential leadership but the scope of foreign and domestic problems and the recurrent emergencies facing a world power simply demand Presidential power — particularly when Congress' foreign policy decisions are so often governed by domestic policies.[71]

Or, as another study of public attitudes expressed it, for most Americans the presidency is "everyone's first resort." Realistically or not, the American people expect the chief executive to be forthright and successful in solving national problems, and they complain vocally about the lack of White House leadership when this does not happen.[72]

The celebrated American comedian Will Rogers once told his audiences, "There's good news from Washington. Congress is adjourned." Such humor always strikes a responsive chord with Americans, for whom the denigration of Congress' deeds and misdeeds sometimes seems a national pastime.[73]

Today, as in the past, the American people are aware that Congress' record has been badly tarnished. "Influence peddling" on Capitol Hill, misuse of campaign contributions, scandalous personal behavior by legislators, and the obstructionist moves by Congress in dealing with national policy issues have become public knowledge. Legislators can be energetic and decisive in dealing with executive wrongdoing, but dilatory and ineffectual in correcting unethical practices, illegal activities, and organizational problems on Capitol Hill.

Public confidence in Congress' performance has fallen steadily in recent years. One poll in 1974 showed that almost half of the American people approved the way Congress was doing its job. By mid-1979, this figure had declined to 19 percent. According to another study of public attitudes, twice as many Americans blamed Congress, as blamed President Carter, for deadlocks between the two branches of the government. The dominant reaction of Americans was that Carter had been "victimized" by the failure of Congress to cooperate with him in solving urgent national problems.[74]

Public attitudes towards national institutions will unquestionably influence Congress' future foreign policy role. Events like the Vietnam War and the threatened impeachment of President Nixon diminished public confidence in the executive branch and aroused deep public concerns about the "imperial presidency." These anxieties did not, however, fundamentally alter the people's confidence in the American constitutional system, nor did they in the long run modify the traditional demand by citizens for dynamic White House leadership. Popular apprehensions about the abuses of presidential power did not automatically translate into heightened public confidence in Congress' performance or leadership potential. Implicit in public criticism of President Carter's lack of leadership was the twofold demand that the White House take charge of the governmental machinery, and that the president exercise more leadership in dealing with Congress to produce unified and effective policies and programs.

Public and Congressional Domestic Concerns. Another factor restraining congressional activism in foreign policy is the low level of public interest in international questions. This has been true of the American society historically. It was a major force, for example, sustaining the "isolationist" approach to foreign relations, and it is no less the case in the contemporary period. Almost invariably, on any list of the dominant concerns of the American people, pollsters have found that internal problems are given highest priority by citizens. Only some 15 percent of the people belong to the "attentive public" — or that minority of opinion which is reasonably interested in, and informed about, foreign relations.[75] The behavior of Congress is inescapably affected by this public opinion trait.

This leads to another closely related factor likely to inhibit a dynamic and sustained role by Congress in the diplomatic field. Constituency-related business ranks as a primary claim upon the time and energies of most legislators. Even with a greatly enlarged staff, most legislators today are hard pressed to meet the diverse demands made upon them by their constituents.[76]

As several of our case studies emphasized, relatively few legislators have the time to acquire expert knowledge of a broad range of complex foreign policy questions. Only a minority of legislators has shown any real desire to receive, and to assimilate, detailed information about the activities of intelligence agencies — although they are legally entitled to it. Similiarly, few legislators are inclined to read and digest voluminous reports from executive officials regarding human rights problems in approximately 150 independent nations.

The high priority accorded to domestic concerns by the American people and their legislative representatives has two specific consequences. First, perhaps even more today than in the past, Congress' approach to foreign affairs is heavily colored by local and domestic considerations vis-à-vis a commitment to the national interest. Late in 1979, one of the nation's most experienced reporters characterized the foreign policy process in the United States in such terms as "chaos" and "an international scandal." To a considerable degree, he blamed Congress for this state of affairs:

> Seldom in memory has it seemed so divided, so concerned with personal, local or state interests and so indifferent to its own Congressional leadership or the disturbing problems of the 1980s.[77]

Second, Congress' involvement in external affairs is likely to be characterized by a short attention span and to be heavily conditioned by the current newsworthiness of a particular foreign policy issue. As our discussion in Chapter 6 illustrated, members of the House and Senate were actively concerned for a time about various misdeeds of the CIA. After a relatively brief period, however, the attention of most legislators had shifted to other issues, leaving only a handful of senators and representatives to monitor intelligence activities on a continuing basis. Summing up a conversation about attempts by Congress to restore its powers, one senator characteristically exclaimed, "I think we've made substantial headlines — I mean headway."[78]

Invitation to Struggle

From the time of George Washington's administration until the present day, the president and Congress have vied for control over foreign relations. And the lively interaction between Congress and the president — the major theme of our study — will continue to be a dominant feature of the American foreign policy process in the future. During some periods (the era from World War II until the closing stage of the Vietnam War), executive authority in the foreign policy sphere has been pre-eminent. In other periods (during the 1930s and the 1970s), the congressional voice has been louder and more decisive.

Continuation of this institutional rivalry in foreign affairs seems assured by two fundamental conditions: the provisions of the United States Constitution and the obligations inherent in America's role as a superpower in a complex and unstable international system. Although many formal and informal changes have been made in the Constitution since 1789, the basic pattern of divided responsibility and power in foreign affairs remains unaltered. The president still serves as commander in chief of the nation's armed forces; he alone has the power to recognize other governments; and only the chief executive and his agents can officially negotiate treaties and agreements with other countries in the name of the United States.

After two centuries, Congress also retains influential prerogatives in national security and foreign affairs. The size and nature of the American military establishment are determined by Congress; funds for current military operations and for the development of new weapons must be provided by the legislative branch. In addition, Congress must authorize and appropriate funds for a host of other programs and governmental activities in the foreign policy field — ranging from the State Department budget, to foreign military and economic aid programs, to the activities of intelligence agencies. Also implicit in Congress' lawmaking function is its power to investigate the operations of executive agencies and the administration of programs it has authorized and funded — a power the House and Senate have used with telling effect on numerous occasions since World War II.

The nature of the contemporary international system also provides incentives for the executive and legislative branches to use their respective powers vigorously in the foreign policy field. Since World War II, the United States has been — and all indications are that it will indefinitely remain — one of the two superpowers in world affairs. As a superpower, the United States has certain inescapable and continuing global responsibilities, and discharging them nearly always requires policies and programs involving participation by executive and legislative officials.

During the closing months of the 1970s, Iran held some 50 Americans hostage in Tehran; the Soviet Union launched a massive military incursion into Afghanistan; and the oil-producing states of the Middle East announced another major increase in the price of this vital commodity. These recent events point to a larger phenomenon: ongoing political upheaval in what is sometimes called the "arc of crisis" or the zone extending from East Africa, through the Arabian peninsula, and curving northeastward through the Persian Gulf area to the borders of India. In this volatile region, the security and diplomatic interests of the United States will assuredly be challenged in the years ahead. From the available evidence, the "arc of crisis" could easily emerge as a zone of highest American diplomatic priority.

If the United States is to use its power and influence to preserve a minimum degree of peace and stability in this area — and to date, its efforts have been less than outstandingly successful — a more effective American strategy is needed. It might include deeper public and official insight into the Islamic culture; military and economic assistance programs; continued progress in resolving the Arab-Israeli conflict; reduced American vulnerability to the threat of an oil boycott by Middle East producers; and the acquisition of new military bases and naval installations in the region, along with the creation of a mobile and combat-ready military "strike force" capable of projecting the nation's military power in crisis situations.

Continuing Disunity in the Policy Process. Since the Vietnam conflict, the executive and legislative branches of the American government have faced comparable problems with respect to their role in the foreign policy process. Stated negatively, the efforts of both branches have often been seriously weakened by the schisms, organizational rivalries, and centrifugal forces impairing their internal cohesion and their ability to arrive at unified positions on major diplomatic issues. Stated positively, policymakers at opposite ends of Pennsylvania Avenue have important and distinctive contributions to make to the American foreign policy process, greater recognition of which ought to guide their diplomatic deliberations.

Our discussion in Chapter 1 called attention to the fact that within the executive branch the traditional authority and premier position of the State Department in the diplomatic field has been steadily diluted by the proliferation of executive agencies playing a major or minor role in contemporary American foreign policy. Since the Nixon administration particularly — with the emergence of the president's national security adviser as a rival to the secretary of state — executive efforts in foreign affairs appear to have become increasingly disunified and uncoordinated.[79] The question which was addressed almost daily to the White House during President Carter's incumbency — Who really speaks for the administration in foreign affairs? — identified an endemic and increasingly serious obstacle to sound decisionmaking within the executive branch.

As our case studies have shown, the role of Congress in contemporary American foreign policy is also beset by comparable difficulties. If the House and Senate have now established — and can be expected to maintain — an influential congressional presence in the foreign policy field, how well are they equipped to continue to play this role? Recent experience indicates that the answer must be: rather poorly and inadequately. To date, in terms of organizational, procedural, and behavioral changes required, few members of Congress have faced up squarely to the necessary implications of their demand for a position of equal "partnership" with the White House in foreign affairs.

As the nation enters the 1980s, Congress appears to be more decentralized, fragmented, and resistant to unifying influences than in any previous period of American history. To date, Congress has supplied little evidence to show that it is prepared to adapt its own organizational structure and internal procedures to the demands of an active foreign policy role its members are determined to play. In the long run, this failure could prove decisive in determining the future of congressional activism in foreign affairs.

In judging the respective claims of the presidency and Congress to leadership in the foreign policy process, the American people are likely to apply their customary pragmatic and eclectic tests. Has the active intrusion of Congress into many dimensions of foreign affairs improved, or detracted from, the ability of the United States to achieve its diplomatic goals? Has congressional assertiveness on foreign policy questions enhanced the domestic well-being of the American society? Has the influence of Congress upon the course of the nation's diplomacy reversed, or has it contributed to, the tendency toward weakened American power and influence abroad? As much as any other single factor, how the American people perceive the answers to these questions will determine Congress' future foreign policy role.[80]

Shared Goals. Executive and legislative officials alike, we may safely assume, ultimately seek the same goal: a unified, rational, and successful foreign policy for the United States. Moreover, all participants in foreign policy decisionmaking would no doubt subscribe to the theoretical proposition that continuing discord, disunity, and competing efforts within the American government — regardless of whether they arise within the executive branch, within Congress, or from conflicts between the executive and legislative branches — nearly always impair the ability of the United States to achieve its diplomatic objectives.

If broad agreement exists in Washington on these propositions, it follows that officials in each branch need to devote greater attention to defining more clearly their respective contributions to the foreign policy process. By virtue of their differing constitutional responsibilities, their experience, and their resources, executive and legislative policymakers ought to make different contributions to the common effort, reflecting what each group is uniquely prepared to supply.

Presidential Role. What contributions are the president and his executive advisers singularly qualified to make? More than any other official of the American government, the president symbolizes and represents the national interest of the United States — both to the American people and to foreign countries. The chief executive alone can speak in behalf of the American society to governments, leaders, and political movements abroad. As commander in chief of the armed forces, only the president is in a position to respond promptly and decisively to external threats.

The president and the executive officials under his jurisdiction also play an indispensable role in policy formulation. Relying upon the State Department's communications system with American embassies overseas, and upon the intelligence community's resources for collecting and analyzing data, the White House remains in an unrivaled position to consider available options and to devise diplomatic strategies and programs for which it will later seek legislative support. Moreover, the president's position as a leader and educator of public opinion is unequaled. When circumstances require it, the chief executive can inform the American people about diplomatic issues and can elicit their support in behalf of the nation's diplomatic objectives. Such presidential appeals seldom fail to rally public opinion behind the White House.

Contribution of Congress. Congress also brings certain distinctive powers to bear in foreign policy decisionmaking. First, there is the legislative power to grant or to withhold funds for foreign policy ventures and programs. Although Congress has possessed this power since 1789, only since the closing stage of the Vietnam War has it relied regularly upon its control over the purse strings to determine the course of American diplomacy. As the internal and external demands upon the financial resources of the American government continue to escalate — and there is no reason to anticipate a reversal of that tendency in the near future — Congress will be challenged as never before to use the power of the purse wisely and effectively in allocating funds to a variety of foreign policy undertakings.

Second, Congress makes an essential contribution in supplying a base of legitimacy to American foreign policy. For a democracy, this vital element — a pervasive public belief that the nation's diplomatic goals are rational, are attainable at reasonable cost, and are consonant with the American society's cherished values — is a prerequisite for diplomatic success. Since the Vietnam War, even executive officials have acknowledged this legislative contribution to the foreign policy process. Thus, as the United States prepared to enter the 1980s, one State Department official called attention to the important need after Vietnam and Watergate "to legitimize American foreign policy." Referring to President Carter's decision to sell arms to certain nations in the Middle East, this spokesman observed, "If the President had made the Middle East arms sales decision on his own, he could have been run out of town on a rail. But the congressional vote legitimized the sale."[81]

Third, as our discussion of legislative activities with regard to the intelligence community illustrated, Congress can make a positive contribution to foreign policy decisionmaking — and to the future of American democracy — by scrutinizing the activities of executive agencies and by imposing more stringent guidelines upon their operations. Owing in no small measure to Congress' efforts, the CIA and other intelligence agencies are no longer seemingly "out of control" and engaging in activities at variance with American legal and ideological traditions. Continuing oversight by the House and Senate has gone far towards restoring popular confidence in the intelligence agencies and giving them a necessary base of public support. How intelligence agencies can operate effectively while respecting democratic norms is a related question which has still to be resolved by national policymakers.

A fourth essential and distinctive contribution of Congress to the foreign policy process was brought into sharp focus by our analysis of its role in the disposition and control of the armed forces. Relying upon its constitutional prerogatives over the military establishment, Congress can prescribe limits to the president's use of armed force for foreign policy ends. By doing so, Congress creates powerful restraints upon diplomatic adventurism, upon a tendency by the United States to become overextended abroad, and upon the tendency to intervene indiscriminately in the affairs of other countries.

Efforts by the House and Senate to impose more stringent controls over the president's use of the armed forces abroad make another singular contribution to American foreign policy. They serve to remind executive policymakers that, although the United States is a superpower, it is not omnipotent. Even superpowers must base their diplomacy upon a set of priorities. They must define and continually redefine their diplomatic vital interests with care and discrimination. As Walter Lippmann cautioned Americans many years ago, success in foreign policy lies in arriving at and maintaining a balance between what the nation would *like* to accomplish abroad and what it is *able* to accomplish on the basis of the power available to it. Failure to preserve an approximate balance between these elements can result in a kind of "diplomatic bankruptcy."[82]

The executive and legislative branches of government would do well to concentrate upon the unique contributions each is equipped to make in the foreign policy process. Too often in the past each branch has jealously guarded and asserted its own powers in foreign affairs, while endeavoring to exercise or usurp those properly belonging to the other. A clearer sense of a division of labor in the diplomatic field by officials on both ends of Pennsylvania Avenue would go far toward achieving the goal of a more unified, stable, and successful American approach to external problems in the years ahead.

NOTES

1. See the views of Ambassador Peter Jay, as quoted in William D. Rogers, "Who's In Charge of Foreign Policy?" *New York Times Magazine,* September 9, 1979, p. 49. The author is a former State Department official, but he is not to be confused with ex-Secretary of State William P. Rogers.
2. *The New York Times,* January 25, 1975, dispatch by Bernard Gwertzman.
3. "Second Annual Report to the Congress on United States Foreign Policy," *Public Papers of the Presidents of the United States: Richard M. Nixon, 1971* (Washington, D.C.: U.S. Government Printing Office, 1972), p. 345.
4. I. M. Destler, "Treaty Troubles: Versailles in Reverse," *Foreign Policy* 33 (Winter 1978-79): 53.
5. For President Ford's view on Congress' activities in foreign affairs, see Gerald R. Ford, *A Time to Heal* (New York: Harper & Row and the Reader's Digest Assn., 1979), pp. 138-139, 150; Ford's views are also quoted in Marvin Stone, "Presidency: Imperial or Imperiled?" *U.S. News & World Report,* 86 (January 15, 1979): 88.

6. Lee H. Hamilton and Michael H. Van Dusen, "Making the Separation of Powers Work," *Foreign Affairs*, 57 (Fall 1978): 29.

7. Nicholas DeB. Katzenbach, "Foreign Policy, Public Opinion and Secrecy," *Foreign Affairs*, 52 (October 1973): 18.

8. For the views of John V. Lindsay, former member of Congress and mayor of New York, see "For a New Policy Balance," *Foreign Affairs*, 50 (October 1971): 1.

9. For a detailed analysis of the "legislative explosion" witnessed since World War II, see James McClellan, "The State of the American Congress," *Modern Age*, 21 (Summer 1977): 227-239.

10. *The New York Times*, September 21, 1979, dispatch by James Reston.

11. *The New York Times*, January 9, 1979, dispatch by Richard Burt; see also the views of Senator Frank Church as reported in *The New York Times*, May 23, 1979.

12. Marvin Stone, "Proxmire's Well-Placed Jab," *U.S. News & World Report*, 87 (September 10, 1979): 84.

13. See the views of Professors Thomas Franck and Edward Weisband in *The New York Times*, November 29, 1976.

14. McClellan, "The State of the American Congress," p. 237. See also the study by Susan W. Hammond, "Congressional Change and Reform: Staffing the Congress," in Leroy N. Rieselbach, ed., *Legislative Reform: The Policy Impact* (Lexington, Mass.: D. C. Heath and Co., 1978), pp. 183-193.

15. See Dean Acheson, *Sketches from Life of Men I Have Known* (New York: Harper & Row, 1961), pp. 124-125. For historical background, see Holbert N. Carroll, *The House of Representatives and Foreign Affairs* (Boston: Little, Brown & Co., 1966).

16. See the views of Representative Paul Findley in *The New York Times*, October 6, 1966.

17. U.S., Congress, House, Committee on International Relations, *Congress and Foreign Policy*, 94th Cong., 2d sess., 1977, p. 19. See also the dialogue between executive and legislative officials on the role of public opinion in foreign affairs in William O. Chattick, *State Department, Press, and Pressure Groups* (New York: John Wiley & Sons, 1970), pp. 43-45.

18. See the views of Senator Frank Church in *The New York Times*, January 9, 1979, dispatch by Richard Burt.

19. *The New York Times*, July 28, 1978, dispatch by Adam Clymer.

20. For detailed analyses of changing American attitudes toward foreign affairs, see John E. Rielly, "The American Mood: A Foreign Policy of Self-Interest," *Foreign Policy*, 34 (Spring 1979): 74-87; and Daniel Yankelovich, "Farewell to 'President Knows Best,'" *Foreign Affairs*, (Special Issue 1978): 670-693.

21. *The New York Times*, January 4, 1980, dispatch by James Reston.

22. James Chace, "Is a Foreign Policy Consensus Possible?" *Foreign Affairs*, 57 (Fall 1978): 15-16.

23. U.S., Congress, House, Committee on International Relations, *Congress and Foreign Policy: 1976*, 95th Cong., 1st sess., 1977, pp. 188-189.

24. Ben J. Wattenberg, *The Real America: A Surprising Examination of the State of the Union* (Garden City, New York: Doubleday & Co., 1974), pp. 211-212.

25. See, for example, the views of ex-Senator J. William Fulbright in "The Legislator as Educator," *Foreign Affairs*, 57 (Spring 1979): 723, 727.

26. "What Carter's Aides Really Think of Congress," *U.S. News & World Report*, 85 (August 14, 1978): 15.

27. The quotation is from the Supreme Court's decision in *United States v. Curtiss-Wright Export Corp.*, 299 U.S. 304 (1936).

28. For a general discussion of the increase in foreign lobbying in America, see "Foreign Grab for Influence in Washington," *U.S. News & World Report*, 88 (November 22, 1976): 30.
29. See the article by ex-Senator Dick Clark in *The New York Times*, January 30, 1979.
30. For a detailed study of efforts by the executive branch to influence the deliberations of Congress, see Abraham Holtzman, *Legislative Liaison: Executive Leadership in Congress* (Chicago: Rand McNally, 1970).
31. Alton Frye and William D. Rogers, "Linkage Begins at Home," *Foreign Policy*, 35 (Summer 1979): 55-56.
32. *The New York Times*, February 19, 1979, dispatch by Graham Hovey.
33. See, for example, the views of William P. Bundy in "Who Lost Patagonia? Foreign Policy in the 1980 Campaign," *Foreign Affairs*, 58 (Fall 1979): 1-28. See also the views of Marvin Stone in *U.S. News & World Report*, (September 17, 1979): 88.
34. *The New York Times*, February 17, 1979, dispatch by Hedrick Smith.
35. See the excerpts from majority and minority reports submitted by the Senate Foreign Relations Committee on SALT II, as reprinted in *The New York Times*, November 20, 1979.
36. *The New York Times*, October 12, 1979, dispatch by Charles Mohr.
37. *The New York Times*, September 21, 1979, dispatch by James Reston. For a more detailed discussion of the implications of the problem of intraexecutive conflicts, see Rogers, "Who's In Charge of Foreign Policy?" pp. 44-51.
38. See the article by Theodore C. Sorenson in *The New York Times*, September 21, 1979.
39. 1 U.S. Statutes-at-Large 613 (1799).
40. *The New York Times*, April 14, 1979, dispatch by Hedrick Smith.
41. *The New York Times*, September 21, 1979, dispatch by James Reston.
42. *The New York Times*, November 26, 1979, dispatch by John Kifner; and November 27, 1979, dispatch by Bernard Gwertzman.
43. *U.S. News & World Report*, 85 (February 19, 1979): 52-54.
44. *The New York Times*, March 1, 1979, dispatch by Graham Hovey.
45. See *The Washington Post*, December 14, 1979; and Congressional Quarterly *Weekly Report* 47 (December 15, 1979): 2850.
46. For the views of the Nixon-Kissinger White House on the results of congressional action toward the Vietnam War, see Richard Nixon, *The Memoirs of Richard Nixon* (New York: Grosset & Dunlap, 1978), pp. 744, 888-889; and Henry Kissinger, *White House Years* (Boston: Little, Brown & Co., 1979), pp. 1413, 1461.
47. Kissinger, *White House Years*, pp. 400-401.
48. Ibid., pp. 163-195, 684-788.
49. George W. Ball, *Diplomacy for a Crowded World: An American Foreign Policy* (Boston: Atlantic, Little Brown, 1976), p. 204.
50. "What Carter's Aides Really Think of Congress," p. 15.
51. Fulbright, "The Legislator as Educator," pp. 719, 726.
52. *The New York Times*, July 3, 1977, dispatch by Adam Clymer.
53. For a detailed discussion of the crisis over Soviet troops in Cuba, see "SALT Debate is Complicated by Soviet Troops in Cuba," Congressional Quarterly *Weekly Report*, 37 (September 8, 1979): 1913; and the excerpt from the report of the Senate Foreign Relations Committee on SALT II, in *The New York Times*, November 20, 1979.
54. "Coping with the Soviets' Cuban Brigade," *Time*, 114 (October 1, 1979): 100.
55. See the views of William D. Rogers, in "Who's In Charge of Foreign Policy?"

pp. 44, 47, 50. Basically the same criticism is made of Congress' approach to foreign affairs by ex-Secretary of State Henry Kissinger, who contrasts the difference between the fields of law and diplomacy. See Kissinger, *White House Years*, pp. 940-941.

56. Senator Vandenberg's views are quoted in Ben H. Brown, Jr., "Congress and the Department of State," *Annals of the American Academy of Political and Social Science*, 289 (September 1953): 107.

57. Hamilton and Van Dusen, "Making the Separation of Powers Work," p. 39.

58. See the article entitled, "Too Many Negotiators," by Genrikh Trofimenko, in *The New York Times*, July 13, 1979.

59. Ibid.

60. For an excellent interpretation of the philosophical and cultural values of modern American society, see Christopher Lasch, *The Culture of Narcissism: American Life in an Age of Diminishing Expectations* (New York: W. W. Norton, 1978). See also Steven J. Kelman, "Youth and Foreign Policy," *Foreign Affairs*, 48 (April 1970): 414-427; and the detailed discussion of the cultural values of the 1970s in *Newsweek*, 94 (November 19, 1979): 84-133.

61. For the views of Assistant Secretary of State for Congressional Relations Douglas J. Bennet, Jr., see "Congress: Its Role in Foreign Policy-Making," *Department of State Bulletin*, 78 (June 1978): 35-36; and "Congress in Foreign Policy: Who Needs It?" *Foreign Affairs*, 57 (Fall 1978): 40-51.

62. *The New York Times*, January 18 and February 2, 1979, dispatches by Bernard Gwertzman.

63. *The New York Times*, August 23, 1979, dispatch by Anthony Lewis.

64. The concept of oscillating isolationist and interventionist foreign policy moods by the American people is identified and explained in F. L. Klingberg, "The Historical Alternation of Moods in American Foreign Policy," *World Politics*, 4 (January 1952): 239-273.

65. For more detailed discussion of bipartisan collaboration during the Truman administration, see Cecil V. Crabb, Jr., *Bipartisan Foreign Policy: Myth or Reality?* (New York: Harper & Row, 1957), pp. 1-156; and Arthur H. Vandenberg, Jr., ed., *The Private Papers of Senator Vandenberg* (Boston: Houghton Mifflin Co., 1952), pp. 172-581.

66. Acheson, *Sketches From Life Of Men I Have Known*, pp. 123-146.

67. James L. Sundquist, "Congress and the President: Enemies or Partners?" in Lawrence C. Dodd and Bruce I. Oppenheimer, eds., *Congress Reconsidered* (New York: Praeger Publishers, 1977), p. 222.

68. *U.S. News & World Report*, 87 (August 27, 1979): 20.

69. See the dispatch by Barry Sussman, as reprinted from *The Washington Post*, in the Baton Rouge *Morning Advocate*, August 5, 1979.

70. Elizabeth Drew, "Why Congress Won't Fight?" *New York Times Magazine*, September 23, 1973, p. 83.

71. The findings of Professors Thomas E. Cronin and Lawrence C. Dodd, are summarized in *The New York Times*, November 18, 1977, dispatch by Tom Wicker.

72. *The New York Times*, October 28, 1979, dispatch by Terrence Smith.

73. For detailed analyses of public attitudes on Congress, see "What Congress Really Thinks of Itself," *U.S. News & World Report*, 88 (January 14, 1980): 39-42; Malcolm E. Jewell and Samuel C. Patterson, *The Legislative Process in the United States*, 3d ed. (New York: Random House, 1977), pp. 315-317; and Roger H. Davidson, David M. Kovenock, and Michael K. O'Leary, *Congress in Crisis: Politics and Congressional Reform* (Belmont, Calif.: Wadsworth Publishing Co., 1971), pp. 38-66.

74. See the survey data presented in *Time*, 114 (October 1, 1979): 25; and *U.S.*

News & World Report, 87 (July 16, 1979): 21.

75. Ralph B. Levering, *The Public and American Foreign Policy: 1918-1978* (New York: William Morrow & Co., 1978), p. 29.

76. John Bibby and Roger Davidson, *On Capitol Hill: Studies in the Legislative Process* (New York: Holt, Rinehart & Winston, 1967), pp. 111-112. See also McClellan, "The State of the American Congress," pp. 229, 237.

77. *The New York Times*, September 21, 1979, dispatch by James Reston.

78. This unnamed senator is quoted in Drew, "Why Congress Won't Fight?" p. 16.

79. For innumerable examples illustrating the decline of the State Department in the foreign policy process during the Nixon administration, see Kissinger, *White House Years*.

80. The influence of pragmatic, trial-and-error criteria in shaping American attitudes are discussed more fully in Wattenberg, *The Real America*, pp. 203-213; and in George W. Ball, *The Discipline of Power: Essentials of a Modern World Structure* (Boston: Little Brown & Co., 1968), pp. 343-358.

81. See the views of Assistant Secretary of State for Congressional Relations Brian Atwood in *The New York Times*, December 24, 1979, dispatch by Martin Tolchin.

82. Walter Lippmann, *U.S. Foreign Policy: Shield of the Republic* (Boston: Little, Brown & Co., 1943); and Lippmann, *The Cold War: a Study in U.S. Foreign Policy* (New York: Harper & Row, 1947).

Suggested Readings

Books

Bathory, Peter D., ed. *Leadership in America: Consensus, Corruption and Charisma*. New York: Longman, 1978.

Berkowitz, Morton, et al. *The Politics of American Foreign Policy: The Social Context of Decisions*. Englewood Cliffs, N.J.: Prentice-Hall, 1977.

Blaney, Harry C. III. *Global Challenges*. New York: New Viewpoints, 1979.

Blechman, Barry M., and Kaplan, Stephen S. *Force Without War: U.S. Armed Forces as a Political Instrument*. Washington, D.C.: Brookings Institution, 1978.

Brown, Peter G., and MacLean, Douglas, eds. *Human Rights and U.S. Foreign Policy: Principles and Applications*. Lexington, Mass.: D. C. Heath, 1979.

Brown, Seyom. *The Crises of Power: Foreign Policy in the Kissinger Years*. New York: Columbia University Press, 1979.

Cohen, Stephen D. *The Making of United States International Economic Policy*. New York: Praeger Publishers, 1977.

Cotton, Norris. *In the Senate: Amidst the Conflict and the Turmoil*. New York: Dodd, Mead & Co., 1978.

Dodd, Lawrence C., and Schott, Richard L. *Congress and the Administrative State*. New York: John Wiley & Sons, 1979.

Editorial Research Reports. *U.S. Foreign Policy: Future Directions*. Washington, D.C.: Congressional Quarterly, 1979.

Feulner, Edwin J. *Congress and the New International Economic Order*. Washington, D.C.: Heritage Foundation, 1976.

Ford, Gerald R. *A Time to Heal*. New York: Harper & Row and the Reader's Digest Association, 1979.

Franck, Thomas, and Weisband, Edward. *Foreign Policy by Congress*. New York: Oxford University Press, 1979.

Hamilton, James. *The Power to Probe: A Study of Congressional Investigations*. New York: Random House, 1976.

Havemann, Joel. *Congress and the Budget*. Bloomington, Ind.: Indiana University Press, 1978.

Heaphey, James J., and Balutis, Alan P. *Legislative Staffing: A Comparative Perspective*. New York: John Wiley & Sons, 1976.

Heclo, Hugh. *A Government of Strangers: Executive Politics in Washington*. Washington, D.C.: Brookings Institution, 1977.

Hughes, Barry B. *The Domestic Context of American Foreign Policy*. San Francisco: W. H. Freeman & Co., 1978.

Joyce, James A. *The New Politics of Human Rights.* New York: St. Martin's Press, 1979.

Kanter, Arnold. *Defense Politics: A Budgetary Perspective.* Chicago: University of Chicago Press, 1979.

King, Anthony, ed. *The New American Political System.* Washington, D.C.: American Enterprise Institute, 1978.

Kissinger, Henry. *White House Years.* Boston: Little, Brown & Co., 1979.

Kommers, Donald P., and Loescher, Gilburt D., eds. *Human Rights and American Foreign Policy.* South Bend, Ind.: University of Notre Dame Press, 1979.

La Feber, Walter. *The Panama Canal: The Crisis in Historical Perspective.* New York: Oxford University Press, 1978.

Lehman, John F. *The Executive, Congress and Foreign Policy: Studies of the Nixon Administration.* New York: Praeger Publishers, 1976.

Levering, Ralph B. *The Public and American Foreign Policy, 1918-1978.* New York: William Morrow, 1978.

Lipsen, Charles B., and Lesher, Stephan. *Vested Interest: A Lobbyist's Account of Washington Powr and How It Really Works.* New York: Doubleday & Co., 1977.

Mueller, John E. *War, Presidents and Public Opinion.* New York: John Wiley & Sons, 1973.

Nash, Henry T. *American Foreign Policy: Changing Perspectives on National Security.* 2d ed. Homewood, Ill.: Dorsey Press, 1978.

Nixon, Richard M. *The Memoirs of Richard Nixon.* New York: Grosset & Dunlap, 1978.

Nuechterlein, Donald E. *National Interests and Presidential Leadership: The Setting of Priorities.* Boulder, Colo.: Westview Press, 1978.

Orbach, William W. *The American Movement to Aid Soviet Jews.* Amherst, Mass.: University of Massachusetts Press, 1979.

Ornstein, Norman J., and Elder, Shirley. *Interest Groups, Lobbying and Policymaking.* Washington, D.C.: Congressional Quarterly, 1978.

Osborne, John. *White House Watch: The Ford Years.* Washington, D.C.: New Republic Books, 1977.

Oye, Kenneth A., et al., eds. *Eagle Entangled: U.S. Foreign Policy in a Complex World.* New York: Longman, 1979.

Palmer, Bruce, Jr., ed. *Grand Strategy for the 1980s.* Washington, D.C.: American Enterprise Institute, 1978.

Pierre, Andrew J., ed. *Arms Transfers and American Foreign Policy.* New York: New York University Press, 1979.

Pious, Richard M. *The American Presidency.* New York: Basic Books, 1979.

Platt, Alan, and Weiler, Lawrence D. *Congress and Arms Control.* Boulder, Colo.: Westview Press, 1978.

Polk, William R. *The United States and the Arab World.* 3d ed. Cambridge, Mass.: Harvard University Press, 1975.

Quandt, William B. *Decade of Decisions: American Policy Toward the Arab-Israeli Conflict, 1967-1976. Berkeley: University of California Press, 1977.*

Ravenal, Earl C. *Never Again: Learning from America's Foreign Policy Failures.* Philadelphia: Temple University Press, 1978.

Reich, Bernard. *Quest for Peace: United States-Israeli Relations and the Arab-Israeli Conflict.* New Brunswick, N.J.: Transaction Books, 1977.

Ryan, Paul B. *The Panama Canal Controversy: U.S. Diplomacy and Defense Interests.* Stanford, Calif.: Hoover Institution Press, 1977.

Said, Abdul A., ed. *Ethnicity and U.S. Foreign Policy.* New York: Praeger Publishers, 1978.

Sarkesian, Sam S., ed. *Defense Policy and the Presidency: Carter's First Years.* Boulder, Colo.: Westview Press, 1979.

Schneider, Jerrold E. *Ideological Coalitions in Congress.* Westport, Conn.: Greenwood Press, 1979.

Stern, Paula. *Water's Edge: Domestic Politics and the Making of American Foreign Policy.* Westport, Conn.: Greenwood Press, 1979.

Szulc, Tad. *The Illusion of Peace: Foreign Policy in the Nixon Years.* New York: Viking Press, 1978.

Wesson, Robert G. *Foreign Policy for a New Age.* Boston: Houghton Mifflin Co., 1977.

Wilcox, Francis O., and Frank, Richard A. *The Constitution and the Conduct of Foreign Policy.* New York: Praeger Publishers, 1976.

Articles

Aspin, L. "The Defense Budget and Foreign Policy: The Role of Congress." *Daedalus,* 104 (Summer 1975).

Burstein, P., and Freudenburg, W. "Ending the Vietnam War: Components of Change in Senate Voting on Vietnam War Bills." *American Journal of Sociology,* 82 (March 1977).

Franck, Thomas M. "After the Fall: The New Procedural Framework for Congressional Control Over the War Power." *American Journal of International Law,* 71 (October 1977).

Gareau, F. H. "Congressional Representatives to the U.N. General Assembly: Corruption by Foreign Gentry?" *Orbis,* 21 (Fall 1977).

Johnson, Loch, and McCormick, James M. "The Making of International Agreements: A Reappraisal of Congressional Involvement." *Journal of Politics,* 40 (May 1978).

Kaiser, Fred. "Oversight of Foreign Policy: The U.S. House Committee on International Relations." *Legislative Studies Quarterly,* 2 (August 1977).

Karns, David A. "The Effect of Inter-parliamentary Meetings on the Foreign Policy Attitudes of United States Congressmen." *International Organization,* 31 (Summer 1977).

Laurance, E. J. "The Changing Role of Congress in Defense Policy-Making." *Journal of Conflict Resolution,* 20 (June 1976).

Livingstone, N. C., and von Nordheim, M. "The United States Congress and the Angola Crisis." *Strategic Review,* 5 (Spring 1977).

Manning, Bayless. "The Congress, the Executive and Intermestic Affairs: Three Proposals." *Foreign Affairs,* 55 (January 1977).

Ornstein, Norman J. "Lobbying for Fun and Policy." *Foreign Policy,* 28 (Fall 1977).

Stevens, C. J. "The Use and Control of Executive Agreements: Recent Congressional Initiatives." *Orbis,* 20 (Winter 1977).

Trice, Robert H. "Congress and the Arab-Israeli Conflict: Support for Israel in the U.S. Senate, 1970-1973." *Political Science Quarterly,* 92 (Fall 1977).

Index

227